The Falklands
& South Georgia Island

Tony Wheeler

Contents

Islands off West Falkland p121

West Falkland p110

East Falkland p89

Stanley p66

Islands off East Falkland p101

South Georgia p143

Lonely Planet books provide independent advice. Lonely Planet does not accept advertising in guidebooks, nor do we accept payment in exchange for listing or endorsing any place or business. Lonely Planet writers do not accept discounts or payments in exchange for positive coverage of any sort.

Destination the Falklands & South Georgia Island

A war and the collapse of communism were the events that combined to put two of the world's most remote destinations on the tourist map.

Until Argentina's military dictatorship made an ill-judged decision to invade the Falkland Islands in 1982, pinpointing the location of the remote cluster of South Atlantic islands was strictly a challenge for trivia enthusiasts. The image, if there was one at all, was of a treeless, windswept wasteland populated by a couple of thousand dour shepherds, outnumbered 300 to one by their woolly four-legged friends. Visitors were strictly 'been everywhere' list-tickers and getting there was very difficult until, in 1977, the Argentines constructed an airport.

The Falklands War suddenly put the islands on the front page, at the cost of roughly 1000 Argentine and British military deaths – almost one for every two islanders. Suddenly the world woke up to the colony's colourful capital of Stanley, the Islands' intriguing history (amply illustrated by Stanley's collection of Victorian-era shipwrecks) and the amazing wildlife (penguins, seals and albatrosses for starters), and even that windswept, treeless terrain had a curious attraction.

The dismemberment of the Soviet Union left a fine collection of Antarctic research vessels (some of them more like spy ships) looking for alternative employment. Many ended up shuttling tourists down to Antarctica, and visitors soon discovered the dramatically forbidding island of South Georgia. The scenery here is spectacular, the wildlife abundant (10 or 20 penguins are fascinating, 10 or 20 thousand are mind-blowing), and over everything lies the legend of Sir Ernest Shackleton and his heroic adventures on the island in 1916.

KERRY LORIMER

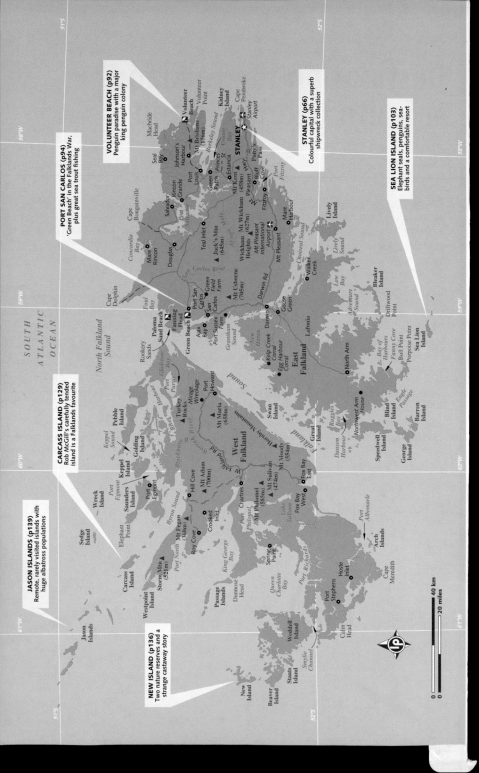

JASON ISLANDS (p139)
Remote, rarely visited islands with huge albatross populations

NEW ISLAND (p136)
Two nature reserves and a strange castaway story

CARCASS ISLAND (p129)
Rob McGill's carefully tended island is a Falklands favourite

PORT SAN CARLOS (p94)
'Green Beach' in the Falklands War, plus great sea trout fishing

VOLUNTEER BEACH (p92)
Penguin paradise with a major king penguin colony

STANLEY (p66)
Colourful capital with a superb shipwreck collection

SEA LION ISLAND (p103)
Elephant seals, penguins, sea-birds and a comfortable resort

SOUTH
ATLANTIC
OCEAN

North Falkland Sound

Jason Islands

Sedge Island

Wreck Island

Elephant Point

Carcass Island

Westpoint Island

Storm Mtn (521m)▲

Port North

Mt Fegan (361m)▲

Roy Cove

Dunnose Head

Passage Islands

King George Bay

Queen Charlotte Bay

Dunmose Head

Spring Point

Weddell Island

Beaver Island

New Island

Staats Island

Calm Head

Smylie Channel

Port Egmont

Saunders Island

Keppel Island

Keppel Sound

Byron Sound

Hill Cove

Mt Adam (700m)▲

Crooked Inlet

Port Howard

Philippa

Fort Chartres

Mt Philomel (585m)▲

Mt Sullivan (474m)▲

Fox Bay West

Fox Bay East

Lake Sullivan

Port Richards

Port Stephens

Hoste Inlet

Cape Meredith

Arch Islands

Port Albemarle

Golding Island

Pebble Island

Port Purvis

Turkey Rocks

Mirage Wreckage

Blackburn River

Warrah River

Mt Maria (658m)▲

West Falkland

Hornby Mountains

Mt Moody (554m)▲

W Falkland Rd

Chartres R

Falkland Sound

Cape Dolphin

Foul Bay

Rookery Sands

Paloma Sand Beach

Fanning Head

Green Beach

Ajax Bay

Port San Carlos

San Carlos

Port Sussex

Grantham Sound

New House

Great Island

Swan Island

Ragdale Bay

Danson Harbour

Speedwell Island

George Island

Blind Island

Barren Island

Cape Bouganville

Concordia Bay

Mare Rincon

Douglas

Salvador

Teal Inlet

Jack's Mtn (645m)▲

Mt Usborne (705m)▲

Darwin Rd

Green Field Farm

Darwin

Goose Green

Egg Harbour Corral

Kelp Creek Corral

Lafonia

North Arm

Northwest Point

Bay of Harbours

Adventure Sound

Low Bay

Choiseul Sound

Walker Creek

Lively Sound

Breaker Island

Driftwood Point

Eagle Passage

Purpose Point

Fanny Cove

Bull Point

Sea Lion Island

Mt Brisbane (176m)

Machride Head

Seal Bay

Rincon Grande

Port Louis

Green Patch

Estancia

Mt Kent (458m)▲

Mt Wickham (627m)▲

Wickham Heights

Mt Pleasant International Airport

Mt Pleasant

Mare Harbour

Lively Island

Volunteer Point

Volunteer Beach

Kidney Island

Johnson's Harbour

Princes St

Berkeley Sound

STANLEY

Stanley Airport

Port William

Bluff Cove

Port Harriet

Port Fitzroy

Fitzroy

Potty's Pass

Cape Pembroke

0 ____ 40 km

0 ____ 20 miles

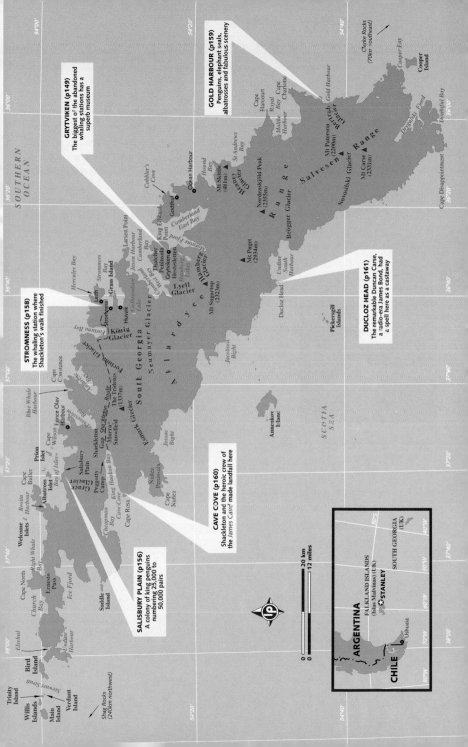

STROMNESS (p158)
The whaling station where Shackleton's walk finished

GRYTVIKEN (p149)
The biggest of the abandoned whaling stations has a superb museum

GOLD HARBOUR (p159)
Penguins, elephant seals, albatrosses and fabulous scenery

SALISBURY PLAIN (p156)
A colony of king penguins numbering 25,000 to 50,000 pairs

CAVE COVE (p160)
Shackleton and the heroic crew of the *James Caird* made landfall here

DUCLOZ HEAD (p161)
The remarkable Duncan Carse, a radio-era James Bond, had a spell here as a castaway

SOUTHERN OCEAN

SCOTIA SEA

South Georgia

Salvesen Range

Allardyce Range

ARGENTINA
CHILE
Ushuaia
STANLEY
FALKLAND ISLANDS
(Islas Malvinas) (UK)
SOUTH GEORGIA (UK)

0   20 km
0   12 miles

Wildlife is the number one attraction for most visitors to the Falkland Islands and South Georgia. It's not that the variety is so great, it's the sheer numbers of certain species that takes visitors' breath away. Walking among a colony of tens of thousands of king penguins is an experience not easily forgotten and the huge colony at the **Bay of Isles** (p156) on South Georgia is one of the most impressive. The king penguin colony at **Volunteer Beach** (p92) on East Falkland is much smaller, but two other species of penguin also breed here (and the trip from Stanley is a classic excursion across the Falklands countryside known as 'camp'). Magnificent albatrosses are a prime attraction for birdwatchers, whether it's the black-browed albatross on **Saunders Island** (p126) in the Falklands or the uber version, the huge wandering albatross encountered at **Albatross Islet** (p156) off South Georgia.

KERRY LORIMER

Witness the mating display of
the wandering albatross (p50)

Enjoy a close-up view of a rockhopper
penguin (p48)

TONY WHEELER

Take in the spectacle of a colony of king penguins in St Andrew's Bay (p159), the largest penguin colony in the world, on South Georgia

GRANT DIXON

Stanley (p66), the capital of the Falklands, is a colourful little settlement with brightly painted buildings, many of them constructed of 'wriggly tin'. Along the Stanley Harbour water's edge are a number of shipwrecks including the historic **Jhelum** (p72) and the magnificent old iron barque **Lady Elizabeth** (p74). Memorials along the waterfront road include the **1982 Falklands War Memorial** (p77), strategically sited on Thatcher Dr, and further along the **1914 Battle of the Falklands Memorial** (p71), dedicated to one of the last great set piece naval encounters. Each of the South Georgia whaling stations is a fascinating snapshot of industrial archaeology, a frozen-in-time reminder of the abrupt ending of the whaling business in the 1960s. **Grytviken** (p149) is the biggest of these abandoned settlements, but they're all fascinating to visit.

See the *Plym* and the *Lady Elizabeth* (p74) at Whalebone Cove, Stanley, East Falkland

TONY WHEELER

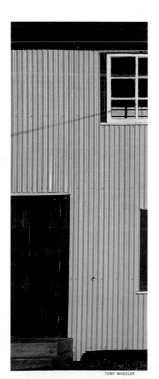

Appreciate the colours and construction of 'wriggly tin' (p67), Stanley, East Falkland

TONY WHEELER

Explore abandoned Grytviken Whaling Station (p149), seen here from King Edward Point, South Georgia

GRANT DIXON

It's hard to get away from Shackleton's influence around South Georgia. If you're lucky your ship may schedule a stop at **Cave Cove** (p160) on King Haakon Bay where Shackleton and his men landed the *James Caird* after their epic voyage from Elephant Island. Further up the bay is **Peggotty Camp** (p160), from where the crossing party started across the island. The manager's villa, where they finally found help, still stands in the abandoned whaling station at **Stromness** (p158). The Shackleton story is recounted in the **South Georgia Museum** (p150) at Grytviken while the finale to his adventurous life is the grave and memorial in the nearby **Whalers' Cemetery** (p152).

TONY WHEELER

Discover Cave Cove (p160), where Shackleton landed on South Georgia

Trek up to Shackleton Gap
from Peggotty Camp on the
Shackleton walk (p145)

TONY WHEELER

KERRY LORIMER

Visit the Stromness whaling station (p158) on
South Georgia

Getting Started

Apart from a handful of intrepid visitors who arrive by yacht, Falklands visitors are either cruise-ship 'day-trippers', as the islanders call them, or fly-in visitors typically staying for a week or two in Stanley and in 'camp'. Camp, from the Spanish word *campo*, is anywhere apart from in Stanley, ie anywhere in the countryside.

During summer (October to April), a steady stream of Antarctic tour ships make their way down to South Georgia, many of them stopping off at the Falklands en route. The wildlife will be an attraction for nearly every visitor, but some will come in search of history and an adventurous handful will be planning to walk in Shackleton's footsteps.

WHEN TO GO

Since the primary attraction in the Falklands and South Georgia is wildlife, the high season is October to March, when migratory birds (including penguins) and marine mammals return to the beaches and headlands. With very long days, December and January are probably the best months to visit – see p166.

See Climate Charts (p166) for more information.

The first cruise ships to South Georgia turn up in early November and the last ones depart around the end of March. The high summer months of January and February can bring better weather, the ice and snow has melted back from the coast and South Georgia takes on its green and less threatening appearance. Visiting ships are carefully managed so it is rare to have two ships in the same vicinity on the same day – you usually feel as though you have the island all to yourself.

There are distinct seasons for wildlife activity, much of which is tied up with breeding cycles. Although species such as king penguins and

---

DON'T LEAVE HOME WITHOUT...

Even in the summer high season the weather is cool and changeable in the Falklands and South Georgia. Visitors should bring good waterproof clothing and warm sweaters. A pair of knee-high rubber boots (Wellington boots, as they're known to the British) can be useful in wet weather. Apart from coping very well with snow and mud, Wellington boots slip on and off very easily, which is convenient because you seem to be forever removing shoes or boots. In the Falklands boots or shoes are never worn indoors, while on ships visiting South Georgia you'll be putting on boots every time you go ashore and taking them off when you come back on board. Older Falklands houses can be draughty places; come prepared for low indoor temperatures.

In the Falklands summer never gets truly hot and the wind can lower the temperature considerably, but the climate does not justify Antarctic preparations. When the sun does shine it can be intense; bring good sun protection and a hat. For trekkers, a *very* sturdy tent with rain fly and a warm sleeping bag are essential. Also, few visitors will want to be without binoculars and cameras.

Summer on South Georgia is not as cold as you might think. The sort of clothing you'd take for a ski trip should be quite adequate. The one difference would be to trade in your ski boots for a pair of Wellingtons.

If you're planning on more energetic activities ashore (hiking or camping, for example), then you need to dress more seriously with multiple layers. Outer layers in Gore-Tex or other hi-tech synthetic fibres, and high quality walking shoes suitable for snow and wet conditions are a must.

On board, the temperatures are usually comfortably warm and the dress code is casual. The sort of clothing you'd wear for lounging around in a ski lodge will be fine.

wandering albatrosses stay year-round on South Georgia, the usual breeding pattern is to arrive at the beginning of the summer and depart at the end. For seals it's a year-long cycle: the pups born at the beginning of the summer are the result of mating in the previous summer. During breeding times South Georgia visitors must take care not to disturb birds and seals – the fur seal breeding season in particular can bring distinct difficulties for visitors. See p169 for more information on how to live with bad-tempered fur seals.

COSTS & MONEY

Cruise ship visitors will have prepaid most things and, apart from the odd purchase in Stanley or Grytviken, will not need to spend anything off the ships.

Visitors staying in the Falklands will find that short-stay, top-end accommodation, which includes full board, ranges from £50 to £100 per person per day. Cheaper alternatives, such as B&Bs in Stanley, start at about £15. In camp, there are low-cost, self-catering cabins for about £10, and opportunities for trekking and camping at little or no cost. Camp families in some isolated areas still welcome visitors without charge.

Food prices are roughly equivalent to the UK, but fresh meat (chiefly mutton) is extremely cheap. Fast food and snacks are available in Stanley. Getting around the Falklands will usually involve flights on the Falkland Islands Government Air Service (FIGAS), the local domestic airline. Depending on where you're going fares vary from roughly £25 to £80.

TRAVEL LITERATURE

It's disappointing there isn't more general travel literature on the Falklands or South Georgia. A delightful exception is *Antarctic Housewife* (1971) by Australian Nan Brown, who married a radio operator and lived for 2½ years on South Georgia during the whaling era in the mid-1950s. Her readable and warm-hearted tale covers not only the housewife aspect but also interesting interludes about a whale catcher and an elephant sealing foray, as well as travels on the island. It even answers the question, 'would a penguin make a good pet?' The answer is yes; she adopts an injured gentoo that follows her around like a pet dog. Surprisingly, this title is still in print, on South Georgia at least, where it can be bought at the museum.

Simon Winchester includes a chapter on the Falklands in *Outposts*, his circuit of the last remnants of the British Empire. With superb timing he managed to arrive in Stanley just before the Argentine invasion, and as a result spent a spell imprisoned in Argentina. Harry Ritchie made a similar circuit of the empire 15 years later, and wrote about the Falklands and other leftovers in his amusing *The Last Pink Bits*. (The British Empire was always coloured pink in British school atlases.)

The travel literature topic that is well covered is, of course, the adventures of Ernest Shackleton, a subject which often deserves its own bookshelf space. *South* (1919) is Shackleton's own account of the *Endurance* expedition (the Elephant Island to South Georgia voyage and the walk across the island).

Shackleton's Boat Journey by Frank Worsley (1940) is an account by Shackleton's indefatigable New Zealand captain of the dangerous boat trip from Elephant Island and the equally daring crossing of South Georgia.

Endurance – The Greatest Adventure Story Ever Told by Alfred Lansing was originally published in 1959 and has had numerous reprints since, including a 2001 paperback edition illustrated with many of Frank Hurley's photographs of the extraordinary journey.

HOW MUCH?

Litre of petrol
35p

Internet access
£3 for 20 minutes

Street snack of hamburger made with mutton
£2.20-3.70

Entry fee to South Georgia
£50

Souvenir knitted woollen sweater
£70

Shackleton at South Georgia by Robert Burton and Stephan Venables (2001) is a short booklet covering Shackleton's time on South Georgia, from the first visit of the *Endurance* en route to its Antarctic destruction through to Shackleton's death and burial at Grytviken eight years later. There's a particularly interesting section on his famous trek, with a detailed account of a modern crossing of the island by William Blake (who was involved with the IMAX Shackleton film) with mountaineers Conrad Anker and Reinhold Messner. The booklet is sold at the Grytviken Museum shop and proceeds go towards the restoration of the Stromness Villa.

Photographic Books
The Falklands and their wildlife are so photogenic it's remarkable there aren't more books showing just how stunning they can be.

Falkland Islands by Paul Hugentobler, Lars Böni and Andreas Butz (2002) is a high-quality, self-published, large-format photographic book produced by three young Swiss photographers who made a lengthy shoestring visit to the islands. They produced only a limited run of this book, but if you find a copy it's well worth a look.

The Falklands by Tony Chater (1993) is written and photographed by a long-term Falklands resident and part owner of New Island. An eclectic mix of local personalities, wildlife, shipwrecks and island life, it concludes with a lengthy section on life during the Argentine occupation.

Falkland Adventure by Andrew Coe (2000) is a pleasantly personal look at the Falklands from the perspective of a vet and his family who spent three years on the island and took every opportunity to explore it.

Antarctic Oasis: Under the Spell of South Georgia by Tim and Pauline Carr (1998) features stunning photographs by a couple who lived aboard their yacht, *Curlew*, at Grytviken and around the island for many years.

Antarctic Encounter: Destination South Georgia by Sally Poncet (1995) describes the island's wildlife and history through the eyes of three boys who explore it with their parents by yacht in 1987–88. The book has many colour photos and a great deal of information on the wildlife.

INTERNET RESOURCES
The Falklands
For a place with a population of roughly 2500, the Falkland Islands are covered by a remarkable number of websites. Some of the most useful include:

British Forces Falkland Islands (www.army.mod.uk/bffi/biffi.htm) Covers the British military presence on the islands.

Discovery Falklands (www.discoveryfalklands.com) This local tour company's site has interesting information on Falklands War battle sites, as well as general information.

Falklands Conservation (FC; www.falklandsconservation.com) The complete story on Falklands wildlife conservation, including wildlife checklists.

Falkland Islands (www.falklandislands.com) Thoroughly covers the islands, and includes facts, statistics, a useful section on tourism and other sections on services, the environment and business – there's even an interactive map of the Falklands.

Falkland Islands Association (www.fiassociation.co.uk) According to the site, it exists to assist Falkland Islanders in deciding their own future.

Falkland Islands Development Corporation (FIDC; www.fidc.org.fk) Somewhat out-of-date business information is contained on this Chamber of Commerce website.

Falkland Islands Fisheries Department (www.fis.com/falklandfish) All about fishing around the Falklands.

Falkland Islands Government (www.falklands.gov.fk) Government information and links to other sites.

TOP FIVE WILDLIFE ENCOUNTERS

■ Witnessing the huge colonies of king penguins at the Bay of Isles, South Georgia, with up to 50,000 pairs (p46)

■ Having your Zodiac escorted into Stanley Harbour by Commerson's dolphins, known locally as 'puffing pigs' (p45)

■ Observing feeding time for the huge but downy chicks of the wandering albatross (p147)

■ Admiring rockhopper penguins – the clockwork-toy punks of the penguin world (p48)

■ Spotting (but keeping clear of) a massive male southern sea lion, with its solid neck and lion-like mane, basking on a beach (p43)

Falkland Islands Museum (www.falklands-museum.com) A developing website about the museum and associated historical sites.

Falkland Islands News Network (www.falklandnews.com) Covers the local news from the Falklands and has links to many other interesting Falklands-related sites.

Falkland Islands Tourist Board (FITB; www.tourism.org.fk) Information about Stanley and the islands, including a comprehensive list of cruise operators and information on the LanChile and Royal Air Force (RAF) flights.

Horizon (www.horizon.co.fk) The Falklands Internet service provider's site includes webcam views of Stanley Harbour and looking down Ross Rd, in case you want to check what the Falklands look like right now.

International Penguin Conservation Work Groups (www.seabirds.org) Includes a useful summary of Falklands birds and other wildlife, with pictures and text.

MercoPress (www.falklands.com) The website of the news agency operating from Montevideo for the southern part of South America and the South Atlantic has news on the Falklands and South Georgia in both English and Spanish.

South Georgia

Since it's virtually uninhabited, the Internet coverage of South Georgia is even more amazing than that of the Falklands.

British Antarctic Survey (BAS; www.antarctica.ac.uk) The BAS operates the two South Georgia research stations, although much of the information on its site has been superseded by the government site.

Foreign & Commonwealth Office (www.fco.gov.uk) Responsible for keeping an eye on Britain's slowly withering collection of colonies, the FCO administers the British Overseas Territories, which include South Georgia.

Government of South Georgia & South Sandwich Islands (www.sgisland.org) A comprehensive site about all aspects of the islands.

International Association of Antarctica Tour Operators (IAATO; www.iaato.org) The industry-sponsored IAATO develops voluntary guidelines for Antarctic tourist and cruise operators.

James Caird Society (www.jamescairdsociety.com) One of the best Shackleton groups has a site loaded with Shackleton info. The site is named after the open boat that carried Shackleton from Elephant Island to South Georgia.

South Georgia Island (www.sgisland.org) Has lots of information about the island and links to other sites. It's a Project Atlantis research project funded by the University of Dundee.

Itineraries

CLASSIC ROUTES

FALKLANDS ISLAND HOPPING

Two Weeks / Stanley, Off-Shore Island & A Stay in Camp

Each of the smaller offshore islands has its own distinct flavour, so from Stanley you could island hop for about a couple of weeks. Start on **Sea Lion Island** (p103), which is particularly popular because of its varied wildlife. On **New Island** (p136) you could investigate the strange story of Captain Charles Barnard, a famous castaway, while **Westpoint Island** (p133) has penguin and albatross colonies. Visit **Carcass Island** (p129) for a taste of family life on an authentic settlement. A couple of nights on **Saunders Island** (p126) will give you time to stay at the remote Portacabin on The Neck and spend some time watching the albatrosses. Or there's **Pebble Island** (p123), with penguins, cormorants and wreckage from the Falklands War. Back in **Stanley** (p66), take time to explore the capital's **Maritime History Trail** (p72) and make a day trip out to **Volunteer Beach** (p92). To really explore camp it's an easy drive from Stanley past Mt Pleasant Airport to **Darwin** (p98) and **Goose Green** (p98), site of the most bitter fighting of the Falklands War. From here you can strike out to **Lafonia** (p99) or **San Carlos** (p96), one of the two landing beaches for the British forces during the war.

Spend a week or so island hopping, then relax in Stanley for a few days, enjoying some easy day trips from the capital.

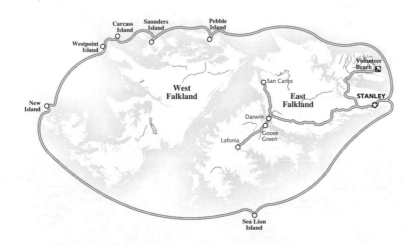

CLASSIC CRUISE

Two Weeks / Ushuaia to Ushuaia

Departing Ushuaia (Argentina) in the late afternoon, there are typically two nights at sea before arriving at one of the smaller islands of the Falklands on the second morning. **Carcass Island** (p129) and **Westpoint Island** (p133), off the northwest corner of West Falkland, and **Sea Lion Island** (p103), off the southeast corner of East Falkland, are especially popular with cruise companies. Alternatively, a company may try to land on a relatively inaccessible island. The **Jason Islands** (p139) are a good example of islands that are very difficult to get to if you're not travelling by sea.

Some cruise companies might include a second stop on a smaller offshore island, but the usual pattern is to travel overnight to arrive in **Stanley** (p66) in the morning for a day in the capital. This allows time for a look around the town, perhaps a bus trip out to **Gypsy Cove** (p84) and a visit to a Stanley pub before returning to the ship in the late afternoon.

From Stanley there are then two days at sea before arriving at South Georgia. Once there, the next four or five days will be spent visiting sites along the coast, usually making two landings per day. **Grytviken** (p149), with its whaling history, and attractions such as **South Georgia Museum** (p150) and the King Edward Point **research base** (p153), will always be on the itinerary. Other possibilities include the **Bay of Isles** (p155), the huge population of king penguins at **Salisbury Plain** (p156) and the wandering albatross colony on **Albatross Islet** (p156). A visit to **Stromness** (p158), where Shackleton concluded his crossing of the island, is always popular. **Ocean Harbour** (p159), **St Andrew's Bay** (p159), **Royal Bay** (p159) and **Gold Harbour** (p159) are possible stops along the north coast. Less frequently, ships make a complete circumnavigation of the island and visit bays along the wilder south coast. Finally there are four or five days at sea en route back to Ushuaia.

Experience a circumnavigation of South Georgia and the Falklands. Your route will vary depending on the cruise company you use and the weather, but it will take up to two weeks.

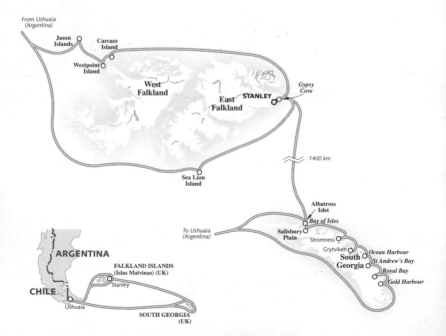

The Author

TONY WHEELER

Tony and Maureen Wheeler's Asia overland trip in 1972 led to *Across Asia on the Cheap*, the very first Lonely Planet guidebook. Over the years Tony has written or contributed substantially to nearly 40 books from Lonely Planet, including the first guide to newly independent East Timor. A visit to Antarctica in the mid-1990s sparked Tony's interest in South Georgia, but the Falklands – with its curious blend of end-of-the-world isolation and end-of-the-empire history – had always been on his 'must visit' list.

My Favourite Trip

From the moment my LanChile flight descended over the two main islands of the Falklands – the country below cut with that hyper-realistic detail which always reminds me of either Antarctica or Tibet – I was entranced. Later that afternoon in Stanley (p66) I spent hours wandering around photographing those brightly painted houses, each of them straight out of some child's paintbox.

My favourite moments in the Falklands were those wonderful moments of isolation, when the world is just you and a thousand birds. Saunders Island (p126) provided the best day of my Falklands stay. I was dropped off at the Portakabin, right by the penguin-populated isthmus accurately known as The Neck. That afternoon I walked the 8km along the coast down to the western end of the island. I was dive-bombed by skuas at one point and sat watching the elephant seals at another. By the time I'd walked another 8km back to The Neck, the afternoon was drawing to a close and I'd seen absolutely nobody all day. I climbed up to the east of The Neck to check out the rockhopper penguins and the black-browed albatross chicks (looking far too big for their nests). Finally I made my way back to the Portakabin as the sun set, cooked up a pleasant meal, which I enjoyed with half a bottle of very drinkable red Chilean wine, and sat there wondering could life be any better?

South Georgia (p143) also exceeded expectations. Of course, the scenery was magnificent, the sheer numbers of seals and penguins were mind-blowing and the abandoned whaling stations were fascinating, but it was an attempt to follow Shackleton's heroic walk across the island that topped the bill.

Snapshot

Surrounded by the South Atlantic Ocean and centuries of controversy, the Falkland Islands lie some 500km east of the South American mainland. The islands support a permanent nonmilitary population of about 2500, most of them in the capital, Stanley. The remainder live on widely dispersed sheep stations in camp.

For the steadily increasing flow of visitors to the Falklands the big attraction is wildlife. The islands' wildlife may not be hugely varied – there are no land mammals and just 60-odd breeding bird species – but it's spectacular. Bird colonies, whether they're gentoo penguins, king cormorants or black-browed albatrosses, are often huge and for some species the Falklands have a disproportionate share of the worldwide population.

Add enormous elephant seals, dolphins, increasing numbers of whales and a number of endemic bird species, and it's easy to see why the Falklands attract so many visitors interested in wildlife. Many, but not all, of the islands' best wildlife sites are on offshore islands where sheep, rats and cats have not had the same impact they have had on the main islands. Rats and cats have completely eliminated some small ground-dwelling birds from the main islands, and for this reason it's on the smaller islands where you'll find most of the tourist accommodation. Some of the most interesting and remote islands have few or no visitor facilities and very difficult access, so opportunities to visit them are well worth jumping at.

The vegetation of the Falklands is remarkably uniform: grass, heath and shrubs are about as much natural vegetation as you'll find anywhere. The Falklands are not treeless but any trees you see have probably been introduced. Despite images of treeless flatness the Falklands are anything but uniform and boring. All of West Falkland and the northern half of East Falkland are distinctly mountainous. They may not be very high mountains, but they often feature impressive rocky ridges and spawn the Falklands' unusual 'stone runs'. In between the mountains there are some relatively short but beautiful rivers, home to pleasingly big sea trout. The coastlines are often spectacular, particularly along the west coast of West Falkland where the country has a tendency to end in high cliffs that simply plummet into the sea.

Ponds and lakes are such a feature of the Falklands' landscape that it's a little surprising to discover that in some places water can be a scarce resource, and that the islands' rainfall is actually comparatively low.

Another 1400km to the east lies the even more remote and lightly populated island of South Georgia. South of the Antarctic Convergence (the weather is far more brutal than in the Falklands) this is one of the most spectacular places on earth. Aptly described as looking like an Alpine mountain range rearing up out of the sea, South Georgia blends awesome scenery with an even greater density of wildlife, backed up by a series of fascinating, though rapidly decaying, abandoned whaling stations and close ties with the heroic adventures of Sir Ernest Shackleton.

FAST FACTS

Falkland Islands

Population – civilians: 2500

Population – military: 1000

Population – sheep: 700,000

Area: 12,173 sq km

Number of islands: 750

South Georgia

Population – people: 10-20

Population – penguins: 2-3 million

Area: 3755 sq km

Percentage of surface covered by glaciers: 57%

Whales killed 1904-66: 175,250

History

THE FALKLANDS

The Falklands were once part of the southern mega-continent Gondwana-land. Fossils dating back nearly 400 million years trace their relationship to Antarctica and the coast of Africa. This ancient connection with Africa is part of the reason for current gold exploration projects. If there's gold in Africa, why not in the Falklands too? Despite ample evidence written in stone, there's not a lot of Falklands prehistory and the islands remain pretty much a blank until the first explorers chanced by.

DISCOVERY & EXPLORATION

Patagonian Indians may have reached the Falklands in rudimentary canoes, but the islands were uninhabited when Europeans began to frequent the area in the late 17th century. The first sighting was probably by the Englishman John Davis on the *Desire* in 1592. Two years later Sir Richard Hawkins named the islands (if indeed he ever sighted them) Hawkins Maydenlande, the maiden being Queen Elizabeth I. Neither early visitor set foot on land; nor did the Dutchman Sebald de Weert, who made the first authenticated sighting in 1600.

Another Englishman, Captain John Strong of the *Welfare*, made the first landing near the site of Port Howard on West Falkland in 1690. Strong called the channel between the two major islands Falkland Sound after Viscount Falkland, later the First Lord of the Admiralty. In turn, Captain Woodes Rogers named the islands Falkland's Land after the channel in 1708 and John Byron named the whole group the Falkland Islands in 1765. French explorers followed the early English visitors, touching on outlying islands like Beauchêne and Sea Lion.

> Renaming Stanley as Puerto Argentina during the Argentine occupation did not go down well with the islanders.

EARLY SETTLEMENT

Although the English Lord Anson reached the Falklands in 1740 and suggested using it as a base for Pacific exploration, no European power established a settlement until the French explorer Louis-Antoine de Bougainville, in command of *L'Aigle* (the Eagle) and the *Sphinx*, sailed from the Channel port of St.-Malo in 1763. The St.-Malo connection led to the name Les Îles Malouines and, in turn, the Spanish derivation Islas Malvinas. On 5 April 1764 de Bougainville landed in Berkeley Sound, East Falkland, and built a garrison at Port Louis, disregarding the 1494 papal Treaty of Tordesillas, which had divided the New World between Spain and Portugal. A variety of place names in the Falklands come from de Bougainville's visit and his name pops up regularly in the South Pacific.

Eight months later, in January 1765, Captain John Byron arrived at Saunders Island with the *Tamar* and *Dolphin*, named the harbour Port Egmont, named the whole group the Falkland Islands and claimed it all for George III. He was unaware of the French settlement but rumours of

> Old Falkland Photos: A View of Life 1880-1940 was compiled by Shane Wolsey (1990) and has some intriguing old photographs, including a slightly worrying series on traditional lamb castration methods: the shepherds bit them off and spat them out.

400 Million Years Ago	1592
Earliest fossils formed in the Falklands	First sighting by European explorers

its existence soon reached England so, 12 months later in January 1766, a second British fleet – the frigate *Jason*, the sloop *Carcass* and the store ship *Experiment* – led by Captain John MacBride established a settlement at Port Egmont.

The years 1766 and 1767 were complicated ones for European diplomacy. In October 1766 the French agreed to sell the islands to the Spanish, although it took time for the news to filter back. Two months

HISTORY BOOKS

The Falklands

The History of the Falkland Islands by Mary Cawkell (2001) is a concise and fairly up-to-date summary of the islands' history.

Based on unpublished materials from Cambridge University archives and other sources, Patrick Armstrong's *Darwin's Desolate Islands: A Naturalist in the Falklands, 1833 and 1834* (1992) is of great historical interest.

Charles H Barnard's misadventures as a castaway are incorporated in the story of *The Wreck of the Isabella* by David Miller. It was the wreck of this British ship, en route from Australia to England, which led to all Barnard's problems. A shorter account of Barnard's Falklands marooning is given in *Castaway in Paradise* (1998) by James C Simmons, which includes Barnard, along with a number of other famous castaways.

French explorer Louis de Freycinet's shipwreck of the *l'Uranie* in 1820 was another well-documented Falklands shipwreck. Although de Freycinet's official report of the mishap makes interesting reading the account by his wife, Rose Marie Pinon de Freycinet, who was smuggled on board his ship just before departure, is most unusual. It appeared in French only in 1927 and an English translation as *A Woman of Courage: The Journal of Rose de Freycinet on Her Voyage Around the World, 1817–1820* did not appear until 1996.

Condemned at Stanley by John Smith (1986) is a handy booklet covering the shipwrecks at Stanley. Unfortunately it's out of print.

Falklands War

There have been many books on the Falklands War, some of them concentrating on particular battles or on ships, aircraft types, weapons or military groups. *74 Days: An Islander's Diary of the Falklands Occupation* by John Smith (1984) is an account of the war from the civilian perspective. It's out of print.

South Georgia

The Island of South Georgia by Robert Headland (1984) is the definitive study of the island's history, geography, exploration and natural history. As well as extensive coverage of the whaling and sealing industries, there is also a detailed history of the 1982 conflict during which the author was captured by the Argentines. As the island's deputy postmaster he had a particular interest in its postage stamps. The book also analyses every surveying expedition and year by year, species by species, records the 175,250 whales caught from South Georgia. Reprinted as a paperback in 1992, it's now out of print.

Log Book for Grace: Whaling Brig Daisy 1912–13 by Robert Cushman Murphy (1947) is an account of one of the last of the old-time sealing expeditions with extensive ornithological studies and material on life ashore on South Georgia. There was also an illustrated edition titled *A Dead Whale or a Stove Boat: Cruise of Daisy in the Atlantic Ocean; June 1912 to May 1913* (1967).

1675	1690
First sighting of South Georgia Island	First landing on the Falklands by European explorer

later MacBride chanced upon the Port Louis settlement and told the French to pack up and depart since they were on British territory, ignoring the fact that the French had claimed the Falklands and planted their settlement almost a year earlier than any British claim and nearly two years before the first British settlement. The French ignored him but, in early 1767, Port Louis was transferred from French to Spanish hands, the settlement became Puerto de la Soledad and the islands became Islas Malvinas.

Place Names of the Falkland Islands by Richard Munro (1998) analyses the origin of place names around the Falklands.

Captain Hunt from the *Tamar* was now in command of the British settlement in Port Egmont and, in September 1769, met a Spanish vessel sailing out of Puerto de la Soledad. This was no doubt something of a surprise to the British, who thought it was the French they had told to get out. The Spanish curtly pointed out that they'd paid good money, £25,000 of it, to buy the islands from the French and suggested that the British depart instead. In 1770, 1600 Spaniards arrived in the Falklands – or Islas Malvinas, depending upon which way you look at it – confirming that this was no empty threat. The small British group decided that retreating to England was the best decision after all. Threats and counter threats almost led to war but, in 1771, the situation was resolved: the Spanish retained Puerto de la Soledad and the British were allowed to re-establish themselves at Port Egmont. It was a short stay for the British; in 1774, without any outside persuasion, they abandoned the small colony. The reasons were probably purely economic, but they left a plaque as a sign that they still claimed the settlement and might return.

The intriguing story of Charles H Barnard's period as a castaway on New Island, off the west coast of West Falkland, from 1813 to 1814, is documented in his own account *Marooned: Being a Narrative of the Sufferings and Adventures of Captain Charles H Barnard*.

For over 30 years the Spanish had Islas Malvinas to themselves – apart from steadily increasing visits by whalers, sealers and wayward explorers. In 1811 the Spanish, facing quite enough difficulties with unruly colonies in Latin America, abandoned what had become a very secure penal colony and from then until 1820 there was no official control over the islands. In the early 1820s the United Provinces of the River Plate, later to become Argentina, dealt itself into the game when it sent a military governor to assert its claim as successor to Spain. Later, the naturalised Buenos Aires entrepreneur Louis Vernet initiated a project to monitor uncontrolled sealers and exploit local fur seal populations in an ostensibly sustainable manner, and to tame the numerous feral cattle and horses that had multiplied on the islands since the Spanish departure. By 1828 Vernet had established a variety of settlements on the islands and was appointed governor.

THE BRITISH TAKEOVER

Vernet's seizure of three American sealers triggered reprisals from hot-headed US naval officer Silas Duncan of the USS *Lexington*, who thoroughly wrecked the Puerto de la Soledad settlement in 1831. At that time the settlement was under the command of Matthew Brisbane who, although he was British, had been appointed by Vernet. Before arriving in the Falklands, Brisbane had sailed with Antarctic sealing captain and explorer James Weddell on some of his pioneering voyages. Duncan shipped him off to Montevideo having announced that the Falklands no longer belonged to anybody and, as far as he was concerned, sealers could do whatever they wanted. The Argentines sent another governor

For information on the islands' history and a lot more, go to the History of the Falkland Islands website at www.history.horizon .co.fk.

1764	1766
French explorer de Bougainville establishes Port Louis	French agree to sell the islands to the Spanish

Darwin left his name on the East Falkland settlement but said that 'the whole landscape has an air of desolation'.

in 1832, who was promptly murdered by mutineers, and in December of that year – after an absence of nearly half a century – the British sailed back into the picture.

Captain John James Onslow on HMS *Clio* re-established the British presence at Port Egmont. In early 1833 he sailed into Berkeley Sound and told José Maria Pinedo, the new Spanish commander at Puerto de la Soledad, that Islas Malvinas were, once again, the Falklands and he should head home to Buenos Aires. After the American depredations of 1831, the enforced departure of Brisbane and the murder of his successor, Puerto de la Soledad was a shambles and Pinedo was probably only too happy to depart. (Vernet, however, pursued claims for property damages in British courts for nearly 30 years, with little success.)

Onslow didn't hang around either, leaving a token force to welcome Charles Darwin and Captain Robert FitzRoy when they visited the islands from March 1833 on HMS *Beagle*. FitzRoy, who later became governor of New Zealand, has a river, a port and a settlement named after him. Despite the British claim, the new Puerto de la Soledad commander was none other than Vernet's man Brisbane, but he was only in control from April to August 1833 before being killed by more mutinous gauchos. The British, chancing by again, arrested the gauchos and left the first officer of HMS *Challenger* and a ship's crew in command.

By the late 19th century the population of the Falklands was approaching 2000.

Real British control came with the arrival of Lieutenant Governor Richard Moody on the *Hebe* in January 1842, but the decision was soon made to abandon Puerto de la Soledad/Port Louis and establish a new settlement at Stanley. In 1844 the first wooden cottages – one of which still stands – were erected and in 1845 Stanley officially became the capital, taking its name from Edward Stanley the 14th Earl of Derby and the Secretary of State for the Colonies.

DECIMATING THE WILDLIFE

While the British, the French, the Spanish and the Argentines squabbled about who owned the Falklands another group got into the more serious business of wiping out the wildlife. Reports from early explorers about the inexhaustible numbers of whales, seals and penguins soon brought men who would prove that inexhaustible was the wrong word.

Whalers headed for the colder waters further south, but the Falklands were an ideal supply base where geese, penguins and their eggs could be gathered to feed ships' crews. Horses and cattle were released on the islands to provide a ready supply of meat. In between hunting for whales, seals could also be killed for their oil, a process which required no great skill: you simply walked up to the animal and clubbed it to death. Fur seals were massacred for their fine fur with ships carrying off more than 10,000 pelts at a time. By the mid-1800s fur seals and elephant seals had virtually disappeared, so attention turned to sea lions; when they became scarce even penguins were fair game. Rendering down eight rockhopper penguins would make a gallon of penguin oil and, in one brief period in the 1860s, 60,000 gallons of oil were shipped out of Stanley – half a million penguins' worth.

The penguin business finally dried up in the 1880s. An attempt to run a whaling station on New Island in the Falklands folded in 1916 (South Georgia was much more successful), but a final misguided attempt to exploit seals – there weren't enough left to be worth exploiting – ran from 1950 to 1953 at Port Albemarle on West Falkland.

From 1848 the California Gold Rush prompted a shipping boom around the southern end of South America as ships shuttled back and forth to the west coast gold fields. Many vessels ran into difficulties (or something harder) rounding Cape Horn and Stanley became the repair centre for troubled ships. It was a seller's market and the Falklands became notorious for leisurely work practices and inflated bills. Over-expensive ship repairs didn't make for a solid long-term economy, but in the mid-19th century sheep began to replace cattle and wool became an important export commodity. Samuel Lafone, an Englishman from Montevideo, was given the first large land grant in 1846, but by 1849 he was heavily in debt and, in 1851, he was taken over by the Falkland Islands Company. The FIC quickly became the islands' largest landholder, owning half the land and dominating the local economy for nearly a century. By the 1870s all other available pastoral land was held in extensive holdings by immigrant entrepreneurs.

English and Scottish immigrants augmented the early population of stranded mariners and holdover gauchos from the Vernet era. Roughly half resided in the new capital and port of Stanley, while the remainder became resident labourers on large sheep stations resembling those in Australia.

A severe lack of trees or other building materials (the local clay doesn't make very good bricks) has always tested Falklands builders. Local ingenuity has found its way around the problem with galvanized iron sheeting (known locally as 'wriggly tin') and the recycling of old ships: even Isambard Kingdom Brunel's pioneering iron steamship the SS Great Britain was turned into a storage hulk after it ended its days in the Falklands.

THE FALKLANDS IN A TIME WARP

The sheep business was very successful and spawned other sheep-based industries on the South American continent. Nothing stood in the way of sheep: the warrah, the island's only native mammal, was wiped out; bounties were placed on birds that were felt to be a threat to sheep; and the native tussock grass was soon devastated by overgrazing. By the late 1800s the island's ecology was tottering and the area of exhausted land needed to sustain each sheep was growing. The deliberate introduction of cats and the accidental introduction of rats devastated small bird populations.

Land use may have brought problems but so did land ownership. From the 1870s through to the 1970s the islands were a near-feudal society with landowners in London – absentee landlords, often exhibiting all the bad qualities those words imply – caring only about the bottom line while the islanders were essentially poorly paid labourers. Since all the land had been parcelled out in the early days of British rule there was no way for islanders to acquire any. Even publicly owned land was minimal; apart from a few outlying islands, the Falklands today are almost devoid of parks and reserves.

Things started to change in the late 1970s when the sale and subdivision of large landholdings was encouraged in order to slow high rates of emigration. Since 1982 change has become even more rapid. Prior to the Falklands War there were only about 35 farms in the whole country, which was suffering a steady population decline. Now there are about 90 owner-occupied farms averaging about 12,000 hectares. Unfortunately, encouraging local farm ownership coincided with a steep and long term drop in the price of wool, so many of the new Falkland land owners have been finding life very difficult. Prior to the war, the seas around the Falklands were unpoliced and open to any fishing fleets that cared to drop their nets. The subsequent expansion of fishing zones has revolutionised

Corrals & Cauchos by Joan Spruce (1992) tells the story of the gaucho era in the Falklands, and explains why so many Spanish words have crept onto Falklands maps and into the islands' vocabulary. It also details where to find the best examples of stone cattle corrals.

1775	1786
Captain James Cook makes first landing on South Georgia	First sealing expedition to South Georgia

NAVAL BATTLES

The Falklands played a part in naval encounters during both world wars. In late 1914, off the coast of Chile, Admiral Graf von Spee's German fleet engaged three British ships under the command of Sir Christopher Cradock and sent HMS *Monmouth* (with Sir Christopher aboard) and HMS *Good Hope* to the bottom with no survivors. Just over a month later, on 8 December 1914, the tables were dramatically turned in the Battle of the Falklands.

Von Spee decided to attack the Falklands on his way back to Germany. He was, however, unaware that a British fleet under Vice Admiral Sir Frederick Doveton Sturdee was waiting for him with the battle cruisers *Invincible* and *Inflexible*, the armoured cruisers *Carnarvon*, *Cornwall* and *Kent*, the light cruisers *Bristol* and *Glasgow* (the only survivor from the earlier encounter) and sundry support vessels. By the time the German admiral realised they were there and turned tail it was too late. His flagship *Scharnhorst* went down with 600 men, including von Spee and his two sons. The *Gneisenau*, *Leipzig* and *Nurnberg* soon followed. In all, 1800 men lost their lives – about twice the death toll from the 1982 Falklands War. The one surviving German ship, the *Dresden*, was cornered by the *Glasgow*, *Kent* and *Orama* and scuttled on 14 March 1915 at Juan Fernandez Island (now Robinson Crusoe Island), off the coast of Chile. The Battle of the Falklands was the last straightforward naval battle slugged out by ships firing at each other at long range; in future, mines, torpedoes and aircraft would come in to the picture.

With WWII barely under way a British fleet bottled up the German pocket battleship *(panzerschiffe)*, *Admiral Graf Spee*, at Montevideo in Uruguay. The *Graf Spee* had taken 20 hits from the British ships and 36 of the crew were killed. The badly damaged vessel limped out to sea with a skeleton crew and was scuttled in the River Plate. Three days later Captain Hans Langsdorff, the *Graf Spee*'s commander, committed suicide in Buenos Aires, lying on his ship's battle flag.

the economy. More recently, oil exploration has found preliminary indications, but so far not commercial quantities, of offshore petroleum. Some gold exploration has also been going on.

During these long years when time stood still, the two world wars were almost the only interruptions. In WWI the Battle of the Falkland Islands was fought southeast of Stanley and in WWII Stanley was the starting point for the Battle of the River Plate.

THE FALKLANDS WAR

Battle for the Falklands by Max Hastings and Simon Jenkins (1983) is one of the best of the books on the war. Max Hastings was in the Falklands with the British forces – he strolled into Stanley ahead of the Argentine surrender and had already knocked back a double whisky at the Upland Goose before the British troops marched in.

Although Argentina has persistently affirmed its claims to the Falklands since 1833, successive British governments never publicly acknowledged their seriousness. This changed in the late 1960s when the Foreign & Commonwealth Office (FCO) began to see the islands as politically burdensome and as an uneconomic anachronism. The FCO and the Argentine military government reached a communications agreement in 1971 giving Argentina a significant voice in matters affecting Falklands transportation, fuel supplies, shipping and even immigration.

Islanders and their supporters saw the Argentine presence as an ominous development. There had been some curious events in the decades prior to the invasion. In 1964 an Argentine Cessna landed on the Stanley racecourse, the Falklands having no airport at the time. The pilot emerged from his light aircraft, planted an Argentine flag, handed over a letter claiming the islands were Argentine, jumped back in his plane and flew home. Having sized up the aviation possibilities of the racecourse,

1811	1820
Spanish abandon Puerto de la Soledad and depart from the Falklands	Argentina sends military governor to take over Spanish claim

in 1966 a group of 20 right-wingers hijacked an Aerolineas Argentinas DC-4 for a repeat performance. This time they grabbed four islanders as hostages, announced they would die rather than surrender and held out until the next day when they changed their minds about death and surrendered to an island priest. A third unofficial flight followed in 1968.

Concerned about Argentina's chronic instability, Falkland Islanders suspected the FCO of secretly selling out to Argentina. Negotiations on the Falklands' situation dragged on for over a decade while Argentina's brutal internal Dirty War gave Falkland Islanders good reason to fear their increasing presence. In 1977 the Argentines even gifted the reluctant islanders with a Trojan horse in the shape of an airport; it was to play an important part in the Falklands War. What was too fast for the islanders was too slow for General Leopoldo Galtieri's desperate military government; his troops invaded the lightly defended islands on 2 April 1982.

Argentines were fed up with the corruption, economic chaos and totalitarian ruthlessness of Galtieri's disintegrating regime, but his seizure of Islas Malvinas briefly united the country and made him an ephemeral hero. Galtieri and his advisers did not anticipate that British Prime Minister Margaret Thatcher, herself in precarious political circumstances, would respond so decisively. In a struggle whose loser would not survive politically, Argentina sought diplomatic approval of the *fait accompli*, while the British organised a naval task force to recover the lost territory.

The military outcome was one-sided, despite substantial British naval losses, as experienced British troops landed on the west coast of East Falkland and routed the ill-trained and poorly supplied Argentine conscripts. The most serious fighting took place at Goose Green and in the assaults on the highpoints overlooking Stanley. The Argentine surrender averted the destruction of the capital.

The Cost

The cost of the Falklands War was horrendous. The Argentines lost more than 700 military personnel, half of them from the *General Belgrano*, while the British lost 252 plus three civilians. There were 12,978 Argentine prisoners of war, against just one British. The Argentines lost more than 100 aircraft and helicopters, while the British lost 10 Harriers and at least 24 helicopters. Including the *Belgrano*, the Argentines lost five ships and the British lost six, with 10 more seriously damaged. The bill ran into the billions of US dollars.

It was a finely balanced war with severely constrained resources on both sides. The British won because the Argentine leadership was hopeless. They made no attempt to harass the British landings and advance, and, until the final assaults on the high ground around Stanley, the only pitched battle was at Goose Green. The British forces were still outnumbered two to one when they took Stanley. The Argentine air force was heroic but their navy played little part, and their unmotivated and poorly trained conscript army faced a highly trained and highly motivated force.

In fact, the war should never have happened. The Argentines certainly would not have invaded if they thought the British really cared about the Falklands or if they had suspected the response would have been so resolute. Galtieri desperately needed some distraction from the chaos he

Falkland Island Shores by Ewen Southby-Tailyour (1985) is by a Royal Marine officer posted to the Falklands prior to the war. After the war his yachting guide, supplemented with material from his experiences during the military campaign, was finally published.

The Falklands War 1982 by Martin Middlebrook (1985) covers the Falklands War in fairly detailed fashion as part of the 'Classic Military History' series.

1831	1832
US Navy officer trashes Puerto de la Soledad	British return to Falklands and re-establish Port Egmont settlement

---

THE 77-DAY WAR

2 February The British Prime Minister, Margaret Thatcher, says 75 Royal Marines in Stanley are enough to keep the Argentines at bay.

18 March An Argentine scrap-metal dealer Constantine Davidoff lands at Leith on South Georgia with 40 men; this intrusion into British sovereignty turned out to be a forewarning of later events.

26–9 March UK intelligence warns that an Argentine invasion is imminent, but the warning is ignored by the British government.

2 April Argentina invades the Falklands.

3 April The British government announces that a task force is to be sent to reclaim the islands. The UN demands that Argentina withdraws.

4–5 April The first ships set out from Britain.

7 April The British government announces a 200-mile Maritime Exclusion Zone. Any ship entering the exclusion zone is liable to be attacked.

9–19 April Alexander Haig, US Secretary of State, tries mediation.

25 April Britain retakes South Georgia.

30 April Ronald Reagan announces US support of the UK position on the Falklands. The Total Exclusion Zone, targeting aircraft as well, comes into force.

1 May A Royal Air Force (RAF) Vulcan long-range bomber attacks Stanley Airport. This is followed by attacks on Argentine strongholds by carrier-borne Harriers.

2 May The Argentine flagship, *General Belgrano*, is sunk by a torpedo from the nuclear submarine HMS *Conqueror*. More than 350 Argentine sailors die, most of them conscripts. The *Belgrano* is well outside the exclusion zone when she is torpedoed. The British point out that the small print says that anything inside the exclusion zone can be sunk, no questions asked, and anything outside can be sunk if they feel it poses a threat. An Argentine spokesman comments, 'Britain may no longer rule the waves but it still waives the rules'. In fact, the real threat is thought to be the aircraft carrier *Veinticinco de Mayo*, which had also served in WWII as HMS *Venerable*. The sinking of the *Belgrano* sidelines the Argentine navy for the rest of the war.

---

had created at home. The cost in lives for the British was much lower than in Malaya, where they lost 525, or in Korea, where they lost 537, or even in Northern Ireland where British army losses are around 500. However, the cost in Argentine lives was enormous. In comparison, less than 300 Americans were lost in the 1991 Gulf War with Iraq and even fewer in the initial stages of the next Iraq invasion. In relation to the Falklands' population of not much more than 2000 the death toll was horrendous.

The USS *Phoenix* survived the Japanese attack on Pearl Harbor only to be sunk 40 years later by a nuclear submarine. Renamed the *General Belgrano* she was the flagship of the Argentine navy, sent to the bottom by a torpedo from the British nuclear sub HMS *Conqueror*.

POSTWAR POLITICS & DEVELOPMENT

Margaret Thatcher, Argentina and the Falklands all got some good out of the Falklands War. Thatcher got re-elected and went on to become Britain's longest-term prime minister. The Argentines got rid of their nasty military dictatorship and moved on to a succession of equally inefficient and corrupt, although far less brutal, civilian governments. It was the Falklands that really won. Suddenly everybody could pinpoint the Falklands on the map, the old sheepocracy got their marching orders, the new economic zones brought in a steady stream of fishing licence money and the boom in Antarctic cruises put the islands on the tourist map. From being a colonial backwater with a declining population and a struggling economy, Stanley was transformed into a South Atlantic boom town. Nevertheless, relations with Argentina are still distinctly cool and

1833	1844
British kick out Spanish and take over Puerto de la Soledad	British abandon Puerto de la Soledad and establish Stanley as new capital

4 May An Argentine Exocet missile sinks the Type 42 destroyer HMS *Sheffield*. Ironically, the Argentines also have Type 42 destroyers, including one that they have not yet paid for. The first Harrier is also shot down by the Argentines.
7 May The exclusion zone is extended to 12 miles from the Argentine coast.
15 May Pebble Island is raided by the SAS, who destroy all the Argentine aircraft on the island.
19 May The UN gives up on a negotiated settlement.
21 May British troops successfully land on East Falklands at Ajax Bay, San Carlos and Port San Carlos, but an Argentine air assault commences on the fleet crowded into San Carlos Water. The frigate HMS *Ardent* is sunk, but the Argentine aircraft come in so low that many of their bombs do not explode.
23 May The frigate HMS *Antelope* is sunk.
25 May The destroyer HMS *Coventry* and the container ship *Atlantic Conveyor* are sunk by the Argentines. The *Atlantic Conveyor* was loaded with helicopters intended to ferry the British landing force forward for the assault on Stanley. The loss of ships is a major blow to the British forces, but the Argentines have lost more than a third of their fighter force and many of their best pilots.
27 May British forces set out south across East Falkland for Goose Green and east to Stanley. Deprived of all but one of the helicopters from the *Atlantic Conveyor* the British troops have to 'yomp' – march across the inhospitable terrain.
28 May Goose Green falls after one of the most hard-fought engagements of the war.
31 May British forces helicopter ahead to take Mt Kent by night. They now overlook Stanley.
4 June Britain vetoes the Panamanian–Spanish cease-fire resolution at the UN.
8 June An attempt to speed the British advance by landing troops at Fitzroy, 25km southwest of Stanley, ends in disaster when the landing ships *Sir Galahad* and *Sir Tristram* are bombed and 50 men are killed.
11 June The battle for Stanley begins. Mt Longdon, Mt Harriet and Two Sisters are taken.
13 June The British take Mt Tumbledown and Wireless Ridge. They now control all the high ground overlooking Stanley.
14 June Argentine forces surrender and the Falklands War is over.
17 June Argentine prisoners of war burn down the Globe Store, one of Stanley's historic old shops. More than 10,000 Argentine prisoners of war are returned to Argentina on the *Canberra* and the *Norland*. The remaining 593 prisoners, mainly officers and specialists, are sent back a month later.

many islanders remain deeply suspicious of Argentine motives; most trade with the South American continent goes via Chile.

In terms of international politics the Falklands remain a colonial anachronism. They are administered by a governor appointed by the Foreign & Commonwealth Office (FCO) in London. This governor is also the commissioner of South Georgia and the South Sandwich Islands. The present incumbent, since late 2002, is Howard Pearce. In local affairs the eight-member, elected Legislative Council (LegCo) exercises considerable power. Five of the eight members come from Stanley, while the remainder represent camp. Selected LegCo members advise the governor as part of the Executive Council (ExCo), which also includes the chief executive and the financial secretary.

Falklands or Malvinas by Conrado Etchebarne Bullrich (2000), president and founding member of Americanos del Sur, is published in English and tries to present an even-handed view of the Falklands dispute from the Argentine viewpoint.

SOUTH GEORGIA

DISCOVERY & EXPLORATION

London-born merchant Antoine de la Roche was probably the first to sight the island. In April 1675, while sailing from Lima to England, his ship was blown south as he rounded Cape Horn; he caught a glimpse of South Georgia's ice-covered mountains and actually took shelter in a bay

1848	1851
Stanley becomes a repair centre for troubled ships during California's Gold Rush	Falkland Islands Company moves to become biggest landowner

---

HMS COVENTRY

Hit by three bombs dropped by Argentine Skyhawks, the Type 42 destroyer HMS *Coventry* capsized and sank with the loss of 19 men. It went down about 15km off Pebble Island in about 100m of water. After the war a team of divers spent six months on the wreck. One theory for this protracted deep-water diving mission was that the *Coventry* should have sunk in a stable manner; the fact that it turned turtle before going down pointed up some serious design flaws, which the divers were investigating. A more colourful explanation was that the *Coventry* came straight to the Falklands from patrol in the Mediterranean, without time to stop in Britain en route to remove the nuclear depth charges it was carrying. These went to the bottom along with various NATO code books and, this explanation insists, the divers were retrieving the wayward weapons. For 20 years this was merely a wild rumour, but in late 2003 the British government admitted that ships did set out for the Falklands with nuclear weapons on board but, the Ministry of Defence claimed, they were transferred to other ships and returned to Britain before entering the war zone. Perhaps in another 20 years the real story will emerge.

---

for 14 days. It's thought the bay may have been Doubtful Bay or Drygalski Fjord near Cape Disappointment at the eastern end of the island. Unfortunately, the original records of la Roche's voyage have been lost and even the name of his ship is unknown, but it's likely that he made no attempt to land while he sheltered in the bay.

The island was seen again in 1756 by Spaniard Gregorio Jerez, sailing in *Leon*, a vessel chartered by French merchants; one of them, Nicholas-Pierre Guyot, recorded his impressions of the island and named it Île de Ste Pierre, Isla de San Pedro in Spanish. Guyot was later Louis-Antoine de Bougainville's second in command when he circumnavigated the world.

Captain James Cook made the first landing on 17 January 1775 at Possession Bay; he named it the Isle of Georgia after King George III and claimed the island in the name of his majesty. George Forster, one of the naturalists on board the *Resolution*, noted that the ceremony of taking possession of South Georgia involved firing several muskets into the air and that 'the barren rocks re-echoed to the sound, to the utter amazement of the seals and penguins, the inhabitants of these newly discovered dominions.'

Although Cook's description of South Georgia was somewhat less than glowing ('savage and horrible') his account, when published in 1777, included descriptions of fur seals, which set off a stampede of sealers.

Cast-iron pots called trypots were used for boiling down penguins – a number of them can be seen on Falkland beaches, as can the stone corrals where the hapless penguins were herded.

SEALING

British sealers began arriving in 1786, American sealers soon followed and within five years there were more than 100 ships in the Southern Ocean taking fur seal skins and elephant seal oil. The British sealer *Ann* took 3000 barrels of elephant seal oil and 50,000 fur seal skins from South Georgia in 1792–93. In that same season, an American sealer hit upon the idea of taking fur seal skins to the market in China, circumnavigating the globe in the process.

South Georgia's rock-filled waters proved treacherous for ships, and many were wrecked or sank near the island. These include: *Sally* (1796),

---

1904

Grytviken whaling station established

1914

Battle of the Falklands decimates German naval fleet

Regulator (1799), *Canada* (c 1800), *Earl Spencer* (c 1801), *Admiral Colpoys* (1817), *Hope* (1829), *Fridtjof Nansen* (1906) and *Ernesto Tornquist* (1950).

An amazing 57,000 fur seal skins were taken in 1800–02 by American sealer Edmund Fanning, in what was probably the most profitable sealing voyage ever made to South Georgia. Sixteen other British and US sealers worked at South Georgia that season but by 1831, the American ship *Pacific*, landing a sealing gang for eight months, found that fur seals were scarce. As late as 1909, when the American ship *Daisy* stayed for five months in what was probably the last fur-sealing visit, only 170 fur seals could be found.

Elephant seals were slaughtered by the thousand for the oil rendered from their thick blubber. A large elephant seal yielded one 170L barrel of oil (though a big bull could produce double that), so the 15,000 barrels taken in 1877–78 by the American sealer *Trinity* show the huge number of seals that one ship could exterminate in a single year. By 1885–86, the American ship *Express* secured just two elephant seals and 123 'sea leopards' (probably Weddell seals), which produced only 60 barrels of oil.

WHALING

Whaling began in 1904, when the Compañia Argentina de Pesca, a Norwegian company based in Buenos Aires, established the first Antarctic whaling station at Grytviken. Using only one whale-catching ship, the Compañia took 183 whales in its first year. This modest start quickly grew into an enormous industry that generated millions of kröner for its Norwegian owners and marked the beginning of South Georgia's permanent occupation.

Eventually six shore stations were built – at Grytviken, Ocean Harbour, Leith Harbour, Husvik Harbour, Stromness Harbour and Prince Olav Harbour – plus an anchorage for floating factory ships at Godthul. Grytviken was the longest-lived, remaining open with a caretaker until 1971 although whaling actually ceased a year before it did at Leith Harbour. Godthul ran from 1908 to 1917 and from 1922 to 1929. Ocean Harbour, which opened in 1909, closed in 1920. Leith Harbour opened in 1909, closed for a year in 1933 and again during WWII, and closed for good in 1965. Husvik Harbour operated from 1910 to 1931 and again from 1945 to 1960, missing the 1957–58 season. Stromness Harbour operated from 1912 to 1931 and then became a repair yard until it closed in 1961. Prince Olav Harbour operated from 1917 to 1931.

Looking at two seasons in the 1920s it's easy to understand why whales are so scarce today. In the 1925–26 season the five shore stations, one factory ship and 23 whale-catching ships took 1855 blue whales, 5709 fin whales, 236 humpbacks, 13 sei whales and 12 sperm whales. The total catch made it a record year: 7825 whales, which produced 404,457 barrels of whale oil. During the 1926–27 season, the same number of catcher ships took 3689 blue whales (a record), 1144 fin whales, no humpbacks, 365 sei whales and 17 sperm whales. The total catch was 'only' 5215 whales, but they produced a then-record 417,292 barrels of oil. Nevertheless, of the total Antarctic whale catch land stations took only 10%.

In late 1920 Grytviken had its own little replay of the Russian revolution when the whalers, proclaiming themselves Bolsheviks, went out on

During 62 years of operation the South Georgia whaling stations caught more than 170,000 whales. The largest blue whale (of the 41,515 blue whales they butchered) was a 33.5m female, the largest animal ever recorded.

1920	1965
Whalers go on strike in South Georgia	Grytviken is last whaling station to close

strike. However, at this opportune moment, the Royal Navy cruiser HMS *Dartmouth* chanced by, the ringleaders were arrested and deported and the strike fizzled out. The Great Depression from 1929 proved fortuitous for the whales of Antarctica. Combined with a barely nascent realisation that controls were needed, it put the brakes on the booming business. By the 1931–32 season, the economic crisis and severe overproduction the season before forced Prince Olav and Stromness stations to close for good. Husvik also closed but reopened in 1945. Leith closed only for the 1932–33 season and Grytviken never closed.

By 1961–62, the Norwegian companies could no longer make a satisfactory profit. The Japanese took over the South Georgia whaling operations but also found it unprofitable and closed the last shore station, Grytviken, in 1965.

South Georgia's total whale catch from 1904 to 1966 included 41,515 blue whales, 87,555 fin whales, 26,754 humpbacks, 15,128 sei whales and 3716 sperm whales.

Elephant seals were also killed again during the whaling era. Their oil was mixed with inferior-quality whale oil to improve it. Grytviken was able to remain open longer than the other whaling stations in part because it processed elephant seals. From 1905 to 1964 498,870 seals (most of them elephant seals) were killed at South Georgia for their oil.

In the UK, Miles Apart (☎ 1638-577 627, fax 1628-577 874; www.sthelena.se/miles; 5 Harraton House, Exning, Newmarket, Suffolk CB8 7HF) is run by Ian and Alison Mathieson, and has an extensive selection of new and second-hand books about the Falklands, South Georgia and other islands of the South Atlantic.

SCIENCE & EXPLORATION

Science intruded on the 19th century sealing slaughter in 1882–83 when the German International Polar Year Expedition, part of a 12-country polar scientific blitz, set up a station for 13 months at Royal Bay on the southeast coast. Shackleton's connection with the island included his amazing cross-island trek and then his death at Grytviken six years later (see p145).

The *Discovery* investigations in the 1920s brought much additional knowledge of South Georgian waters, but the 1928–29 Kohl-Larsen expedition was the first real exploration of the interior since Shackleton's famous crossing. A serious survey of the interior did not take place until Duncan Carse's 1950s survey visits. (See p161 for Duncan Carse's extraordinary spell as an Antarctic Robinson Crusoe and his role as a radio-era 007.)

GOVERNMENT & POLITICS

In 1908, the British established the Dependencies of the Falkland Islands including South Georgia, the South Orkneys, the South Shetlands, the South Sandwich Islands and Graham Land on the Antarctic Peninsula. Until 1985 South Georgia was governed as part of the Falkland Islands Dependencies, but in that year it was separated from the Falklands to become part of the British Dependent Territory of South Georgia & the South Sandwich Islands (SGSSI). Nevertheless, government control and administration is still managed from Stanley and the island commissioner is also the governor of the Falkland Islands.

From 1908, when Britain formally annexed the island, until 1969 a full-time magistrate was resident at King Edward Point. From then until 1982 the British Antarctic Survey (BAS) was based at King Edward

1982	1982
Argentina invades Falklands, kicking off the brief Falklands War	The Falklands War takes more than 955 lives, including over 700 Argentines

SOUTH GEORGIA & THE FALKLANDS WAR

On 25 March 1982 the Argentine naval vessel *Bahía Paraíso*, later to become infamous for spilling fuel at Anvers Island off the Antarctic Peninsula, arrived at Leith Harbour. On 3 April *Bahía Paraíso*, *Guerrico* and their helicopters landed 200 Argentine forces at King Edward Point and after a two hour battle overpowered the 22 Royal Marines defenders. With the station scientists they were taken as prisoners to Argentina. Fifteen British researchers at four field stations were later relieved by the Royal Navy. Later that month British forces, in a side play to the Falklands War, retook South Georgia, sank the submarine *Santa Fé* and took 185 Argentines prisoner.

Point and its base commander also functioned as the magistrate. After the Falklands War in 1982 a British military garrison was based there and the officer commanding took on the magistrate's role. That ended in 2001 when the military force was withdrawn and new BAS base buildings were constructed.

During the period between 1982 and 2001 BAS personnel operated only on Bird Island and other field stations. In 2001 they returned to King Edward Point to once again manage the administrative roles as well as their scientific duties. The BAS station commander is also magistrate and BAS personnel wear the hats of harbour master, customs and immigration officer, postmaster and fisheries liaison officer.

1980s	1985
After the war, Stanley is transformed into a South Atlantic boom town	South Georgia becomes part of the British Dependent Territory of South Georgia & the South Sandwich Islands

The Culture

THE NATIONAL PSYCHE

Britain and Argentina – they're the two countries that bookend everything for the Falkland Islanders. The islanders look towards Britain and shy away from Argentina (the 'Argies' are viewed with deep suspicion, and discussions about restarting regular air connections between the Falklands and Argentina are treated with disdain by many members of the community).

Margaret Thatcher remains a national hero in the Falklands.

Of course a strong link with the 'Mother Country' and distrust of Argentina was the norm even before the Falklands War, but in many ways the war has made dramatic changes to the national psyche. For a start Falkland Islanders are much more outgoing, much more connected with the outside world and much wealthier. Prior to the war the Falkland Islands were slowly grinding to an economic halt. The sheep business was in steady economic decline and, in any case, the money had always been made in London, not Stanley. The unfortunate islanders were landless labourers, toiling for absentee landlords.

The sheep business is still pretty dire but it has been superseded by a number of other activities including fishing licences, which bring in the big bucks. Some Falkland Islanders have become very wealthy indeed and the money has trickled down almost everywhere. The Falklands are now much better known to the outside world, prompting a steady flow of visitors, and the regular air connections have made the outside world much more accessible to Falkland Islanders. Despite their suspicion, Falkland Islanders are more likely to jet across to the South American mainland on shopping trips or en route to Britain or other places overseas. Chile, however, has replaced Argentina as the important South American neighbour.

The Falklands by Tony Chater (1993) is written and photographed by a long-term Falkland Islands resident and part owner of New Island. An eclectic mix of local personalities, wildlife, shipwrecks and island life, it concludes with a lengthy section on life during the Argentine occupation.

Today's Falkland Islands is a much more cosmopolitan place than its pre-Falklands War predecessor but some big problems remain. Prior to the war there was concern about a declining population. Today, quite apart from the military contingent, there are even immigrants, mainly from St Helena, who do the work Falkland Islanders can no longer be bothered with. Although fears of a population decline may have been arrested, the growth is all in Stanley – it's a bigger problem than ever in camp. It takes less people to raise sheep and as a result the camp settlements are fading away. It's the same story everywhere and numbers are just a fraction of their level even five or 10 years ago.

LIFESTYLE

There are two lifestyles in the Falklands – life in Stanley and life in camp. Stanley today is not very different from a small town in Britain: there's everything from a library, a bank, a municipal swimming pool and a well-stocked supermarket to a choice of pubs, and restaurants with menus featuring the latest food fashions.

Check out the website of the Falklands' own R&B band, the Fighting Pig Band, at www.fighting pigband.com. The Fighting Pig Band reveals it can play 'Mustang Sally', but it won't.

Life in Stanley may have changed remarkably since the Falklands War but in camp everything still revolves around raising sheep. The sheep business may not be much of a money spinner – wool prices have been low for years and attempts to raise Falklands sheep for meat have never been successful – but it's still a major employer. However, shepherds no longer live in remote 'outside houses'; it's easier to zip out to inspect the flock by motorcycle; shearing is usually done by a visiting team; and commuting into Stanley by road or air is much quicker. As a result camp populations have plummeted and life in camp is no longer so totally isolated.

MIND YOUR MANNERS

The islanders are down-to-earth farming folk but there are some social pitfalls to beware of:

Ask Permission There's very little public land in the Falklands so walking almost anywhere means crossing somebody's land. Wherever possible ask permission first.

Be Careful about Argentina Even 20 years after the Falklands War the relationship with Argentina can still be, well, a minefield. Feel your way carefully before expressing strong opinions.

Leave the Gates Getting anywhere in camp inevitably involves a succession of opening and closing of gates. Make sure you always close the gate securely, unless it's already open – in which case leave it that way. Mastering the sometimes tricky 'fence' gates, which use a star picket or a pole to tension the fence, is a sure sign that you've served your camp apprenticeship.

No Shoes As in Japan, houses are shoe-free territory. It can be muddy outside so outdoor shoes are always removed at the front door. In places where unknowing outsiders may be regular visitors you may encounter warning signs, but whether it's signposted or not always take them off.

Sign the Book Every Falklands hotel, guesthouse, B&B or whatever has a visitors' book and not to sign it is unthinkable.

In fact the Falklands have a third lifestyle, the military one, sequestered away at Mt Pleasant. For most visitors the only sign of the military, apart from at arrival and departure, will be the throb of a passing helicopter or a glimpse of a Royal Air Force (RAF) aircraft roaring overhead.

POPULATION
The Falklands

The 1996 census recorded a Falklands population of 2564, three-quarters in Stanley and the remainder in camp (including nonmilitary personnel at Mt Pleasant). About 60% of the permanent residents are native-born, some tracing their ancestry back six or more generations. The great majority of the remainder are immigrants or temporary residents from the UK. Falkland Islanders' surnames hint at a variety of European backgrounds, but English is the language of the Falklands. A few people speak Spanish. The handful of South American immigrants are nearly all from Chile.

Because of the islands' isolation and small population, Falkland Islanders are proud of their versatility and adaptability. Falkland Islanders are extraordinarily hospitable, often welcoming visitors into their homes for 'smoko' (the traditional mid-morning tea or coffee break) or for a drink. This is especially true in camp, where visitors of any kind can be infrequent. When visiting people in camp, it is customary to bring a small gift – rum is a special favourite. Stanley's several pubs are popular meeting places.

A thousand or more British military personnel, commonly referred to as 'squaddies', reside at the Mt Pleasant airport complex. Civilian–military relations are generally cordial, if now rather distant. There are increasing numbers of professionals. In recent years there has been a large influx from St Helena, another British colony in the South Atlantic; many of these people work in Stanley's expanding tourist business in hotels and restaurants.

In the Falklands there are about 150 sheep for every person, including the military – which beats even sheep-saturated New Zealand where 60 million sheep computes to only 15 sheep per person.

Camp Census (May 2000)

	People	Sheep
East Falkland	213	374,350
West Falkland	129*	253,312
Outer Islands	29	42,143
Total	371	669,805

* Since the census the population in West Falkland has fallen to less than 100.

South Georgia

By the early 1800s it's probable that a number of sealers had over-wintered in South Georgia or even stayed for a year or more. The German International Polar Year Expedition also stayed for more than a year in 1882–83, but it was not until the establishment of the whaling station at Grytviken in 1904 that South Georgia had a real permanent population.

More whaling stations quickly followed Grytviken and a census in 1909 recorded a summer population of 720; 80% of them Norwegian, 93% of them Scandinavian. Only three of them were female and there was only one child. During the height of the whaling era the summer population of South Georgia could have been as high as 2000.

Today there's just the British Antarctic Survey (BAS) base at King Edward Point and a smaller outbase on Bird Island, along with the handful of people at Grytviken. Altogether the total summer population is perhaps 18, dropping to less than 10 in winter.

ECONOMY
The Falklands

After the shake up delivered by the Falklands War the real money started to come from fishing – a business that could easily fit the traditional Falklands pattern of overexploitation and decline. The sheep business is still the main employer, but its economic contribution is essentially negative; it costs more to raise the sheep than the £5 million they're sold for. Oil production could be a money spinner one day but nothing commercially exploitable has yet been found. The search for gold is a very low key activity. Tourism is still small scale and suffers from local ambivalence. There are real fears that tourism to this isolated part of the world could be fragile and easily damaged through overexploitation.

Like many small countries the Falklands produces some colourful postage stamps, but philately is in decline worldwide. Some local crafts, including high-quality knitwear, are sold to visitors.

Michael Mainwaring's *From the Falklands to Patagonia* (1983) is a worthy historical work on pioneer sheep farming in the South Atlantic, based on private correspondence.

SHEEP

For most of the past 150 years the Falklands have truly ridden on the sheep's back: a sheep even appears on the Falklands' flag. Sheep were introduced and farming developed from about 1850 on East Falkland and 1867 on West Falkland. By the end of the century numbers had peaked at 750,000 and have been in gradual decline ever since.

The predominant sheep breed is Corriedale but Polwarth, Romney, Cormo and Comeback sheep are also bred. In recent years, there has been a great deal of effort made to improve wool quality; and after a period of low wool prices they seem to be strengthening, taking wool income back towards £5 million.

Mutton has been nowhere near as successful. Frozen mutton exports were first suggested by Governor Thomas Callaghan in 1883 but nothing further happened until 1907, when a German firm's attempt to export frozen mutton failed. In 1910 two meat canning operations were set up and by WWI 90,000 sheep had found their way into a can, most at a 2-acre canning factory at Goose Green. Most of that canned sheep was sent off to England, but the operation was never economic and the factory was abandoned. Frozen mutton was on the agenda again after WWII. A site was chosen at Ajax Bay on Falkland Sound but it took four years to build the plant and cost twice as much as planned. After processing only 40,000 sheep in its first two years, the venture collapsed. Remarkably, in 2001 an abattoir opened, despite misgivings that this might be another financial disaster. Due to EU regulations, the Mt Pleasant military base could not purchase meat locally without a slaughterhouse that met EU standards. Whether the Falklands market is big enough to justify the expenditure remains to be seen.

OTHER FARMING
Periodically other animals have been tried out, but nothing has come close to replacing sheep. Cattle and pigs are raised for local consumption and a small programme exists to raise cashmere goats for their valuable wool. Recently, small herds of reindeer have been introduced from South Georgia. Guanacos, closely related to llamas, have been introduced from South America and small numbers of miniature horses are raised. Turkeys have also been unsuccessfully trialled. In recent years greenhouse production of hydroponically grown vegetables has been quite successful.

FISHING
In 1987 the Falklands' economic zone of 3 nautical miles from shore was extended to 200, thus revolutionising the islands' economy. In recent years squid fishing licences have brought in more than £25 million annually, a per capita cash infusion of more than £10,000. This is five to 10 times as much as wool brings. In addition there is some income from looking after fishing boats and their crews, and from local investment in fishing operations.

Two species of squid are caught in Falklands' waters. The smaller *Loligo gahi* is caught by European stern trawlers, mainly from Spain. The larger *Illex argentinus* is caught by East Asian squid jigging boats, the largest fleet coming from Korea. Fishing boats have also been managed from the Falklands and this has created new wealth.

The only problem is that squid numbers have fallen dramatically in recent years. It may be simply a short-term climatic or current change, perhaps an Atlantic version of the Pacific's El Niño cycle. However, it may be a real decline due to overexploitation.

TOURISM
Falkland Islanders seem surprisingly ambivalent about tourism. There are two categories of tourist. Annually 30,000 to 40,000 visitors arrive on 50 to 60 ships. Many come in small Antarctic 'expedition ships', sometimes with less than 50 passengers, sometimes with as many as 200. Larger, more conventional cruise ships may have 500, 1000 or even more passengers. Cruise ship visitors are known to the islanders as 'day-trippers' and for the big cruise ships, which can often land passengers only at Stanley, the stay will indeed be just a day.

Most expedition ships will incorporate a Falklands visit with other stops on the Antarctic Peninsula or South Georgia. The government charges larger 'Stanley only' ships with more than 120 passengers a £10 a head landing charge. Smaller ships stopping at the outer islands are usually charged £10 to £15 a head by the island owners.

The other visitor category is much smaller. Perhaps 2000 visitors a year stay on the islands, usually arriving on the RAF TriStar flight or the weekly LanChile flight, then travelling to islands and settlements by Falkland Islands Government Air Service (FIGAS) flights. These visitors typically stay at least a week, although it takes two or three weeks to see a reasonable amount. They will usually be interested in the wildlife, particularly the birdlife, but Falklands War history and fly fishing are other specialist attractions.

At one time there was an attempt to introduce mink farming, but fortunately these animals didn't have a taste for culled sheep – an escape could have made serious inroads into local bird populations.

Locals refer to those islanders enjoying the new-found wealth derived from squid as the 'squidocracy', a new version of the 'sheepocracy'.

SHEEP SHEARING

Sheep and sheep shearing play such an important role in Falklands history it's disappointing to find that many of the shearers are short term visitors from Australia or New Zealand. Patrick Berntsen was an exception, a genuine 'kelper' who had taken his shearing skills on a worldwide tour.

'I woke up one day and realised I didn't have any more names for them,' Patrick explained, 'so I quit. In 10 years from the mid-70s I reckon I'd sheared about 300,000 sheep.' Today Patrick, with his partner Pat, runs a crafts shop in Stanley, but for years sheep shearing was his ticket to see the world.

'It was never just a way of making money', he explained. 'Shearing was more like a sport. You were always competing with the guy in the next stall and there was lots of camaraderie, with other people doing it for the travel and the life.' That competitive element is easy to pick up in sheep sheds anywhere in the world. The top scores, typically more than 400 sheep a day, are chalked up on the wall. Furthermore, it's a very mobile profession with gangs of shearers moving from shed to shed, country to country – wherever there are sheep to be shorn. The sheep also have to be moved in and out, and the wool has to be packed and baled; it's a busy little team.

'Norway was the highest-paid place I worked,' Patrick explained. 'We sheared the sheep at a government abattoir before they were slaughtered, but in the evening there would be farmers around the town with small flocks to be shorn. They'd send a taxi to pick you up from your hotel and take you out to the farm. You'd shear 30 or 40 sheep and take the taxi back.

'I sheared in the US, mainly in Montana and Wyoming. Back then you couldn't get a work permit so you had to work illegally – there weren't enough shearers and the Americans were all in their 60s and heading towards retirement. In other countries shearing was a young man's pursuit, but in America at that time it was an old man's.

'England would have been profitable as well, but the flocks were so small you simply couldn't get enough sheep to shear and you wasted a lot of time travelling from farm to farm. Plus the farmers were so disorganised. You'd turn up and the sheep were still wandering around in the fields and had to be rounded up. In other countries they'd be in the pens, ready to go.

'Of course, I never saved any money from my shearing years,' Patrick concluded. 'I spent it all on living and travelling but it took me all over the world. I even represented the Falklands in a world sheep-shearing contest in New Zealand.'

Tourism probably brings in as much as £5 million, making it more important than sheep, although it's way behind the fishing business. However, fishing doesn't create a lot of employment and tourism not only generates jobs, it makes them in camp – precisely the place where they're most needed.

There are visitor categories that have been hardly touched. For instance, Ushuaia in Argentina has boomed as a jumping-off point for Antarctic cruise ships. Although the Falklands are limited by infrequent flights, there's still potential for more Antarctic and South Georgia visitors to start and/or finish in the Falklands. If some of those visitors stayed for a few days before or after their trip it could make a major difference to the Falklands economy. However, visitors come to the Falklands looking for isolation and wildlife, so there's a real danger that too many tourists could spoil the loneliness or, even worse, scare off the wildlife.

South Georgia

The old South Georgian economy was heavily based on the whaling station leases. Fortunes were won and lost in the whaling business until it all ground rapidly to a halt in the early 1960s. From then until 1982, when the Argentines invaded as a sideshow to the Falklands War, scientific research was the only real activity on the island although colourful and attractive South Georgian stamps kept some money flowing into the administration's accounts.

Things have changed dramatically since 1982; fishing and tourism are now the main components of the island's economy. Fishing is overwhelmingly the larger. The South Georgia Maritime Zone (SGMZ) extends 200 nautical miles around the island and fishing licences must be applied for at King Edward Point. A four month licence costs about £150,000, an observer is placed on each fishing boat and there's a patrol boat to keep unlicensed boats away.

Longline fishing is usually for Patagonian toothfish *(Dissostichus eleginoides)*, known as Chilean sea bass when it features on a restaurant menu. Mackerel icefish *(Champsocephalus gunnari)* is the other prize catch. There is also fishing for squid *(Martialia hyadesi)* and krill. Typically there will be 15 to 20 licensed South American, Japanese, Korean and Spanish fishing boats operating in South Georgian waters. Krill boats again include the Koreans, along with Russian and Polish.

Compared with the big fishing money, tourism income is very small, but steadily growing and potentially more sustainable. There's a £50 entry fee for every passenger along with the various harbour fees. In the 2002–03 season 44 ships called in, most of them expedition cruise ships. Typically these ships have 40–100 passengers, although some larger ships may have up to 200. In the 2002–03 season a 500 passenger cruise ship was permitted for the first time – although ships this large are only allowed to land passengers at Grytviken.

For visiting vessels, whether they are yachts, tourist cruise ships or fishing boats, there are charges for harbour entry and harbour dues, clearance and customs attendance, charges for taking on fresh water, trans-shipping fees and so on. Of course, those colourful South Georgian postage stamps are still available and the increasing tourist flow means the King Edward Point Post Office is kept busy.

Pesca by Ian Hart (2001) tells the complete story of South Georgia's whaling and sealing operations from establishment to final collapse. The author was part of the small team that established the museum at Grytviken in 1992.

RELIGION

Falkland Islanders are overwhelmingly Anglican (Church of England), although Stanley also has places of worship for Roman Catholics and for followers of the United Free Church, Baha'i Faith, Jehovah's Witnesses and a number of other small communities.

Environment

THE LAND
The Falklands

The Falklands lie about 500km east of South America. They have a land area of 12,173 sq km, which is broken up into two main islands and no less than 748 smaller ones. Only a handful of islands are populated. The Falklands' land area is a smidgen smaller than Northern Ireland or the state of Connecticut, USA, but because there are so many scattered islands the actual distances are much greater than such comparisons might indicate. From Stanley in the northeast to New Island in the southwest is about 240km.

Except for Lafonia, the low-lying southern half of East Falkland, the terrain is generally hilly to mountainous, although the highest peak, Mt Usborne on East Falkland, is a mere 705m; West Falkland's highest point, Mt Adam, is only a few metres lower at 700m. Among the most interesting geological features are the unique 'stone runs' (see the boxed text opposite). The higher elevations are mainly devoid of vegetation, being just scree, stones and eroded peat, and there are few trees anywhere on the islands. The climate discourages the growth of anything beyond grass, heath and small shrubs, although in settlements where trees have been successfully planted they seem to do fine.

It's estimated that 85% of Falklands' land is covered in peat, and this can make cross-country travel slow and subject to frequent interruptions when vehicles become bogged. About 45% of the land is described as 'soft camp' – soggy black peat where the water table rises to just below the surface. The stonier highlands make up 'hard camp'. The numerous bays, inlets, estuaries and beaches present an often spectacular and extremely long coastline, with many excellent anchorages. As you fly over the islands you will clearly see many pools and ponds, but real lakes and rivers are far fewer in number. Surprisingly, parts of the islands suffer from water shortages.

> Anywhere outside Stanley is known locally as 'camp', from the Spanish word *campo* (countryside).

THE ANTARCTIC CONVERGENCE

Today scientists prefer the term Polar Front for the region between 40°S and 60°S where the colder waters of the Antarctic meet the warmer waters of the northern oceans. The resulting collision brings strong currents, winds and a dramatic change in not only the sea temperature but also its salinity and its inhabitants. Before more accurate measuring systems developed, scientists could tell which side of the convergence they were on by the types of krill they encountered. The huge depths and flows of water at the convergence make this the planet's largest ocean current and the persistent westerly winds bring not only the biggest waves on earth but also violent winds and storms. Sailors talk of the 'Roaring Forties' followed by the 'Furious Fifties'. Antarctica begins south of the convergence, so South Georgia is an Antarctic island, the Falklands are not. Ship passengers bound for South Georgia usually run a book on when the first iceberg will be spotted and when the Antarctic Convergence will be crossed.

There is no northern hemisphere equivalent of the Polar Front because the continental landmasses north of the equator interrupt any round-the-world current flow. This difference in flow also accounts for the dramatic difference in the sea ice covering between the southern hemisphere (where the ice-covered size of the Antarctic continent effectively doubles from summer to winter) compared to the northern Arctic regions where the ice cover increase is much less dramatic.

STONE RUNS

The 'rivers' of stones that tumble across the landscape are the most noticeable feature of Falklands topography. They were commented on in the journals of Antoine Joseph Pernetty, a French naturalist at the Port Louis settlement in 1764; and at greater length by Charles Darwin, who called them 'streams of stone', following his visits to the islands in 1833 and 1834.

It's thought the stone runs are a relic of the last ice age, when successive cycles of freezing and thawing cracked blocks of quartzite until they broke apart and slid down the hillsides. Stone runs are found in upland areas of both East and West Falkland, but the most spectacular are along the Wickham Heights, the chain of mountains and peaks running east–west across East Falkland. Stone runs are not unique to the Falklands, but they are unusual for their great number and impressive size. The biggest stones are found at the top of a run and they decrease in size as you move down.

Stone runs vary from short affairs as little as 1m wide to the 6km-long 'Princes Street', 20km northwest of Stanley and described by Darwin as a 'valley of fragments'.

South Georgia

Many visitors rank South Georgia's 'Alps in mid-ocean' physical appearance as one of the most spectacular on earth. The 'alps' are part of the partially drowned mountain range named the Scotia Ridge, after the Scottish National Antarctic Expedition of 1902–04. This ridge runs from the tip of South America in a great curve to the Antarctic Peninsula, and other parts above seas level include the South Sandwich and South Orkney islands.

Crescent-shaped South Georgia is about 170km long and 40km wide at its broadest, and covers 3755 sq km, an area roughly equivalent to Rhode Island, the smallest US state. Well over half the island is permanently covered in snow and ice and, despite the global retreat of icefields, there are many glaciers dropping right down to the sea. All the whaling stations were built along the northeast coast, where the many bays and fjords are protected from the prevailing westerlies by mountains. The south coast has more severe weather and more glaciers, and its smaller numbers of fjords and bays don't afford many safe anchorages. Far fewer cruise ships visit the south coast of the island, especially the very wild and rugged eastern end.

Many of the smaller islands are of particular interest because they have managed to remain free of the plague of introduced rats that has decimated smaller birdlife on the main island. The most notable islands situated well away from the main island include Bird Island and the Willis Islands, off South Georgia's northwest tip; Annenkov Island, off the southwest coast; and Cooper Island, off the southeast coast. Further a field the spectacular Shag Rocks soar out of the sea 250km northwest of the main island, while the Clerke Rocks lie 70km southeast.

Two main ranges, the Allardyce and Salvesen Ranges, form the island's spine. The highest point is Mt Paget (2934m), but there are more than a dozen other peaks over 2000m, including Nordenskjold Peak (2355m), Mt Carse (2331m), Mt Sugartop (2323m) and Mt Paterson (2200m). Glaciers descend into valleys and, where they meet the sea, often calve icebergs and smaller chunks of ice just like on the Antarctic continent.

The only flat areas of any size are Hestesletten (Horse Plain) in Cumberland East Bay and Salisbury Plain in the Bay of Isles. The whaling stations are generally built on small areas of flatter land at the heads of some of the bays. South Georgia has 20 or so lakes and a great many

The Falklands are a long way south of anywhere in Australia or New Zealand. Stewart Island, to the south of New Zealand, doesn't quite reach 47°S, while the Australian state of Tasmania is north of 41°S. On the other side of the equator, London, at 51.5°N, is as far north of the equator as the Falklands are south.

South Georgia's nearest inhabited neighbour is the Falkland Islands, 1400km away to the northwest. South Georgia lies about one-third of the way between South America and Africa, 2050km from Cape Horn and 4800km from the Cape of Good Hope.

pools and ponds, most of them along the northwest coast. There are many streams and rivers in the valleys and some spectacular waterfalls after the spring thaw, but there are only two named rivers: the Hope River at Undine Harbour on the south coast and the Penguin River at Cumberland Bay.

Glaciers cover 57% of South Georgia, but have generally been in retreat since the 1880s.

WILDLIFE
Animals
The Falklands' fauna is abundant, accessible and remarkably tame – much like that of Ecuador's Galápagos Islands. Four species of penguin and many other fascinating birds breed in the Falklands including beautiful black-browed albatrosses, curious striated caracaras (known locally as 'Johnny Rook') and endemic flightless steamer ducks. Many species form large and impressive breeding colonies and are easy to photograph. Elephant seals, sea lions and fur seals breed on the beaches, and dolphins and killer whales (orcas) are often seen offshore.

South Georgia's fauna may lack variety, but this is more than made up for by overwhelming quantity. Fur seals live here in their millions and single colonies of penguins can number in the tens of thousands. The island's birdlife is particularly impressive with interesting species at both ends of the size scale: the tiny South Georgia pipit is one of only two land birds found in Antarctica (the other is also in South Georgia), while the awesome wandering albatross is the 747 of birdlife with the widest wingspan of any bird.

Charles Darwin was an early visitor to the Falklands and although he found the landscape somewhat depressing his name is attached to one of East Falkland's main settlements. He also named the island's longest stone run after Princes St in Edinburgh where he had studied medicine.

Plants
Grasslands and low-standing shrubs dominate the Falklands' flora; there are no native trees. At the time of European discovery, extensive stands of native tussock grass dominated the coastline and provided nutritious livestock fodder, but it proved highly vulnerable to overgrazing and fire. Today, very little tussock remains on East or West Falkland, although well-managed farms on offshore islands have preserved significant areas. Tussock once covered 220 sq km of the Falklands, but today only about 50 sq km remains and less than 1 sq km of that is on the two main islands. Most of the native pasture is rank 'white grass' (see p64), which supports only about one sheep per hectare.

Although it lies south of the Antarctic Convergence there is much more flora on South Georgia than anywhere on the Antarctic mainland or other islands further south. In the summer months the lower slopes of the island's impressive mountains are cloaked in green. Nevertheless, the native flora is very restricted even in comparison to the Falklands. There is a lot of tussock grass.

See p40 for more information on wildlife of both areas.

NATIONAL PARKS
For many years all land in the Falklands was privately owned and even today there are no formally designated national parks. However, there are many outstanding wildlife sites and some offshore islands are protected as wildlife sanctuaries and nature reserves operated by the government, private owners or by organisations like Falklands Conservation (FC).

The island of South Georgia is essentially one big reserve and certain offshore islands enjoy even stricter environmental controls. Run by the government of the British Dependent Territory of South Georgia and the South Sandwich Islands (SGSSI), it has essentially the same regulations for wildlife protection as Antarctica.

The Falkland Islands Association (☎ 020-7592 0022; Douglas House, 16-18 Douglas St, Westminster, London SW1P 4PB) is a political lobby group that publishes a quarterly newsletter on the Falklands with much useful information.

FALKLAND ISLANDS COUNTRYSIDE CODE

■ Always ask permission before entering private land.

■ Always give animals the right of way. Remember not to block the routes of seabirds and seals coming ashore to their colonies.

■ Be aware of the high fire risk throughout the islands. Be extra careful if smoking; take cigarette butts with you.

■ Do not disfigure rocks or buildings.

■ Do not drop litter. Take your rubbish away.

■ Do not touch, handle, injure or kill any wild bird or other animal.

■ Keep to paths whenever possible. Leave gates open or shut as you find them.

■ Never feed any wild animals.

■ Some plants are protected and should not be picked. Wildflowers are there for all to enjoy and should be left where they are found.

■ Try to prevent any undue disturbance to wild animals. Stay on the outside of bird and seal colonies. Remain at least 5m away. When taking photographs or filming stay low to the ground. Move slowly and quietly. Do not startle or chase wildlife from resting or breeding areas.

■ Whalebones, skulls, eggs or other such items may not be exported from the Falkland Islands. They should be left where they are found.

ENVIRONMENTAL ISSUES

Most birds and certain mammals are protected. This is a major contrast with earlier attitudes when bounties were placed on many animals out of a fear that they would compete with the all-important sheep. The *warrah* (Falklands fox) was deliberately driven to extinction in 1876. Today nature-oriented tourism is very actively encouraged and is rapidly growing.

The Falklands and South Georgia both face some severe environmental issues owing to deliberate or accidental introductions of exotic animals, particularly sheep in the Falklands and rats on both islands. The sheep have wiped out the native tussock grass over a large part of the Falklands, while the rats have decimated populations of small birds on both the Falklands and South Georgia. Whale, seal and penguin populations have also suffered from unbridled exploitation, which kicked off with the arrival of seal hunters in the late 18th century and did not finally halt until whaling ended in the 1960s. Commercial fishing, which has increased dramatically in the waters around the Falklands and South Georgia since the Falklands War, could be the next case of over-exploitation and there are concerns that fishing success may be to the cost of other wildlife populations. Penguin numbers in the Falklands have dropped dramatically in recent years and the causes are still unknown (see the boxed text p47).

Falklands Conservation is a nonprofit organisation based in both London (☎ 020-8343 0831; www.falklandsconservation.com; 1 Princes Ave, Finchley N3 2DA) and Stanley (Map pp70-1; ☎ 22247; fax 22288; conservation@horizon .co.fk; Jetty Centre). Membership costs £20 per year.

Natural History

The Complete Guide to Antarctic Wildlife by Hadoram Shirihai (2002) is a hefty and lavishly photographed 500-page guide to the birds and mammals of the Antarctic Continent and Southern Ocean.

The sub-Antarctic region is a rich environment but short of land. Huge quantities of krill, squid and fish in the chilly waters around the Antarctic Convergence (see the boxed text p36) support enormous populations of birds, seals and, once upon a time, whales. Many of the seabirds and seals spend a large part of their lives at sea. Petrels and albatrosses, for example, rarely come to land except during the summer months. At some time, however, all these pelagic (ocean-going) species do come ashore to breed and, when they do, there's not much land available. Consequently, what land there is tends to be heavily populated – hence those huge albatross colonies on Beauchêne or Steeple Jason Islands in the Falklands; the dense crowds of fur seals on many beaches on South Georgia; and the huge penguin colonies on both islands.

MAMMALS

INTRODUCED MAMMALS
The Falklands

Although there are no native land mammals in the Falklands there are a number of introduced species, apart from sheep. The most troublesome introduction is the common domestic cat, which has made huge inroads into populations of small birds. Islands in the Falklands that are cat- and, equally important, rat-free have much larger populations of small birds.

THE WARRAH, THE YAHGAN & THE DISCOVERY OF THE FALKLANDS

Who discovered the Falklands? Opinions depend, it seems, on who's speaking and what that person's native language is. Spanish speakers argue forcefully that a ship from Magellan's 1520 expedition wintered at the islands, while English speakers strongly assert that privateer John Davis discovered them in 1592. Unfortunately, no Yahgan speakers remain to tell us whether the 'Canoe Indians' of Tierra del Fuego might have been the first to set foot on the islands.

The evidence, admittedly, is slim and the idea seems at first glance unconventional and unlikely. The Yahgans navigated the waters of the Beagle Channel and the Strait of Magellan in simple beech-bark canoes held together with whalebone and shredded saplings. By all accounts, these leaky vessels required constant baling, but the Yahgans did use sealskin sails in favourable winds. In these canoes they certainly arrived at Staten Island, at the eastern tip of Tierra del Fuego, and some speculate that they travelled more than 800km northeast to the Falklands. Early settlers found canoes washed up on the shores of West Falkland, but the most concrete evidence, for at least a temporary Indian presence, was the islands' only native land mammal, the warrah, or Falklands fox (Dusicyon australis).

There were no people in the Falklands when Europeans first landed, but the warrah (its name probably derived from the Australian aboriginal word warrigal, used to describe the dingo) aroused the interest of visitors such as Darwin. Writing about his 1834 visit to the Falklands in Voyage of the Beagle he accurately predicted their eventual demise:

These wolves are well known from Byron's account of their tameness and curiosity, which the sailors, who ran into the water to avoid them, mistook for fierceness. To this day their manners remain the same. They have been observed to enter a tent, and actually pull some

Rabbits and hares were also deliberately introduced as a source of meat, but fortunately have not become an unstoppable pest. Rabbits are widespread but not common, while hares are found only in certain areas of East Falkland.

The brown rat, black rat and house mouse were not introduced deliberately, but have also spread widely and caused great damage. Extermination projects have managed to clear rats off a number of smaller islands.

Three other mammals were brought from South America. The guanaco, a relative of the llama, was introduced in several locations and small herds survive on tiny Staats Island, off the southwest corner of West Falkland.

Attempts are being made to eradicate the Patagonian fox, which is also found on Staats Island as well as on nearby Weddell, Beaver, Tea, River and Split Islands. The Patagonian fox was introduced to Tierra del Fuego as recently as 1951 in order to control introduced rabbits; perhaps it was brought to the Falklands with similar intentions. Sea otters were introduced in the 1930s and, although nobody has seen one for years, they like strong winds, rough seas and lots of seaweed and kelp – all of which the Falklands can readily supply. Finally, reindeer have recently been introduced from South Georgia, where they were also an introduction. The main herd is on Beaver Island (p136).

Antarctica – A Guide to the Wildlife by Tony Soper, with beautiful illustrations by Dafila Scott (1994), is a guide to the main fishes, birds, seals and whales of Antarctica, many of which are also found around the Falklands and South Georgia.

South Georgia

There are no native land mammals on South Georgia but, as with the Falklands, there are a number of introduced species. Fortunately cats and rabbits have not established themselves – the weather is simply too severe. Brown rats and house mice have proved hardier, and in the two centuries since their first arrival have spread along most of the northeast

meat from beneath the head of a sleeping seaman. The Gauchos also have frequently in the evening killed them by holding out a piece of meat in one hand, and in the other a knife ready to stick them. As far as I am aware, there is no other instance in any part of the world, of so small a mass of broken land, distant from a continent, possessing so large an aboriginal quadruped peculiar to itself. Their numbers have rapidly decreased; they are already banished from that half of the island which lies to the eastward of the neck of land between St Salvador Bay and Berkeley Sound. Within a very few years after these islands shall have become regularly settled, in all probability this fox will be classed with the dodo, as an animal which has perished from the face of the earth.

Other observers also remarked on the animal's extraordinary tameness, a characteristic which would support British biologist Juliet Clutton-Brock's conclusion that the *warrah* was a feral dog or a cross of feral dog and South American fox. Studying specimens in the British Museum, she concluded that, like the Australian dingo, the *warrah* had been domesticated and most likely brought across several hundred kilometres of open ocean in Yahgan canoes.

Was this possible? The Yahgans were a hardy people and a canoe or two might have ridden the prevailing winds and currents from the Strait of Lemaire to the Falklands. If, as was usual, they carried a dog or two, perhaps a pregnant bitch, those animals might have bred on the islands. Whether these presumed discoverers of the Falklands were able to return to Tierra del Fuego is even more speculative, but European 'discovery' might just be a myth.

As Darwin predicted, the *warrah* itself did not survive European settlement – perceived as a threat to sheep, the last individual was shot on West Falkland in the 1870s. The two remaining stuffed examples are in museums in Belgium and Sweden.

coast. Rats have had a terrible effect on local bird populations, particularly on pipits and burrowing petrels.

Most of South Georgia's offshore islands are still rat-free and visitors are asked to take particular care that they do not take uninvited hitchhikers to new locales. Keeping food containers closed, ensuring there are no stowaways in supplies taken ashore and making sure that hatches are closed at night are all ways of keeping the rat problem under control. Attempts are being made to eradicate rats at a number of South Georgia sites, but there is continuing concern that they could cross sea ice to offshore islands.

A small group of reindeer was brought from Norway in 1910 or 1911 with the intention of providing meat and something to shoot at for the whaling station personnel. There are now more than 2000 of them in two separate herds distributed from Royal Bay to Fortuna Bay; heavy grazing has caused problems with the fragile plant habitat. Take care during the March–April rutting season, when reindeer can become aggressive.

The Island of South Thorgia (1984) by Robert Headland ranks the damage caused by introduced mammals and wryly notes that 'man should be included in the list but it is difficult to decide whether he should come before or after rats'.

SEALS & SEA LIONS

Marine mammals around the Falklands and South Georgia have had a hard time of it over the years. Seals were the first target for modern exploitation and in a remarkably short period European and North American sealers managed to devastate the populations of fur seals, which were hunted for their fur; and then of elephant seals and sea lions, which were hunted for their oil. The focus soon shifted to whales, which were targeted with equally furious zeal. Remarkably, fur seals on South Georgia have enjoyed a population explosion in recent years and have reached such huge numbers that they're beginning to cause problems (see p155).

Seal type	Falklands	South Georgia	World population
South American fur seal	15,000	-	750,000
Antarctic fur seal	-	1.8 million	2 million
Southern sea lions	6000	-	250,000
Southern elephant seal	1000	350,000	750,000

South American (Arctocephalus australis) & Antarctic Fur Seals (Arctocephalus gazella)

Fur seals can be found on most of the southern islands – in very large numbers at some of them. Fur seals breed in harems, and males can be formidable opponents to rivals and human visitors alike. Males come ashore in November to stake out their breeding territory; the females follow and pupping takes place in December. The pups are fed for four months, but the breeding males have mated and gone back to sea by mid-January. While they are ashore during the breeding season they fast, devoting all their time to mating with the cows and seeing off challengers. Their diet consists of squid, fish and crustaceans such as krill.

In the 19th century sealers called male fur seals 'wigs' and female fur seals 'clapmatches'.

Sealing began in the late 18th century and at first the pelts ended up in China, where a technique had been developed to remove the outer guard hairs and leave the fashionably valuable under-fur. Fur seals are now showing a remarkable recovery on South Georgia, where at some localities they are displacing breeding albatrosses and killing vegetation – leading to conservation dilemmas.

South American or Falklands fur seals are usually not migratory and suckle their pups for eight months to as long as two years. Females weigh about 50kg and the much heavier males up to 160kg. Around the Falklands fur seals are generally found on rocky cliffs or isolated rocky outcrops; an exception is New Island (p136) off the southwest end of West Falkland which, as a result, is very popular with cruise ships.

The Antarctic fur seal occurs further south than its close and slightly smaller sub-Antarctic relatives, but their ranges overlap and the two species sometimes interbreed. Males, at over 200kg, far outweigh females, which weigh less than 50kg. Apart from size the two species can also be distinguished by their fur colour: about one in 800 fur seals are of the 'blonde' variety, with markedly yellow or cream-coloured fur.

Fur seals were virtually wiped out in not much more than 50 years from the late 18th century.

Southern Sea Lion (Otaria flavescens)

Like the fur seal, huge numbers of sea lions were killed by sealers – unfortunately their numbers have not recovered to anywhere near the same extent. It's estimated the Falklands' sea lion population today is less than 3% of peak numbers. Males establish beach territories in December and are followed soon after by the females, which pup between mid-December and early February. Mating takes place less than a week after the pups are born. Typically a male will corral a harem of 15 or more females; keeping this group together (and intruding males away) is so time-consuming that there is little time for eating or sleeping during the summer months.

The 'lion' comes from the male's solid neck and lion-like mane. Males weigh up to 350kg and females are lighter coloured, smaller and sleeker at up to 140kg. Unlike fur seals, which prefer rocky coastlines, sea lions are usually found on sandy beaches, where they sprawl sociably in tightly packed groups of females and pups. Diving sea lions can stay down as long as 12 minutes, with deeper-diving females reaching depths of over 400m. Although sea lions normally feed on krill, fish, squid and octopus they will sometimes take unwary penguins.

Sea lions can move very fast and be surprisingly aggressive on land – it's wise to make a large detour around a seemingly basking sea lion on the beach (see p169).

Southern Elephant Seal (Mirounga leonina)

The southern elephant seal is the world's largest seal. Males can attain a weight of 3.5 tonnes and a length of 5m; females weigh up to 900kg and can reach 3m in length. Only the male has the inflatable nose that gives the species its name. It reaches full size at about eight years of age and can be inflated to an even more imposing volume during the breeding season. Snorting, honking and grumbling into this echo box make an impressively fearsome noise designed to warn off intruding rival males.

Males spend the winter at sea, haul out in August and then fight to see who will be beachmaster, with mating rights to a 'harem' of females. The females turn up from September and most pups are born from mid-September through October. At birth an elephant seal pup weighs 40 or 50kg, but during their first 20 to 25 days they guzzle down enough of their mother's super-rich, 50%-fat milk to put on up to 4kg a day. During this time the mother does not feed at all, but after she mates with the beachmaster the pups are abruptly weaned when the female elephant seal abandons them and heads out to sea. By this time the pups have tripled or quadrupled their birth weight. They will now lose up to a kilogram a day before they too depart from the beach after about 50 days.

The beachmasters have also been fasting, devoting all their time to mating or fighting off other males. When a beachmaster spots a potential intruder – or a receptive female – nothing gets in his way. Ploughing across the beach, the ungainly monster will charge right through groups of females and can actually crush and kill unwary pups. The competition

A Field Guide to the Wildlife of the Falkland Islands & South Georgia by Ian J Strange (1992) is a handy guide to just about everything that lives on and around the islands, vegetable as well as animal.

for beachmaster status is so intense that most males will never get to mate, but even the biggest, toughest bull will be unlikely to maintain his position for two seasons. Finally, around mid-November, the dominant males, having fasted for three months and mated with as many as 100 females, also head out to sea, vacating the beaches for nonbreeding seals to come ashore and moult. Breeding females return to the beach in late summer, followed by the dominant males in early winter.

At sea, the adults' diet is predominantly squid, caught during very deep (sometimes more than a kilometre, although the average is 500m to 800m) and long (up to two hours!) dives. During these dives they lower their heart rate to as little as a single beat per minute, separated by remarkably short periods at the surface.

Elephant seals, especially males, were heavily exploited for their oil during the 19th and early 20th centuries by sealers. They were still taken on South Georgia until the 1960s and it was only the abandonment of the whaling stations that ended sealing operations. Population recovery has been erratic and in locations where the numbers have declined the trend may be linked to climatic change affecting food supplies.

The Falklands population now stands at about 500 breeding females, a 90% decline since 1982. Sea Lion Island (p103) is virtually the only breeding site for elephant seals in the Falklands today. South Georgia (p143), with about half of the world's elephant seal population, appears to be one of the sites where populations are growing.

Guide to Birds of the Falkland Islands by Robin Woods, and illustrated by Franklin D Coombs (1988), is said to be the best guide to the islands' birds.

Other Seals

The sleek leopard seal *(Hydrurga leptonyx)* is the largest true seal, after the elephant seal, and has a large head and huge gape, making it a fearsome predator. Neither the Falklands nor South Georgia have permanent populations or breeding colonies, although occasionally breeding may take place on South Georgia.

Weddell seals *(Leptonychotes weddellii)* are found in a single, small colony in Larsen Harbour off the Drygalski Fjord (p160), at the southeastern end of South Georgia. These seals prefer life in frozen Antarctic waters further to the south, so this group of less than 100 is an aberration. Crabeater seals *(Lobodon carcinophagus)* are very occasional visitors to South Georgia.

WHALES & DOLPHINS

Cetaceans – from the Greek word for 'large sea creatures' – are divided into two suborders: Mysticeti and Odontoceti. The large Mysticeti (baleen whales) feed on the tiny sea creatures known as zooplankton, which they filter from the water with comb-like plates called baleen. The smaller toothed whales (Odontoceti), which include dolphins, porpoises, killer whales (orcas) and the sperm whales, live off larger prey. Usually that means fish or squid, but killer whales also hunt penguins, seals and even other whales. Whatever the size of their prey, all whales are carnivorous, air-breathing, warm-blooded mammals. Thick layers of insulating blubber allow them to cope with the low temperatures of Antarctic waters; and their often extreme size is another factor in coping with the cold: the larger the body the larger its mass relative to its surface area and therefore the lower the heat loss. While most baleen whales – the minke is an exception – move north during the southern winter, the toothed whales are more likely to stay in the colder waters year-round. Whales were hunted both for the oil from their blubber and for the strong and flexible baleen, which found many uses until plastics came along.

The current population of blue whales is thought to be just 1% of original numbers.

Whales have become a little more common around the Falklands in recent years. Killer whales (which approach the islands when seal pups are first taking to the water) have always been more common. Around South Georgia 60 years of whaling did a pretty good job of eliminating them, but they have started to reappear in greater numbers, particularly southern right whales and humpback whales along the northeast coast where the concentration of krill is greater.

The larger whales that you might see include humpback whales *(Megaptera novaeangliae)*, recognisable by enormous flippers that can reach one-third of their total body length; they are noted for their extended 'songs'. Southern right whales *(Balaena glacialis)* were the 'right' whale to hunt because they are slow-moving and obligingly stayed afloat after they had been harpooned. The sperm whale *(Physeter macrocephalus)*, with its enormous head and narrow tooth-filled jaw, is the whale of *Moby Dick* fame.

The sei whale *(Balaenoptera borealis)* is the third-largest whale in the Southern Ocean and, like humpback, blue and fin whales, was over-exploited through greed to the point of 'commercial extinction'. The fin whale *(Balaenoptera physalus)* is even larger and formed the largest part of whalers' catches after WWII. Both sei and fin whales were heavily hunted right into the 1960s. The blue whale *(Balaenoptera musculus)* is the largest animal that has ever lived. At the other end of the scale, the minke whale *(Balaenoptera acutorostrata)* is the smallest of the great baleen whales, although with a maximum length of 10m and a weight of up to 8 tonnes, it's still a very large animal. A few hundred are currently (and controversially) killed by Japanese whalers each year, ostensibly for scientific purposes, although their meat is sold for human consumption in Japan.

You are more likely to see members of the dolphin family in the region.

Dolphins

Two small dolphin species are regularly encountered around the Falklands. Commerson's dolphin *(Cephalorhynchus commersonii)*, with a distinctive white band extending from its lower surface across the top, is typically less than 1.8m long. They're often found in sheltered waters, and frequently accompany visiting Zodiacs to the jetty in Stanley Harbour and play in the waters of Port Howard.

The larger and less active Peale's dolphin *(Lagenorhychus australis)* reaches 2.5m in length and is often seen around kelp beds. Unlike Commerson's dolphins, they don't often venture into sheltered waters and their white undersurface doesn't extend across the top.

Killer Whale (Orcinus orca)

Also known as orcas, killer whales are the largest of the dolphin family and are unmistakable, with distinctive black-and-white markings and tall dorsal fins (especially in the adult male). Males reach 9m and females nearly 8m; large specimens can weigh nearly 9 tonnes. Killer whales occur in all seas, but are more abundant in colder waters. They travel in schools (pods) of up to 50 individuals. Pods have their own 'dialect' of discrete calls and are presumably made up of closely related animals. Maturity is reached from 12 years of age in females and 14 years in males. They feed on squid, fish, birds and marine mammals; they have been seen swallowing king penguins whole and tipping up small ice floes to get at resting seals. Sea Lion Island (p103) in the Falklands is a prime viewing spot for killer whales; they're often seen in November and February, hoping to catch unwary elephant seal or sea lion pups.

Commerson's dolphin are known locally as 'puffing pigs' from the noise they make when surfacing to breathe, and because of their small, stocky appearance.

Female blue whales (the largest baleen whale) can grow to more than 30m long. Male blue whales are only half the size of females. It's the other way round with sperm whales (the largest toothed whale). Males can reach up to 18m in length, females are only half the size.

Long-finned Pilot Whale (Globicephala melas)

The short-finned pilot whale is closely related to the long-finned pilot whale, but the short-finned tends to stick to warmer waters.

The relatively small pilot whales have a maximum size of about 7m for males and 5m for females. Males weigh up to 3.5 tonnes but females reach only about 1.3 tonnes. Pilot whales are found in northern and southern polar waters, but also in temperate and tropical seas. In the southern hemisphere they tend to be about 30% to 40% larger than their northern relatives. Pilot whales primarily feed on squid. They move in groups, typically of about 40 individuals. In recent years there have been a number of pilot whale strandings in the Falklands.

BIRDS

PENGUINS

The Falklands and South Georgia are home to enormous numbers of penguins. Five species (the king, gentoo, rockhopper, Magellanic and macaroni penguins) breed in the Falklands and four species breed regularly on South Georgia – as in the Falklands there are kings, gentoos and macaronis, but there's also a small population of chinstrap penguins. Rockhoppers sometimes breed on South Georgia, and emperor, Adélie and Magellanic penguins make the odd visit.

Apart from the equatorial Galápagos penguin, these fascinating, flightless birds are found only in the southern hemisphere.

Penguins are extremely gregarious birds, always breeding in colonies that sometimes number in the tens of thousands. Rockhopper and Magellanic penguins spend most of the year at sea, only coming ashore in the spring to breed. On the other hand, king and gentoo penguins remain in the islands year-round.

	Falklands (pairs)	South Georgia (pairs)	World population (pairs)
king penguin	1000	200,000	1 to 1.5 million
gentoo penguin	70,000	100,000	300,000
rockhopper penguin	350,000	-	3.5 to 4 million
macaroni penguin	50	2,500,000	10 million
Magellanic penguin	100,000	-	1.5 million
chinstrap penguin	-	2000	4 million

King Penguin (Aptenodytes patagonicus)

The world's second-largest penguin is a bit shorter and much lighter than the closely related emperor penguin. Its instantly recognisable gold-yellow plumage on the neck and throat makes this the most striking penguin.

Breeding occurs in often very large colonies close to the shore on rocky terrain. The parents take turns incubating a single egg on their feet during summer; it takes 55 days to hatch. They can shuffle along slowly with their eggs – to avoid lumbering southern elephant seals, for instance. Chicks are reared right through the winter (huddling together to keep warm) and only fledge the following summer. Thus, annual breeding is impossible and kings breed every two years in three.

Unlike most seabirds, penguins do not use their feet to propel themselves under water; instead, they literally 'fly' under water using their short, stiff wings like fins.

After they have hatched, large groups of chicks may be left in crèches, watched over by only a handful of adults while other penguins travel huge distances – sometimes hundreds of kilometres – to find food. The king penguins' diet includes fish and squid, caught by dives up to several hundred metres deep and lasting as long as 15 minutes. King penguins can be found in their rookeries year-round, so visitors in the summer may see penguins involved in courtship, eggs being incubated, small chicks or

RED TIDE?

It's clear that penguin numbers often fluctuate alarmingly in the short and long term. Rockhopper numbers, for example, suffered a serious crash in the Falklands during the mid-1980s, but have also been in a steady decline for many years. At the same time king penguin numbers seem to be increasing. There is concern in the Falklands that the increased number of fishing boats may be making inroads into the penguins' food supply. Sudden drops in squid or krill numbers can result in many penguins starving to death. When penguins come ashore to moult they fast until the moult is completed and they can return to the sea. If they come ashore without sufficient reserves of fat they may complete their moult and then simply drop dead, not having enough energy to return to sea.

In 2002–03 in many parts of the Falklands there were dramatic population drops, particularly in the gentoo and Magellanic penguin colonies (although the problem was much worse in some areas than others). It was widely speculated that the deaths resulted from an algal bloom in waters around the islands, a form of 'red tide' that is usually found only in enclosed freshwater areas. Red tide blooms had led to the closure of shell fisheries zones along the Patagonian coast around the same time. Stricken penguins appeared to be partially paralysed and simply dropped dead on the beaches. The jury's still out on whether the numbers have recovered; gentoo penguins had a very good breeding season in 2003–04 but it was only average for rockhoppers.

newly hatched, and larger chicks. Because males are involved in raising the chicks for about a month longer than females, she will normally have moved on to a new partner before she is ready to breed again.

Kings were once hunted for their oil, but their numbers have been increasing at a number of sites. The Falklands are on the very northern edge of the king's range and the 1000 breeding pairs in the islands are almost all found at Volunteer Beach (p92). On South Georgia kings are found in huge colonies at the Bay of Isles (p155), where there are 25,000–50,000 pairs; St Andrew's Bay (p159), with as many as 50,000 pairs; and Royal Bay (p159), which has 9000 pairs. There are also about 30 smaller colonies.

Gentoo Penguin (Pygoscelis papua)

This attractive species has an orange bill and a white flash above and behind its eye. There are an estimated 300,000 breeding pairs worldwide, more than half of them on South Georgia and the Falklands. About 90% of gentoos return to the same partner in the following year. In the Falklands gentoos breed in winter, laying two eggs as early as July. On South Georgia the eggs are laid in October in bulky tussock grass nests and the parents take day-by-day turns at incubating the eggs. The chicks hatch in late November and stay in the nests for a month before grouping together in large crèches.

In contrast to the adult king penguin, the downy and dowdy dark-brown chick was once described as the 'woolly penguin', a species of its own!

Pursuit dives for prey can go deeper than 100m, reaching the bottom in inshore waters, but most dives are probably shallower. Their diet includes krill and fish (mainly lantern fish and squid). Both parents make a fishing trip each day, usually within just a few kilometres of the colony, so the chicks are fed twice daily.

Gentoo populations are showing some alarming decreases at their sub-Antarctic breeding localities. On South Georgia the small gentoo colonies are found in sheltered bays and fjords, a contrast to the huge colonies of macaronis on exposed sites. Gentoo penguin colonies are always very active, with penguins squabbling over stones and other nest-building material or older chicks chasing their parents around, demanding to be fed.

PENGUIN PEBBLE PROSTITUTION

In their tightly packed colonies gentoo penguins often squabble over ownership of stones and rocks used to build up their nests – they'll even steal them if given a chance. Scientists have observed male gentoos can actually buy the favours of a female gentoo with the offer of a nice pebble.

Rockhopper Penguin (Eudyptes chrysocome)

At first glance rockhopper and macaroni penguins look very similar, but 'rockies' are smaller and have yellow tassels that do not meet between the eyes. Rockhoppers are sub-Antarctic breeders; the largest population is found in the Falklands where 20 years ago the breeding population was estimated to be 2.5 million (although it's now less than 400,000). Disease, introduced rats and rises in sea temperature have all been implicated, and the continuing downward population trends are worrying.

Rockhoppers breed in summer, laying two dimorphic eggs. The smaller, first-laid 'A' egg is often lost during incubation and even if retained, does not always hatch. Rockhopper rookeries are smaller than those of macaronis, and rockhoppers are able to breed among tumbled boulders on exposed shores, where their hopping abilities are required to enter and emerge from the sea, and to reach their nest sites. Where other penguins may be loyal to their breeding partner, but not concerned about their specific nest site, for rockhoppers the site is all important. The routes from the sea to their nesting sites are often scratched and polished from generations hopping back from fishing trips. Rockhoppers prey upon krill and lantern fish.

Macaroni Penguin (Eudyptes chrysolophus)

Orange tassels meeting between the eyes distinguish the macaroni from the slightly smaller (and lighter-billed) rockhopper. 'Maccies' are the most abundant of the sub-Antarctic/Antarctic penguins and about 2.5 million of the 10 million worldwide population are found on South Georgia. Only about 100 of them breed in the Falklands, which is at the northern limit of their range; they're usually mixed in with rockhoppers.

Macaronis breed in summer in immense colonies sited on steep slopes dropping into the sea. The sites are deserted in winter. Two eggs are laid, the first smaller than the second (which is extremely unusual for birds). The first-laid ('A') egg is usually kicked out of the nest soon after the 'B' egg is laid and only one egg ever hatches. All the eggs in a colony are laid within a two- to three-week period in late November. The chicks hatch in late December and the young penguins depart in mid-February.

Macaronis eat mainly krill, particularly at night when it come to the surface, but also lantern fish, caught by pursuit-diving. Macaronis have decreased at some sub-Antarctic breeding localities – but getting accurate censuses is easier said than done in a million-strong colony.

The macaroni gets it name from London dandies in the 18th century who followed Italian fashions by wearing feathers in their hats. They were known as 'macaronis'.

Magellanic Penguin (Spheniscus magellanicus)

The fairly large Magellanic penguin barely reaches the Antarctic region – the Falklands are at the southern edge of its range, although it does make occasional appearances on South Georgia. Like the other penguins in the genus *Spheniscus*, it has black-and-white bands across its face, neck and chest. It takes its name from the Spanish explorer Magellan, who first noted the species in 1520. Magellanic penguins return to their colonies in September, and by March or April have raised their chicks and moved on. They often nest in burrows dug into the soil.

PENGUIN PERSONALITIES

Gentoos are the suburban penguin, gathering together in large groups and always keen to do a little DIY home improvement by adding yet another stone to their nests. Magellanics are the working-class penguin, living underground it's hard to look your penguin best all the time. That braying call and their shy manner add to the persona. Rockhoppers are the penguin punks with their stylish brush cuts, the bright feathers spiking up at the edge and what looks like a pair of sunglasses perched above their eyes. Their clockwork toy jump up rocky cliff faces, their complete nonchalance towards human intruders and the fact that they don't even bother hanging out with other penguins, seeming to prefer albatross and cormorant colonies, means the tiniest penguins are the biggest personalities. Macaronis are grownup rockhoppers and the style kings – as they should be since they're named after 18th century London fashionistas. The kings? They're the penguin aristocracy, aloof, always immaculately attired and, like the rockhoppers, unconcerned about human visitors. In 1823 the sealer and explorer James Weddell in 1823 commented that the king penguin was 'in pride, perhaps not surpassed even by the peacock'.

Chinstrap Penguin (Pygoscelis antarctica)

The aptly named chinstrap is black-and-white with a distinctive black line running from the black cap to below the chin. Despite their large numbers, including 1.5 million pairs on the little-visited South Sandwich Islands, there are only about 2000 pairs on South Georgia, which is at the northern limit of the species' range. Most of them are found in small colonies at the southeast end of the island. Two eggs are laid in November or December and chicks fledge in late February and early March.

The braying call of the Magellanic penguin accounts for their alternative name: jackass penguin.

ALBATROSSES

The 14 species of albatross are divided into two groups: the 'great albatrosses' (the royal and wandering albatrosses, and the very rare Amsterdam albatross), and the 'small albatrosses' or 'mollymawks'. The word albatross is an English corruption of the Portuguese word for pelican: *alcatra*. Most species of albatross are found south of the equator.

The legendary aura surrounding the albatross comes partly from their impressive size (the wandering albatross's wingspan can be over 3.5m) and partly from the wild and remote regions where they are found. They usually breed in large colonies on isolated islands and spend much of their lives on the wing, often in wild and windy conditions. In fact, albatrosses need windy weather; aloft they are perfect soarers, but without an airstream to ride their flying performance is unimpressive. If there is insufficient air movement albatrosses may actually have to land (usually at sea) and wait for the wind to pick up.

Albatrosses feed mainly on squid, but they also follow ships. Unfortunately, the practice of trailing longlines behind tuna and toothfish fishing boats has led to many losses. It is hoped that recent regulations and new practices, such as only setting lines at night and using *tori* poles with attached streamers to scare birds away from baited hooks, will protect these splendid birds.

Albatrosses are slow to develop; mollymawks do not usually breed until their sixth or seventh year, and the great albatrosses not until their ninth. They mate for life but the process of selecting a mate is also long and time consuming. It often requires two to four years of visits to a breeding site before the right mate is found. Long and involved courtship rituals and displays precede mating, and the actual breeding process is equally time-consuming: in the extreme case of the wandering albatross, from newly

Albatrosses are sometimes referred to as gooney birds, either due to their awkwardness on land or because their lack of fear made them easy prey when they were hunted by humans for their feathers.

laid egg to fledgling takes almost a full year. The albatross chicks are fed so vigorously that they will be much bigger than their parents when they finally leave the nest. Albatrosses breed during the southern summer months (from October to April) and mortality is high for young birds.

Albatross colonies are usually situated on high, windswept cliffs, which are selected to make taking off easier. The black-browed albatross is the only species to breed in the Falklands, although other species, in particular the royal albatross, can be seen around the islands; wandering, grey-headed, black-browed and light-mantled sooty albatrosses all breed on South Georgia.

> Mollymawk is another name for the small albatross.

Black-browed Albatross (Diomedea melanophris)

The black-browed albatross is one of the smaller mollymawks, but with a 2.5m wingspan and a mass up to 5kg it's still a big bird. It can be identified at a distance by its underwing pattern featuring a wide, dark leading edge. At close range, the adult bird's yellow bill with orange-red tip and dark line through the eye make identification easy.

This species is widespread in southern seas and is often seen accompanying fishing boats. There are more than 500,000 breeding pairs of black-brows – and, with nonbreeding birds, the species' population is over two million, making it the most numerous and widespread albatross.

> Albatrosses can live to a remarkable age – often more than 50 years.

An annual breeder, it builds a cone-shaped nest out of mud and vegetation and lays a single egg. It often breeds in vast numbers: Beauchêne Island (p109), off the Falklands, has a colony estimated to be more than 100,000 pairs. The colonies on New Island (p136) and Westpoint Island (p133), off the west coast of West Falkland, are popular with visiting cruise ships, while the Saunders Island colony (p126) is one of the most popular for visitors staying in the Falklands. Black-brows are easy to spot offshore all around the Falklands. They breed in September and October, and by March or April the newly fledged young will have left. They also breed on South Georgia.

Black-brows eat squid, fish and crustaceans, caught at the sea's surface or by shallow dives. Interactions with fisheries, especially longliners fishing for tuna and toothfish, are a cause for concern.

Wandering Albatross (Diomedea exulans)

The wandering albatross is a bird of superlatives – for many visitors, it is *the* bird of the Southern Ocean. To see one glide past your vantage place on a ship, just a few metres away as it watches you with its soft brown eyes, is to experience a thrill not for 'lesser mortals'. The species is distinguished from the smaller mollymawks albatrosses by its huge size – its wingspan can reach 3.5m. It's hard to tell the wandering albatross from the royal albatross *(Diomedea epomophora)*, which breeds mainly off New Zealand.

> Young wandering albatrosses may not return to land for five years or more, staying at sea the whole time.

The latest population estimates are 21,000 annual breeding pairs at 10 island groups in the Southern Ocean. The bird's more than year-long breeding season means that, even if successful, it breeds only every second year, so the total breeding population is nearly twice this figure. South Georgia has a breeding population of about 4000 pairs but it is in steady decline. The bird is at serious risk from being caught by longline vessels fishing for tuna – an ignoble death by drowning for such a splendid animal. Much research is currently being done into ways of reducing this mortality, and perhaps as a result some populations have stabilised.

Diet is mainly squid and fish caught, it is thought, by predation at night and scavenging by day. Satellite tracking has revealed that wanderers can cover vast tracts of the Southern Ocean, flying up to several thousand kilometres on a single foraging trip.

Grey-headed Albatross (Diomedea chrysostoma)

The grey-headed albatross is identifiable by its greyish head, broad, dark leading edge to the underwing and orange stripes on both upper and lower mandibles. This species is slightly smaller than the black-browed albatross and only breeds every two years. The world population is around 200,000 breeding pairs and there are large colonies on South Georgia. Grey-heads breed in colonies on cliff ledges, sometimes alongside black-browed albatrosses, as on Bird Island (p154) off the western end of South Georgia. Like all albatrosses, they lay only one egg. Both parents share incubation and chick-feeding. Interactions with longline fishing vessels remain its most serious conservation problem, although the grey-head does not follows ships as much as other varieties.

Sooty (Phoebetria fusca) & Light-mantled Sooty Albatrosses (Phoebetria palpebrata)

It's difficult to distinguish the uniformly chocolate-brown sooty from the light-mantled sooty, even though it has a contrasting pale back. When viewed close up (impossible at sea unless the bird flies right alongside your vessel), the sooty has a yellow stripe (the sulcus) along its lower mandible, whereas the light-mantled sooty has a blue one. Their long, pointed tails and narrow wings make these two species easily distinguishable at sea from giant petrels, which have broader, shorter wings.

Light-mantled sooties tend to occur further south and reach the edge of the pack ice. This is mirrored by their breeding distribution: sooties generally breed further to the north and only light-mantled sooties breed at South Georgia, where they nest in small colonies on cliffs. Their remarkable paired courtship flights and haunting calls around misty cliffs make up one of the quintessential experiences for visitors to the Southern Ocean.

Annual breeding populations are about 16,000 pairs for sooties and 23,000 pairs for light-mantled sooties. They eat squid, fish, crustaceans and small seabirds, such as prions and diving-petrels. Exactly how these last are caught remains unknown, but the species' agile flight and dark colouration suggest predation at night. These albatrosses do not seem to get caught as often on longlines as other albatross species.

CORMORANTS (SHAGS)

Although there may be as many as seven species of cormorant (or shag, to give them their other commonly used name) on the southern islands and the Antarctic Peninsula, there are just two of real interest in the Falklands and South Georgia.

Cormorants breed in summer, forming colonies of nests made of seaweed and terrestrial vegetation on cliff tops and ledges directly above the sea. Up to five eggs are laid. They eat mainly benthic (bottom dwelling) fish, caught by deep and long dives from the surface. The blue-eyed cormorant, with plumage similar to the king cormorant, is also found on South Georgia.

Cormorant chicks hatch naked, which is unique among southern seabirds.

Rock Cormorant (Phalacrocorax magellanicus)

Also known as the rock shag or black shag, there are around 60,000 breeding pairs in the Falklands. The rock cormorant stays in the Falklands year-round and is not found on South Georgia. Rock cormorants form small colonies, sometimes with their nests precariously perched on cliff ledges, but also on piers, jetties and even on the shipwrecks of Stanley Harbour. Their two to five eggs are laid in November and the chicks fledge in January and February. They're relatively weak flyers so they are usually seen close to shore and their presence alongside a ship is a sure sign of approaching land. They dive to a maximum of 15m and particularly like kelp beds. The rock cormorant is slightly smaller than the king cormorant and easily distinguished by its black throat and red face patches.

King Cormorant (Phalacrocorax atriceps)

The king cormorant also has a Falklands population of around 60,000 breeding pairs and stays in the islands year-round, but unlike the rock cormorant is also found on South Georgia. They breed in packed colonies on cliff tops, sometimes with their rock cormorant cousins clinging to the cliff edge below them. The colonies are often intermingled with rockhopper penguins and black-browed albatross colonies. King cormorants lay two to four eggs in November and their chicks fledge in February. Unlike rock cormorants, which tend to stay close to shore, king cormorants make long flights in search of small fish, which they catch in shallow dives. King cormorants are slightly larger than rock cormorants and their throat is white right up to the head, unlike the black-throated rock cormorant.

PETRELS

The order of 'tube-nosed' seabirds includes petrels, storm-petrels, prions, diving-petrels and albatrosses. The name 'petrel' comes from the storm-petrel's ability to 'walk on the water'. The 'storm' may have come about because they are often seen around ships in stormy weather or because stormy weather can blow them inland, where they are known as 'wrecks'.

Giant Petrels

Because they are the largest of the petrel family, giant petrels can be mistaken for albatrosses, although they do not have the effortless soaring grace of the larger birds. Northern (Macronectes halli) and southern giant petrels (Macronectes giganteus) are closely related and not easy to distinguish. Giant petrels can be seen in all parts of the Southern Ocean, with southern giant petrels occurring further south – indeed, some breed on the Antarctic Peninsula. Both species are found on South Georgia, although this is at the southern edge of the northern's range; only the southern is found in the Falklands. Southerns breed in colonies, while northerns breed singly or in scattered groups. Genetic isolation is helped by the fact that northerns commence breeding earlier. Both species are annual breeders. Worldwide there are an estimated 12,000 breeding pairs of northerns and 36,000 pairs of southerns.

Watching blood-stained giant petrels squalling and fighting over a seal carcass is not for the faint-hearted. Indeed, old-time whalers used to call them 'breakbones'.

Unlike albatrosses, giant petrels (nicknamed 'Nellies' or 'stinkers') forage on both land and sea. On land, they kill birds as large as king penguins and scavenge in seal colonies. At sea, they eat fish, squid and crustaceans, and scavenge dead cetaceans and seabirds. The birds have a raffish charm that appeals to some and they are undeniably magnificent fliers.

Giant petrels are caught by tuna and toothfish longline fishing vessels in the Southern Ocean. Several populations of the southern species are decreasing, probably as a result. Northerns are faring better, with some increases recorded, perhaps because increasing seal populations are creating more opportunities for scavenging. Giant petrels are liable to abandon their nests if disturbed, so visitors should give them a wide berth. Their habit of spewing a jet of foul-smelling stomach oil at intruders is another reason to keep clear!

Snow Petrel (Pagodroma nivea)

These unmistakable, pure-white petrels have a black bill and small black eyes, and are truly creatures of the ice. Their flight is more fluttering than most petrels. They breed at hundreds of sites on South Georgia, on rocky slopes and in crevices among boulders on nunataks (rocky peaks surrounded completely by ice) and sea cliffs. They are very much denizens of the pack-ice zone, where they roost on icebergs (the Falklands are too far north).

Snow petrels eat primarily krill, fish and squid, caught mainly by surface-dipping while on the wing. They can regurgitate their stomach oil as a defence mechanism. Snow petrels are nervous at the nest and will desert their eggs if overly disturbed.

Cape Petrel (Daption capense)
The Cape petrel's speckled appearance gives it its other common name, pintado petrel – *pintado* means 'painted' in Spanish. Interestingly, its generic name *Daption* is an anagram of pintado and has no meaning otherwise. The old name 'Cape pigeon' is singularly unhelpful and has thankfully gone out of use: no pigeon can fly the oceans the way a petrel can. As an assiduous ship-follower, the cape petrel eats just about anything edible thrown overboard. In the days of whaling, it was seen in vast noisy numbers around South Georgia's whaling stations and it still breeds on South Georgia. Although they may be seen around the Falklands they do not breed there.

Storm-petrels are the smallest and lightest seabirds in the world. The Wilson's storm-petrel weighs only 35kg to 45g.

Blue Petrel (Halobaena caerulea)
The small blue petrel breeds on a number of islands including South Georgia, but not the Falklands, although their distribution extends that far north. Although there are about 70,000 breeding pairs on South Georgia they've been seriously affected by fur seals destroying the tussock grassland where they nest.

Wilson's Storm-Petrel (Oceanites oceanicus)
'Willies' breed on the more southerly sub-Antarctic islands, including South Georgia (600,000 breeding pairs), where they nest mainly on rocky scree slopes, and in the Falklands. They have been regarded as the world's most abundant seabird, possibly even the most numerous bird on land or sea; there are certainly several million of them, but despite their large numbers they are not often seen. They only come ashore to breed at night, because in daylight they would be easy prey for skuas and other predators.

Willies nest in burrows and rock crevices in cliffs, rocky slopes and scree banks. They eat mainly planktonic crustaceans, including copepods, krill and amphipods, as well as small squid and fish, caught while skimming and pattering with their feet over the sea's surface. Storm-petrels are regular ship followers.

Other Storm-petrels
The small and distinctively marked grey-backed storm-petrel *(Garrodia nereis)* breeds in the Falklands and very occasionally on South Georgia. It nests in coastal grassland among tussock and in hollows among rocks. It feeds by pattering over the sea's surface, and by dipping and shallow-plunging. Black-bellied storm-petrels *(Fregetta tropica)* breed on South Georgia in loose colonies in burrows on steep cliffs above the sea. Foraging is by pattering and dipping.

Prions
Also known as whalebirds, prions are small grey-blue and white birds. They can be distinguished from blue petrels by their black terminal band to the upper tail. All have a vague 'M' shape visible on their upperparts in flight.

Broad-billed prions *(Pachyptila vittata)*, affectionately known as 'Donald Ducks' in some quarters, have the broadest bills, with lamellae for straining out food, analogous to the baleen plates of the great whales. The fairy prion *(Pachyptila turtur)* and thin-billed prion *(Pachyptila belcheri)* have narrow bills. Prions may burrow, or they may breed in crevices among boulders and at the base of cliffs in scree slopes. They can be seen in all areas of the Southern Ocean north of the pack ice to continental waters, often in very large flocks. Like most burrowing petrels of the southern islands, prions have suffered from predation by introduced cats and rats.

Superstitious sealers and whalers called Wilson's storm petrels 'Mother Carey's chickens', from 'Mater Cara' (the Virgin Mary) because they believed that the birds came to collect the souls of dead sailors.

White-chinned Petrel (Procellaria aequinoctialis)
White-chinned petrels breed in the Falkland Islands and South Georgia and, although cats have reduced breeding success on some islands and they're also caught on longline hooks, white-chins are the only burrowing petrel that has not been seriously affected by rats.

Shearwaters
The sooty shearwater *(Puffinus griseus)* is all brown, apart from its silvery underwings, which are obvious in flight. They're found from the pack ice fringe north past the equator and in the Falklands they breed on Kidney Island (p88), just north of Stanley at the entrance to Berkeley Sound. In New Zealand and Australia they're known as muttonbirds and although hundreds of thousands are taken annually by the Maori and on Tasmania's Bass Strait islands, their population runs into the millions. The handsomely marked great shearwater *(Puffinus gravis)* breeds in small numbers on Kidney Island near Stanley and on other tussock islands off East Falkland.

Diving-Petrels
These small seabirds have stubby wings that seem to whir like wind-up toys as they fly fast and low above the sea. Diving-petrels are not usually seen at great distances from their breeding sites. The South Georgian *(Pelecanoides georgicus)* breeds on South Georgia, while the very similar common *(Pelecanoides urinatrix)* sticks to the Falklands and other southern ocean islands. The Falklands' breeding sites are on remote islands so the birds are rarely seen. As with practically all the burrowing petrels, introduced cats and rats have severely reduced some populations of diving-petrel.

White-chinned petrels, the largest of the burrowing petrels, have been called 'Cape hens' and 'shoemakers', because their call resembles the sound of a cobbler hammering shoes.

GEESE
The Falklands' three varieties of geese are easy to distinguish because they tend to stick to their own territory (kelp geese like kelp-strewn coast while upland geese head for the uplands) and because they're almost always seen in pairs. So although you might confuse a ruddy-headed goose with a female upland goose, put two of them together and they're easy to distinguish. The Falklands also have a fair number of feral geese – regular domestic geese that have gone wild.

Upland Goose (Chloephaga picta leucoptera)
With something like 60,000 breeding pairs and habitat spreading to almost every corner of every island, it's hard to get away from the upland goose in the Falkland Islands. You can sometimes step out of the Upland Goose Hotel, Stanley's best known hotel, and see upland geese across the road on the waterfront Victory Green. Upland geese like grassland and it was felt at one time that they competed with sheep for grazing. In the late 1800s farms paid 15 shillings for 100 goose beaks and from 1905 there was an official government bounty of 10 shillings per 100 and an official

'collector of goose beaks'. Fortunately there's a more enlightened attitude today and research has shown sheep and geese can co-exist quite happily, although farmers still look at them askance. The upland goose has, however, long made a minor contribution to Falklands cuisine.

Upland geese lay five to eight eggs in September or October and the chicks are mobile soon after hatching. Many chicks are taken by birds of prey; those that aren't fledge in January or February. The Falklands upland goose is a unique subspecies of the smaller South American variant. Male birds have a white head and breast but females have a brown head and therefore can be mistaken for the ruddy-headed goose. It's usually very easy to identify upland geese, however, because they're almost always seen in pairs. When flying the wings of males and females have a black bar down the centre of the wing, ending in a black wingtip.

Ruddy-headed Goose (Chloephaga rubidiceps)

At a glance ruddy-headed geese look remarkably like female upland geese, but there are far fewer of them (perhaps 3000 breeding pairs) and since they are usually seen in pairs they're quite easy to distinguish. Ruddy-headed geese lay five to eight eggs in October and the chicks fledge in January or February. These geese are closely related to South American ruddy-headed geese, which are very close to extinction.

Kelp Goose (Chloephaga hybrida malvinarum)

This species is also usually seen in pairs; the male is completely white while the female has dark grey and black feathers and a barred breast. They're usually seen on rocky, kelp-strewn coasts since they feed on green seaweed. Kelp geese nest close to the shore and lay four to seven eggs from late October to early November, a month later the chicks hatch, fledging in February. Falklands kelp geese are larger than the South American variety. There are about 15,000 breeding pairs in the Falklands.

Robin and Anne Woods wrote, and Geoffrey McMullan illustrated, *An Atlas of Breeding Birds of the Falklands* (1997), which covers the birds that actually breed in the Falklands.

DUCKS & OTHER WATERFOWL

The numerous ponds and small lakes around the Falklands are home to a large variety of waterfowl, although one of the most interesting and common, the flightless steamer duck, is generally seen along the seashore. South Georgia has one endemic duck (the South Georgia pintail), one of only two land birds found in Antarctica.

Steamer Ducks

The Falklands have two steamer ducks – one that cannot fly and one that can, but would prefer not to. Other than that they're virtually indistinguishable, although the very solid and substantial flightless steamer duck *(Tachyeres brachypterus)* tends to be larger and more heavily built. It looks like flying would be a very difficult proposition. The flightless variety is the most common marine duck in the Falklands and breeds in bays, inlets and beaches all around the coast. Each breeding pair jealously guards a stretch of coastline, chasing off any other intruding steamer ducks. Five to 10 eggs are laid in a nest close to the shoreline between September and December, and the ducklings fledge from January to March.

In the Falklands they are known as logger ducks. The flying steamer duck *(Tachyeres patachonicus)*, also known as the canvasback, is not so keen on the sea, preferring freshwater lakes. They are also much more timid than the flightless variety. There are an estimated 30,000 breeding pairs of the endemic flightless steamer duck; the flying type is much less numerous although it is also found in South America.

Other Ducks

The crested duck *(Anas specularioides specularioides)*, known locally as the grey duck, is one of the most common ducks in the Falklands and is found on both lakes and the sea. It's also one of the noisiest: groups of crested ducks spend a lot of time quacking at each other. The yellow-billed pintail *(Anas georgica spinicauda)* is not particularly numerous but is very widespread. Locally known as the grey or coast teal, it's easy to confuse with the smaller speckled or yellow-billed teal.

The speckled (also known as yellow-billed or Chilean) teal *(Anas flavirostris)* is the smallest of the Falkland ducks and is quite common. It has an exceptionally long breeding season (August to April). It can be distinguished from the superficially similar yellow-billed pintail by its smaller size, tendency to gather in groups, preference for freshwater locales rather than the sea, and bolder disposition.

The steamer ducks' name comes from the way it 'steams' across the water, using its wings with a curious paddling motion when it's in a hurry.

The silver teal *(Anas versicolor fretensis)* and Chiloé wigeon *(Anas sibilatrix)* are both attractive birds that prefer freshwater to salt and are most prevalent on the pools and ponds of Lafonia (p99), the southern half of East Falkland. Neither duck is very enthusiastic about human intruders. Locally known as the pampa teal, the silver teal is widespread but not particularly numerous. It likes ponds with well-established vegetation and is easily recognised by its very distinctive plumage and colouring. The Chiloé wigeon, locally known as the black-and-white wigeon, also has distinctive plumage and colouring.

A variety of other ducks make occasional visits to the Falklands.

South Georgia Pintail (Anas georgica georgica)

Endemic to South Georgia, this pintail is a subspecies of the Falklands' yellow-billed pintail and one of only two land birds found in Antarctica (the other is the South Georgia pipit; see p63). It has been dubbed the world's only carnivorous duck having been sighted pecking at seal carcasses – but, in fact, ducks are not unhappy with consuming other smaller animal life, such as insects and worms.

Black-necked Swan (Cygnus melancoryphus)

With their white bodies and black neck and head, the black-necked swan is like a combination of Australia's black swan and the northern hemisphere's white swans. Black-necked swans breed on large freshwater ponds and despite the plethora of ponds in the Falklands not all of them meet their requirements. Large nests are made close to the water's edge in August and September; the four to seven eggs hatch in late October or early November and the chicks fledge by February. Black-necked swans stay in the Falklands year-round and although they're fairly easy to find they're very wary of any approach and immediately move away.

Grebes

Two varieties of grebe breed in the Falklands and both are very active birds, frequently diving for small fish and aquatic plants. The silvery grebe *(Podiceps occipitalis)* is found only in the south of South America and the Falklands. Although there are only about 500 breeding pairs in the Falklands, they are widely distributed: they prefers ponds and slow-moving streams close to the coast, and in winter can also be found on kelp beds. The more common white-tufted grebe *(Podiceps rolland)* is found in similar habitat to the slightly smaller silvery grebe. Its breeding season begins a little earlier and, like the silvery grebe, it often feeds in kelp beds during the winter months.

Another species, the great grebe *(Podiceps major)*, is a regular visitor from South America and about twice the length of the two resident Falklands grebes.

HERONS, EGRETS & IBISES

Known as the 'quark' in the Falklands, the black-crowned night heron *(Nycticorax nycticorax falklandicus)* is found in the Americas, Europe, Africa and South Asia; the Falklands subspecies is endemic to the islands. They hunt after dusk, stealthily grabbing fish from rock pools and shallow kelp beds. They nest in tussock grass, under piers and jetties and in trees; the settlement at Carcass Island had a famous colony of night herons in the trees beside the house until they were hunted out by striated caracaras. Two to four eggs are laid between October and November, and the birds remain in the Falklands year-round.

The other herons, egrets and ibises seen around the Falklands are either annual visitors or occasional vagrants from South America.

RAPTORS

Spotting a peregrine falcon or a red-backed hawk is a thrill, but it's the comic antics of the striated caracara, known locally as 'Johnny Rook', which are the big attraction. Five species of raptor breed in the Falklands.

Striated Caracara (Phalcoboenus australis)

'Johnny Rook' is one of the Falklands' most interesting birds and also one of the most endangered. Although this large bird of prey is also found on remote parts of the South American mainland, its chances of survival are highest in the Falklands, which is estimated to have as much as three-quarters of the world population.

Charles Darwin, during his time in the Falklands in 1833 and 1834, noted in *Voyage of the Beagle* that the bird was 'exceedingly numerous' and that it 'constantly haunted the neighbourhood of houses'. He added it was also 'extraordinarily tame and fearless' and 'very mischievous and inquisitive, quarrelsome and passionate'. It was not a good combination of characteristics, because when the Falklands developed its sheep focus anything that threatened the well-being of sheep was an enemy, and being 'tame and fearless' made the bird an easy target. With a bounty on its head from 1908, the unfortunate Johnny Rook soon faced a 'a remorseless process of extermination' and by 1922 numbers were very low. Bounty payments soon ceased, but the relationship between the unfortunate bird and Falklands sheep farming continued to be an unhappy one.

Until they reach breeding age Johnny Rooks tend to hang out in rowdy bunches, like teenage gangs.

Two centuries of human contact hasn't made the bird any more cautious. Falklands Conservation (FC) notes that visiting birders 'are amazed when they first encounter a Johnny Rook. They admire the handsome markings of the adults, the impudence of the immatures, their agility on the ground and in the air. As a large bird of prey, it is a powerful predator yet it is ridiculously tame and very vulnerable to persecution.' Johnny Rooks are now protected, with fines of up to £3000 for killing a bird, but a survey from 1997 to 1998 estimated the total breeding population in the Falklands to be only about 500 pairs. Breeding generally takes place on remote, uninhabited islands but nonbreeding birds flock to settlements in autumn to scavenge, and to prey on geese and, if they're available, frail or sickly sheep or lambs. On some remote islands they've taken to staying up at night to pick off petrels returning to their burrows after sunset. See p168 for Johnny Rook warnings.

Crested Caracara (Polyborus plancus plancus)

Known locally as the *carancho*, the handsome crested caracara is found all over the Falklands, but nowhere in great numbers and, unlike Johnny Rook, it's shy and retiring. Big, untidy nests are made for the two or three eggs laid in September or October. Like the striated caracara, it's principally a carrion eater, but quite happy to kill live prey if it's available. The breeding population is probably similar to the striated caracara at around 500 breeding pairs. The crested caracara is the national bird of Mexico where it is known as the Mexican eagle.

Red-backed Hawk (Buteo polyosoma)

Known in the Falklands as the red-backed buzzard or, in the case of the male, as the grey-backed, there are about 500 breeding pairs of these handsome predators. They're found throughout the islands and are able to use a wide variety of nesting sites. They're often spotted perched on fence posts or other suitable outcrops, spying for prey. They catch small birds, and introduced rabbits and rats have provided them with a wider food supply. Their colours are quite variable, but only the slightly larger female has the distinguishing red back; males are blue-grey.

Peregrine Falcon (Falco peregrinus cassini)

Although it's widespread in the Falklands, the peregrine falcon is not abundant and there are only about 300 breeding pairs. Known locally as the sparrowhawk or Cassin's falcon, they make simple nests on steep cliffs on the coast, or on rocky crags further inland. Peregrine falcons prey mainly on smaller birds, particularly prions, which they carry back to their nests to eat.

Turkey Vulture (Cathartes aura falklandicus)

Although they're scavengers rather than hunters, the Falklands' largest and most numerous bird of prey is not popular with Falkland farmers. There is no longer a bounty paid on each turkey vulture head, but concerns that they will attack stranded or weak sheep adds to their image problem. With their wrinkled red head and solid black plumage, being downright ugly doesn't help either. Sometimes known in the Falklands as the plain turkey, it is found all over the island and is regularly seen high overhead searching for carrion – even seal and sea lion placentas and faeces will suffice. Turkey vultures nest on rocky crags, in caves and on tussock islands.

WADERS, SHEATHBILLS, GULLS, TERNS & SKUAS

The seemingly diverse group of birds in the order *Charadriiformes* includes 10 species that breed in the Falklands. Sheathbills, which are common around the Falklands, actually breed on South Georgia. The Antarctic tern, kelp gull and skua breed on both the Falklands and South Georgia, although there are different types of skua in the two locales.

Magellanic Oystercatcher (Haematopus leucopodus)

The Magellanic (or pied) oystercatcher (or seapie) is very common on Falklands' shorelines whether they're sandy, rocky or muddy. Their white underparts, black upper body and pink-red bill are extremely distinctive, and this colouring has led to another name – black-and-white curloo. Like other waders, the young leave the nest soon after hatching, but spend a long time under parental supervision. Magellanic oystercatchers have a characteristic whistling call.

When danger, such as a human intruder, approaches a Magellanic oystercatcher's nest it will feign injury and stagger away, hoping to entice the interloper to follow them. On the other hand they'll fight off predators with great vigour.

Black Oystercatcher (Haematopus ater)

Although looking remarkably like a Magellanic oystercatcher without the two-tone colour scheme, the black oystercatcher is slightly shyer. Since it likes rocky shores, where it blends in well and can find the mussels and limpets that are its main food, it is less likely to be seen than the Magellanic oystercatcher. Like its close relative, it nests in a shallow scrape close to the top of a beach.

Two-banded Plover (Charadrius falklandicus)

Known in the Falklands as the beach lark, this wader is very common on Falklands estuaries and sandy beaches, rarely venturing far from the coast. Its chicks can often be seen on beaches, carefully watched over by their parents. Plovers prefer to run from danger, even though they're strong flyers. The male is easily distinguished by the two bands across its white breast; females are less conspicuously marked. Two-banded plovers hunt small invertebrates by making short runs, then stopping to check where things are. Rufous-chested dotterels have a similar technique.

Rufous-chested Dotterel (Charadrius modestus)

This very common bird can be seen everywhere from estuaries to grassland. During the breeding season they have an easily identified chestnut brown breast, but its colours, and soft, trembling song, are much less noticeable the rest of the year. Most of the Falklands' population migrates to South America for the winter and its return in September marks the start of the Falklands spring. The young hang around with their parents for a long time.

In spring, Magellanic snipe perform aerobatic displays, making an eerie drumming sound with their tail feathers.

Magellanic Snipe (Gallinago magellanica magellanica)

Snipe are found in grassland and heaths all over the Falklands and can be very tame, particularly when they're out hunting for food with their young. They probe peat bogs with their long bill, hunting for invertebrates like worms and grubs. Like other birds in this group the young remain under parental supervision for a long period. When danger presents they respond by staying completely still, trusting their camouflage to hide their position.

White-rumped Sandpiper (Calidris fuscicollis)

Although they do not breed in the Falklands, white-rumped sandpipers flock there in such numbers that they are the most common wader around the islands during the summer months. In the winter they migrate all the way to the Arctic coasts of North America to breed during the northern summer. With grey-brown upperparts it's not a very conspicuous bird compared to the local waders.

Snowy Sheathbill (Chionis alba)

Sheathbills are odd birds in a number of ways. They're not seabirds (for example, their feet are not webbed), but are placed in their own family, allied to waders. They cannot be mistaken for anything else as they strut and squabble around penguin colonies. Also known as the greater, American or pale-faced sheathbill, the snowy sheathbill occurs on South Georgia and migrates north to the Falklands in winter, although it can be found there year-round. Sheathbills nest in crevices in summer, usually near penguin colonies, where they scavenge widely on eggs, spilled food being fed to chicks and carcasses killed by giant petrels. They also feed on intertidal life and on invertebrates in the peat.

Kelp Gull (Larus dominicanus)

The kelp, or Dominican, gull breeds on South Georgia and the Falklands and is resident year-round. It's the more common gull around the islands. Like most southern seabirds, kelp gulls breed in summer. Chicks can leave the nest soon after hatching, but are still fed by their parents until after they can fly. Diet includes scraps scavenged from giant petrel kills and, in penguin colonies, terrestrial invertebrates such as earthworms and moth larvae, and intertidal shellfish such as limpets. There are about 30,000 breeding pairs in the Falklands and, although they breed far away from settlements, they may be seen around Stanley, where they drop mussels on the waterfront Ross Rd to open them.

Other Gulls

Other gulls seen around the Falklands include the dolphin gull *(Larus scoresbii)*, known locally as the red-billed gull. There are about 4000 breeding pairs in the Falklands, a large part of the world population. They nest in small colonies and are generally scavengers rather than predators. Less numerous, although it also breeds in the Falklands, the brown-hooded gull *(Larus maculipennis)* is also smaller than the kelp and dolphin gull. All these gulls are enthusiastic about humans when it comes to looking for food sources but do not like to breed anywhere near settlements.

Terns

The Antarctic tern *(Sterna vittata)* breeds on both South Georgia and the Falklands while the South American tern *(Sterna hirundinacea)* is found only in the Falklands. They are similarly sized, slender, long-winged, grey-and-white birds. Terns breed in summer, laying mottled eggs in open nests in loose colonies. They eat mainly small fish caught at the surface or by shallow dives within sight of land, often within the kelp bed zone. Terns are very easily scared away from their nests and any tern colony should be approached with great caution. Like skuas, they will defend their nesting sites fiercely, but may completely abandon them if overly disturbed. There are about 10,000 breeding pairs of South American tern in the Falklands, all generally located well away from any settlement.

Skuas

Large, heavily built, gull-like birds, skuas are mainly brown but with conspicuous white flashes in their wings. Falkland skuas *(Catharacta skua antarctica)* are known locally as sea hens. They're marginally smaller than the Antarctic (or brown) skuas *(Catharacta skua lonnbergi)*, which are found on South Georgia, and have paler plumage. Their flight is heavy, with relatively little gliding and much flapping.

At sea, skuas chase smaller seabirds to force them to regurgitate or drop their prey (kleptoparasitism), often retrieving it spectacularly before it hits the water.

In winter, both species leave their breeding localities and spend time at sea, occasionally even reaching the Northern Hemisphere. Both breed in summer, generally laying two mottled eggs in open nests on the ground. Breeding birds are strictly territorial and will quickly chase off intruders, not hesitating to fly – clawed feet outstretched – right at the head of any human who comes too near their nest.

Skuas prey upon the eggs and chicks of penguins and other colonial seabirds (including adults of the smaller species), but also clean up any carrion. Any colony of penguins or cormorants will have skuas lurking around, often brazenly landing right among their potential victims. They also feed on Antarctic krill, squid and fish.

OWLS

These nocturnal birds are not common in the Falklands, but there's not a lot of owl-friendly habitat. There are only a dozen or so breeding pairs of the nocturnal barn owl *(Tyto alba)* which, because of the short nights during the summer months, often have to resort to hunting during daylight hours. The short-eared owl *(Asio flammeus sanfordi)* is a subspecies unique to the Falklands and rather more common than the barn owl, although that still amounts to only about 100 breeding pairs. It generally lives on offshore islands (although it has been seen on Kidney Island near Stanley), where it preys on prions and petrels, and will also take rodents and insects.

A few years ago the FC website reported that a barn owl had taken up residence in an old freezer store at Grytviken on South Georgia. The report said it may have been blown there by a storm, but there was certainly no shortage of resident rats to feed this unusual Antarctic visitor.

PASSERINES

Perching birds – the so-called passerines – collectively form an order that includes wrens, thrushes, larks, swallows and sparrows, among others. There is only one passerine, the South Georgia pipit (p63), on South Georgia, but a wider variety is found in the Falklands. Many of these birds are unique subspecies of similar South American species, indicating that perhaps they came to the islands by accident, blown off course by winds, and have not maintained contact with the larger populations on the continental mainland. The Falklands' passerines are more often heard than seen – they're not always easily spotted simply by sitting and waiting for them to appear.

A Visitor's Guide to the Falkland Islands by Debbie Summers (2001) is a nicely produced colour guide for cruise-ship visitors, with excellent maps of many of the islands and wildlife sites popular with cruise ships.

The lack of trees means many of these small birds nest on the ground, where they have become easy prey for introduced cats and rats. The devastation of the coastal fringe of tussock grass, particularly on the main islands, has also deprived them of much ground cover. As a result the population of these small birds is much stronger on outlying islands, particularly those that have remained cat- and rat-free. The Cobb's wren is a handy test: if an island has rats it doesn't have these tiny birds.

The common house sparrow can also be found in the Falklands, mainly around Stanley although its numbers seem to be steadily increasing. It was almost certainly not introduced deliberately to the islands; sparrows probably arrived as stowaways on cargo ships.

Cobb's Wren (Troglodytes cobbi)

Locally known as the rock wren, the endemic Cobb's wren is found only on certain generally uninhabited islands around the Falklands – on the main islands it has been exterminated by rats. The Cobb's wren nests on boulder-strewn or rocky beaches or among tussock grass; it builds a hollow ball-shaped nest of grass with an entrance hole, lined with feathers. Something between 2000 and 6000 breeding pairs survive in the Falklands, many of them on Sea Lion (p103), Carcass (p129) and Kidney (p88) Islands. When you walk along the shoreline these tiny birds hop out from under rocks as you approach, disappearing just as adroitly as you get closer.

Falkland Grass Wren (Cistothorus platensis falklandicus)

The smaller grass wren is much more widespread than the Cobb's wren and manages to survive on islands with rat populations, probably because it spends more time in thick vegetation and above ground level. Nevertheless, they're more successful on rat-free islands. A subspecies found only in the Falklands, the grass wren is known locally as the short-billed marsh wren. The ball-shaped nest is built well above the ground in tall grass or reeds.

Dark-faced Ground Tyrant (Muscisaxicola macloviana macloviana)

The dark-faced ground tyrant is related to flycatchers. It lives on moths and other insects, caught on the wing, as well as other invertebrates found among rocks, grass and even seaweed. The dark-faced ground tyrant is found on open grassland and heath all the way from the coast to hill tops. It's keen on settlements because of the easy availability of insects. The Falklands population is a locally unique subspecies of about 20,000 breeding pairs. This small bird builds a nest lined with feathers and wool.

The dark-faced ground tyrant is called the 'news bird' from its habit of hopping up to visitors as if it was about to have a chat.

Tussock Bird (Cinclodes antarcticus antarcticus)

More correctly called the blackish cinclodes, this small bird doesn't survive on islands with rats or cats. However, on rat-free islands it's common along sandy or rocky shorelines and amazingly tame. Tussock birds feed on invertebrates found along the shoreline and any other tasty scraps. This small grey-brown to dark-brown birds nest under dense vegetation.

Black-throated Finch (Melanodera melanodera melanodera)

The 'sparrow', as it's known in the Falklands, is another subspecies found only on these islands. The male has a handsome blue-grey head with black marks on the face, but the female plumage is much less dramatic; in fact, it does look pretty much like a common sparrow. Black-throated finches are found all over the Falklands, particularly in coastal regions, and build down-lined grass nests hidden close to ground level. These finches use their heavy bill to feed on a wide variety of seeds. There are about 10,000 breeding pairs in the Falklands, a much healthier population than the South American variant.

Black-chinned Siskin (Carduelis barbata)

There are about 1000 breeding pairs of this bird in the Falklands; it is also found in southern South America. In the Falklands it's found on islands with tussock grass and its survival has been helped by the planting of trees and shrubs around settlements. It is often heard rather than seen, despite its yellow-and-brown plumage and, on the males only, black cap and chin. In the Falklands it's sometimes referred to as the canary.

Falkland Pipit (Anthus correndera grayi)

Yet another subspecies endemic to the Falklands, the 'skylark', as it's known to the islanders, is the most common small bird on open grasslands, although it's shy and not frequently seen. Between October and December, the Falkland pipit lays two to four eggs; it usually raises two or even three broods each year. There are about 15,000 breeding pairs in the Falklands and it feeds on insects, spiders and worms.

Tussock birds will hop right up to you and perch on your shoes if you stop for more than a few moments – they're hoping you'll scare up something interesting to eat.

Falkland Thrush (Turdus falcklandii falcklandii)

Fairly common throughout the Falklands, the thrush has adapted to a wide range of habitats and co-exists quite happily with humans. It feeds on insects, worms, berries and seeds, and accepts handouts from households. This middle-sized bird is brown-grey with a distinctive yellow bill, legs and ring around the eye.

Long-tailed Meadowlark (Sturnella loyca falklandica)

It's easy to see why the meadowlark, with its bright red breast, is known locally as the 'robin' or 'military starling'. It's found particularly along the coast and around settlements, where it can often be seen perched on fenceposts or other convenient lookouts. Only the males have the distinctive red breast, but both sexes are easily identified by their long tail and beak. Food includes worms, insects and even small marine invertebrates found along the shoreline. The female does all the hard work, building the nest, sitting on the eggs and feeding the young.

South Georgia Pipit (Anthus antarcticus)

This rather dowdy and sparrow-sized bird is found only on South Georgia, either on rat-free outlying islands or on isolated rat-free sections of the south coast of the main island. South Georgia's only passerine and the Antarctic's only songbird, it typically lays four eggs in a nest of dried grass in tussock grass. During the summer months the South Georgia pipit lives on insects and spiders, but in winter, when snow blankets the ground, it feeds on beach debris.

MARINE LIFE

KRILL

The shrimp-like Antarctic krill *(Euphausia superba)* is a 6cm-long planktonic crustacean that occurs in sometimes enormous swarms south of the Antarctic Convergence. Krill is sifted out of the water by baleen whales, and eaten by many species of southern seabirds (especially penguins), squid, fish and crabeater seals, which have specially adapted teeth for this purpose. Without krill, the ecosystem of the Southern Ocean would collapse; at the end of the food chain there's almost always something which eats krill.

The name krill comes from Norwegian and translates as 'very small fish' or 'whale food'.

It has been estimated that there are 3.5 billion tonnes of krill in the sea, about 10% of which is consumed by whales, seals, seabirds, fish and squid each year. Another estimate is 650 million tonnes in the Southern Ocean. Whales eat an estimated 30 million tonnes of krill annually, but before whaling drastically reduced their numbers they consumed much more. The reduction in whale numbers has increased the availability of krill, which in turn has led to increases in numbers of certain types of seabird and seal.

Ice krill *(Euphausia crystallarophias)* is a smaller species that has been the target of fisheries for a number of years. Krill is difficult to process for human consumption as the fluorine in the exoskeleton contaminates other parts of their structure soon after they are killed. Most krill fishing has been by Russians (who use krill for animal feed and as an ingredient in sausages and fish balls) or by Japanese (who use it in flavourings, soup mixes and as other food additives). Catches peaked in the early 1980s at over 400,000 tonnes a summer season, but have subsequently dropped to around 100,000 tonnes. Quotas are now set by the Commission for the Conservation of Antarctic Marine Living Resources (CCAMLR), which also encourages research on krill and its predators.

Icefish are notable for having no haemoglobin in their blood.

SQUID

Forming the mainstay of the fishing fleets that work the Falklands' maritime zone, squid provide a substantial proportion of the islands' annual income. The Patagonian squid, also known as loligo *(Loligo gahi)*, is found particularly off the eastern side of East Falkland, with especially high concentrations off Beauchêne Island. The small squid grows to only about 30cm and is pursued by black-browed albatrosses and rockhopper penguins, as well as Spanish stern trawlers. Apart from the fact that there are lots of them not a great deal is known about the squid's life cycle.

The larger Argentine short-finned squid, also known as illex *(Illex argentinus)*, grows to around 40cm and is popular with albatrosses, penguins and fur seals, as well as east Asian squid 'jiggers', particularly from Korea. Little is known about this squid's natural history either, although it is believed both types complete their life cycle in a year.

FISH
The Falklands

Robin Woods covers the Falklands' plant life in *Flowering Plants of the Falkland Islands* (2000).

For an island nation with an extremely long coastline the Falkland Islanders, like the Irish, have historically shown little interest in fish. Nevertheless, fly fishing has become a major tourist attraction in the islands. The sea trout *(Salmo trutta)* was introduced to the Falklands in 1940 (see p163 for more about the development of fly fishing), but its spread has pushed the smaller local zebra trout *(Aplochiton zebra)* back to the most remote corners of the islands. There are three species of Falklands minnow; and the Falklands mullet *(Eleginops maclovinus)* is also popular with fly fishers.

South Georgia

Fishing licences have also assumed great importance for the South Georgian economy, but in South Georgian waters it's fish rather than squid that are pursued. About a dozen species have been fished since the start of large scale fishing around South Georgia in the late 1960s. Some species have already been severely affected including marbled rock cod *(Notothenia rossi)*, which only lasted two years. Patagonian toothfish *(Dissostichus eleginoides)* is the most-prized of the Antarctic cod varieties, and is marketed as Chilean sea bass. Other popular catches include lanternfish *(Electrona guntheri)* and mackerel icefish *(Champsocephalus gunnari)*.

VEGETATION

THE FALKLANDS

Along with scurvy grass, sea cabbage was eaten by early visitors to the Falklands to ward off scurvy.

The lack of trees is one of the most immediately noticeable characteristics of the Falklands' landscape. The islands have a fairly simple vegetation, much of it related to South America, particularly Patagonia and Tierra del Fuego, although some Falklands plants are also found in Australia and New Zealand. There are more than 160 species, of which 14 are endemic.

Much of the rolling landscape is dominated by white grass *(Cortaderia pilosa)* – see the boxed text p64. At one time tussock grass *(Parodiochloa flabellata),* also known as tussac, would have fringed almost every coastal area. Grazing activities quickly wiped it out in many areas, although it is making a recovery as farmers fence off coastal areas to keep grazing stock out. Some farmers are actually replanting tussock, but the erosion that can occur after tussock has disappeared can make it difficult to regenerate.

WHITE GRASS

White grass *(Cortaderia pilosa)* is the most common vegetation across the main Falklands islands, particularly in the 'soft camp' areas where drainage is poor. The low-lying Lafonia area in the south of East Falkland is blanketed in white grass. White grass is not so prevalent in the better drained areas of 'hard camp' and it does not appear very often on the smaller islands. White grass is indeed whiteish to light brown in colour.

Diddle-dee *(Empetrum rubrum)* is a very common dwarf shrub found from sea level to mountain tops. It adds some colour to the often uniform grey-green landscape when it blossoms from August to mid-October. Female plants have bright-red berries, which ripen in the autumn and can be used as preserves. The less common tea berries *(Myrteola nummularia)* are a delight in their natural state, although they're time consuming to collect. There's also a native strawberry. Balsam bog *(Bolax gummifera)* is another Falklands favourite; it forms in rounded yellow-green mounds or like hard cushions on rocky, drier soils. Darwin called it 'living rock'.

The small booklet *Wild Flowers of the Falkland Islands* was written by TH Davies and JH McAdam (1989).

Scurvy grass *(Oxalis enneaphylla)* is found near the coast and has white flowers from November to January. It was used by early seafaring visitors for protection against scurvy. Sea cabbage *(Senecio candicans)* has velvety grey-green leaves and grows on beaches and dunes. Wildflowers include the endemic pale maiden *(Sisyrinchium jubatum)* and the arrow-leaved marigold *(Caltha sagittata)*, which flowers in November and December in wet areas near water.

Two native bushes are found in the Falklands, apart from introduced gorse. Native boxwood *(Hebe elliptica)* is grown as a windbreak while fachine *(Chiliotrichum diffusum)*, now comparatively rare, has suffered from overgrazing. Gorse *(Ulex europaeus)* was introduced as a windbreak around settlements and is wonderfully colourful when flowering between October and March. Most trees in the Falklands are also introduced and they're often found around settlement houses; the settlement on Carcass Island has a particularly fine stand. At Hill Cove on West Falkland there's a real forest.

Environmental Management Plan for South Georgia by Dr Elizabeth McIntosh and Dr David WH Walton (2000) is full of useful information about the Island, Its administration, economy and, of course, its fascinating natural history. The report is available on the BAS website at www.antarctica.ac.uk /News_and_Information /Press_Releases/1999 /sgemp.pdf.

SOUTH GEORGIA

If the Falkland Islands' vegetation is fairly simple, that of South Georgia seems positively black-and-white. Tussock grass, moss and lichens predominate, but, in fact, there are 26 native species of higher plants including five different types of grass. There are 100 species of mosses and lichens, and more than 50 toadstools and other fungi. Nowhere further south is there this diversity of vegetation.

Kelp

The giant kelp beds that fringe much of the Falklands and South Georgia are very evident both from the air and at sea level. Giant kelp can reach more than 50m in length.

Stanley

Stanley, the Falklands' capital, is little more than a village which, by historical accident, has acquired a political status totally out of proportion to its size. Despite the rapid growth since 1982 the old part of the town retains its quaint and colourful charm. Bricks were expensive to ship and difficult to make locally while the local stone proved tricky to quarry, so Stanley's builders developed their own building methods incorporating timber from shipwrecks, metal cladding, wide use of corrugated ('wriggly') iron for walls as well as roofs – all of it painted in bright colours.

Flower-bedecked gardens and the odd patriotic flag add to the vivid colours, which make a startling contrast with the surrounding moorlands. Kitchen gardens and the occasional shed full of cut peat hint at an older Stanley lifestyle, although these days most food will come from the supermarket, and the sweetish fragrance of burning peat rarely hangs over the town. The old pubs are reminders that some Falklands traditions have remained unchanged.

If the weather cooperates, Stanley's picturesque and compact layout make it an excellent place to explore on foot. The litter of old shipwrecks along the waterfront provides interest for a waterfront stroll or with more time you can climb to the highpoints around the harbour – many of the hills around Stanley were the scene of fierce fighting in the closing days of the Falklands War in 1982. Just west of the town the Falkland Islands Museum provides an excellent introduction to an often colourful history. Stanley is also the jumping off point for exploring all other centres in the Falklands, whether it's heading out to camp (anywhere in the Falklands outside Stanley) by 4WD or off to West Falkland and the outer islands on the small Islander aircraft of the Falkland Islands' airline FIGAS (Falkland Islands Government Air Service).

HIGHLIGHTS

- Walking Stanley's **history trail** (p75) and soaking up some of its colourful past
- Drinking with the locals in **pubs** (p81) that could easily have been transported from Britain
- Exploring the Falklands' shipwreck history along the **Maritime History Trail** (p72)
- Climbing the **hills** (p86) around the capital, the final battlegrounds of the Falklands War
- Visiting the superb **Falkland Islands Museum** (p71)

★ Stanley
  Township

POPULATION: 2000

STANLEY

HISTORY

In 1844 the colonial office ordered the move of the Falklands' capital from Port Louis, on Berkeley Sound, to the more sheltered Port Jackson, which has since been renamed Stanley Harbour. The new site was more accessible from the sea, had plenty of peat for fuel and a good supply of fresh water from Moody Brook. Originally a tiny outpost of colonial officials, vagabond sailors and British military pensioners, the town grew slowly as a supply and repair port for ships rounding Cape Horn en route to the California Gold Rush. Some damaged vessels limped into port, their cargoes legitimately condemned and sold, but ships began to avoid the port when others were scuttled under such questionable circumstances that the town acquired an unsavoury reputation. Only as sheep replaced cattle in the late 19th century did Stanley begin to grow more rapidly as the trans-shipment point for wool between camp and the UK.

As the wool trade grew so did the influence of the Falkland Islands Company (FIC), which was already the islands' largest landowner. FIC became the town's largest employer after acquiring the property of JM Dean, its only commercial rival, in 1889. Over the next century FIC's dominance was uncontested; it ruled the town no less absolutely than the owners of the large sheep stations ruled camp. The company's relatively high wages and good housing provided a paternalistic security, although these 'tied houses' were available only so long as an employee remained with the company.

During the 1982 conflict, the capital escaped almost unscathed, despite being occupied by thousands of Argentine troops. The two major exceptions were both ironic: a British shell hit a house on the outskirts of town, killing three local women; while Argentine conscripts rioted against their officers after the surrender and burned the historic Globe Store, a business whose Anglo-Argentine owner had died only a few years earlier.

Stanley remains the service centre for the wool industry, but since the declaration of a fisheries protection zone around the islands it has become an important deep-water fishing port. Many Asian and European fishing companies have offices here. The potential oil boom promises further changes, while the proliferation of shops and tour operators indicate the Falklands' growing importance as a tourist destination.

ORIENTATION

On a steep hillside on the south shore of Stanley Harbour, Port William's sheltered inner harbour on East Falkland, Stanley is surrounded by water and low hills. To avoid the prevailing southwesterlies, the town has sprawled east and west along the harbour rather than onto the exposed ridge of Stanley Common to the south.

Ross Rd, running the length of the harbour, is the main street, but most government offices, businesses and interesting old houses are within a few blocks of each other in the compact town centre. The old town of Stanley is almost all on the western side. As you move east towards the FIPASS (Floating Interim Port and Storage System) floating dock and Stanley Airport the new houses, colourfully painted so they fit the

---

PEAT SLIPS

Twice during the late 19th century Stanley suffered unusual semi-natural disasters – peat slips. Flying over the Falklands you will see long rectangular ditches, often water-filled, where peat has been cut for fuel. In the late 1800s peat cutting in the hillsides above Stanley had made some of the slopes dangerously unstable. On 30 November 1878 a slurry of peat over a metre deep slid down through the town, effectively dividing it into eastern and western halves. Fortunately no great damage was caused and there were no injuries.

The story was not so straightforward when a second peat slip occurred on 2 June 1886. This time the runaway peat destroyed houses, killed two people and caused so much damage to the Exchange Building that it was declared unsafe. This prominent building, with its high central clock tower, was built in 1854 as a meeting place for the town's colonists and ship masters; it housed Stanley's school in one wing and the Holy Trinity Church in the other. The loss of the church prompted the construction of the current cathedral (p70), which opened six years later.

old Stanley context at a glance, are in fact much bigger and more luxurious than those in the old town. They're a clear reminder of the watershed between the old (pre-1982) Falklands and the new (postwar) Falklands. The new Stanley has also spread west of the old centre.

INFORMATION

Stanley's a fairly quiet little town most of the time, but things really change when there's a big cruise ship in town. Some of them can carry over a thousand passengers and on occasion two of these monsters contrive to turn up on the same day. Take the arrival of a big ship as the signal to get out of town. Smaller expedition-style cruise ships, often with less than 100 passengers, are a very different story.

Bookshops

Beauchêne Supermarket (Map pp70-1; Beauchêne Shopping Centre, John St) Books and some magazines can also be found here.

Capstan Gift Shop (Map pp70-1; Ross Rd) Has a varied range of books and maps on the Falklands, Antarctica and the South Atlantic, including many titles you're unlikely to readily locate elsewhere.

FIC West Store (Map pp70-1; Ross Rd) Books (and some magazines) can also be found here, right across the road from the Capstan.

Emergency

Fire and Rescue (Map pp70-1; ☎ 27333; St Mary's Walk)

Police (Map pp70-1; ☎ 27222; Ross Rd)

Police, fire and ambulance (☎ 999)

Laundry

Trigger's Laundry Service (Map pp70-1; ☎ 22704; Davis St East; per kg £2.40) In the Lookout Industrial Estate, opposite the car wash. It does pick-up and delivery of laundry and dry-cleaning, and you can get it back the next day if it's not too busy.

Libraries

Lighthouse Seamen's Centre (Map p84; ☎ 22780; beside FIPASS entrance; ⏰ 10am-5pm Tue-Sun, until 9pm if fishing boats in port) Has a good selection of books you can browse; see p80.

Stanley Public Library (Map pp70-1; ☎ 27147; Reservoir Rd; ⏰ 8.45am-noon & 1.30-5.45pm Mon-Fri, 10am-noon & 2-5pm Sat) In the Falkland Islands Community School. It keeps a large selection of specialist papers and books relating to the Falklands.

Medical Services

Hospital dispensary (☎ 27315; St Mary's Walk; ⏰ 9.30am-12.30pm & 1.30-5pm Mon-Fri) Stanley has no commercial pharmacy, but this dispensary at the hospital, below, fills prescriptions.

King Edward VII Memorial Hospital (Map pp70-1; ☎ 27328 appointments, ☎ 27410 emergencies; St Mary's Walk) A joint military–civilian facility. This is probably the best in the world for a community of Stanley's size. Dental services are also excellent. Since care is on a fee-for-service basis, be certain to have insurance.

Money

Most Stanley businesses readily accept travellers cheques and some places accept credit cards. See p172 for more information.

Standard Chartered Bank (Map pp70-1; ☎ 21352; Ross Rd; ⏰ 8.30am-3pm Mon-Fri) The only bank in the Falklands. There is no ATM machine, but the bank changes foreign currency and travellers cheques. It also cashes personal cheques drawn on several UK banks with the appropriate guarantee card.

Post

Post Office (Map pp70-1; ☎ 27180; Ross Rd at Barrack St; ⏰ 8am-noon, 1.15-4.30pm Mon-Fri) Has a Philatelic Bureau (p82).

Telephone & Fax

In Stanley there are public phones situated on Philomel St close to the tourist office, outside the FIC West Store, outside the post office, at the Cable & Wireless PLC office, the Lighthouse Seamen's Centre and FIPASS.

Cable & Wireless PLC (Map pp70-1; ☎ 20804; Ross Rd; ⏰ 8am-noon & 1.15-4.30pm Mon-Thu, 8am-noon & 1.15-4.15pm Fri) Easily identified by its satellite dish, it operates the Falklands' phone, telegram, telex and fax services, and sells phonecards. Limited Internet (p171).

Tourist Information

Falkland Islands Tourist Board (FITB; Map pp70-1; ☎ 22215, 22281; manager@tourism.org.fk; Jetty Centre; ⏰ 9am-5pm Mon-Fri, 10am-4pm Sat & Sun, 10am-3pm Tue, Thu, Sat, Sun in winter) At the Public Jetty, the Jetty Centre tourist office distributes a newspaper-style guide to Stanley and other useful brochures, including a booklet listing accommodation throughout the islands. Office hours are longer if there's a cruise ship in port.

Travel Agencies

See p78 for information on tour operators within the Falklands and p82 for information on airline agencies.

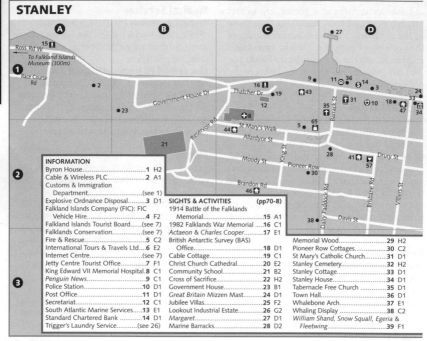

SIGHTS
Christ Church Cathedral

The great peat slip of 1886 (p68) wiped out Stanley's Holy Trinity Church. The foundation stone for its replacement was laid in 1890 and the new church opened in 1892. The massive brick-and-stone **Christ Church Cathedral** (Map pp70-1) with its brightly painted, corrugated-metal roof and attractive stained-glass windows is undoubtedly the town's most distinguished landmark. Plaques along the walls honour the memory of local men who served in the British Forces in WWI and WWII, as well as the great and good of the Falklands.

The stained glass windows are the church's most vivid feature. As you enter from the main door you face the Post Liberation Memorial Window with the Falklands crest and the islands' motto 'Desire the Right'. Below are the crests of the various British forces involved in the 1982 conflict and, below that, illustrations of three features of the Falklands and South Georgia: the Cathedral and Whalebone Arch represent Stanley; a typical farm settlement represents

camp; and the Grytviken Church and surrounding mountains are for South Georgia. At the other end of the same (south) wall is the charming Mary Watson window, dedicated to a much-loved district nurse standing with her bicycle at the ready.

For the Cathedral's centenary in 1992 members of the congregation stitched pictorial hassocks. The collection, picturing many aspects of life in the Falklands, has grown to more than 50 of the cushioned 'kneelers'.

On the small grassy square next to the cathedral, the **Whalebone Arch** was built in 1933 to commemorate the centenary of British rule in the Falklands. The arch, made from the jawbones of two blue whales, was presented by the South Georgia whaling stations.

Government House

Home to London-appointed governors since 1845, the rambling **Government House** (Map pp70-1) was briefly occupied by the Argentine commander Menendez during the 1982 occupation. Once it was traditional for all visitors to the Falkland Islands to sign the register of visitors, but this custom has

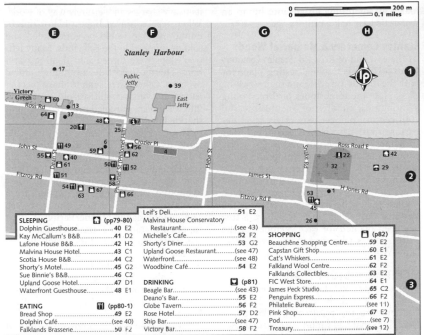

ended since numbers increased in 1982. Once a very minor posting, the governorship is currently much more significant. Government House is set back about 50m from Ross Rd West by a lush green, flower-decked garden rolling back to the glassed-in conservatory, which houses a famous grapevine. The house has had an interestingly varied architectural history with numerous revisions, and various rooms tacked on and later chopped off.

Just past Government House a satellite dish marks the communication centre of Cable & Wireless PLC, the Falklands telecom provider. After the shift from Port Louis to Stanley in 1844 the original wooden Government House stood on this site.

1914 Battle of the Falklands Memorial

This obelisk (Map pp70-1) just past Government House commemorates the WWI naval engagement. Vice-Admiral Maximilian Graf von Spee, who had earlier surprised a British fleet off southern Chile, had the tables turned on him in the Falklands and went down with his fleet (p22).

Falkland Islands Museum

Ironically, the **Falkland Islands Museum** (Map p84, ☎ 27420, www.falklands museum.com; Holdfast Rd; ⏱ 9.30am–noon & 1.30-4pm Mon-Fri, 2-4pm Sat & Sun; admission £2.50) building was constructed for the Argentine representative of LADE (Lineas Aereas del Estado; an airline operated by the Argentine air force), which until 1982 operated air services between Comodoro Rivadavia and Stanley. For several years after the Falklands War it was the residence of the British military commander; after his move to Mt Pleasant it became the new home of the local museum. The museum is south of Ross Rd West, just beyond the Battle of the Falklands Memorial.

The museum contains a professionally presented collection of artefacts from everyday life in the Falklands, plus natural history specimens and a fine collection relating to the islands' numerous shipwrecks. Outside displays include the Reclus Hut, originally fabricated in Stanley then shipped to Antarctica and set up on the Reclus Peninsula in late 1956. Forty years later it was dismantled and brought back to the Falklands, where it makes an interesting insight into life in an Antarctic base half a century ago.

Stanley Cemetery & Memorial Wood

At the east end of Ross Rd, **Stanley Cemetery** (Map pp70-1) is the final resting place for both the islands' tiny elite and their working class. Note the tombstones of three young Whitingtons, children of an unsuccessful 19th-century pioneer, whose eventual departure must have been a sad one. Other surnames, such as Felton and Biggs, are as common in the islands as Smith and Jones are in the UK. The cemetery is fronted by the **Cross of Sacrifice**, a memorial to islanders who lost their lives in WWI and WWII.

Immediately beyond the cemetery is the **Memorial Wood** (Map pp70-1), where a tree has been planted for each member of the British forces who died in the 1982 Falklands War.

MARITIME HISTORY TRAIL

There are over 300 shipwrecks in Falklands waters, but not all the hulks around Stanley Harbour are the result of wrecks. Some were ships that had simply passed their use-by date and were abandoned, but others suffered that most depressing of shipping fates – they were 'condemned'.

In 1848 Stanley was less than five years old when the California Gold Rush prompted an explosion of shipping trade around Cape Horn. Inevitably, many ships ran into trouble rounding that notoriously storm-wracked corner and put into Stanley for repairs. Not all damaged ships could be repaired, but a despairing owner reported that Stanley was 'dreaded by shipmasters being notorious for

---

BOAT OR SHIP?

Definitions for some of the more common sea-going vessels are as follows:

Barque A three-masted vessel, like a ship, but carrying triangular fore-and-aft sails rather than square ones on its mizzen mast, the furthest aft of the masts.

Brig Shortened from brigantine, a two-masted square rigger.

Schooner A vessel with two or more masts carrying triangular fore-and-aft sails.

Ship A vessel with three or more masts carrying square sails.

---

its heavy charges and leisurely way of work'. When repairs proved impossible or uneconomic the ship would be condemned and sold or dumped in the Falklands. Many left-over ships were turned into floating warehouses to store wool bales awaiting shipment overseas. Others were sunk to make piers or jetties and you can still see old ships built into town piers or roofed over to make ramshackle buildings.

The conclusion of the California Gold Rush didn't spell the end for the Cape Horn route. The development of the US and Canadian west coast meant that there were cargoes of grain and timber to carry eastbound, while manufactured goods from Europe and the US east coast moved west. The guano islands off the Peruvian coast supplied a trade in nitrate fertilisers, tea was transported from China, wool clippers started to run to and from Australia and the frozen meat business commenced from New Zealand. Only the advent of reliable steamships around the 1890s began to kill ship repair operations; the opening of the Panama Canal in 1914 was the finale.

Information panels point out some of Stanley Harbour's most interesting wrecks. This wreck tour starts towards the western end of Stanley Harbour and works eastward towards Gypsy Cove.

Capricorn & Philomel   Map p84

A 390 ton, 38m wooden barque, the *Capricorn* was built in Swansea, North Devon in 1859 to trade with the west coast of South America. Rounding Cape Horn in 1882, her cargo of coal spontaneously caught fire and her crew scuttled her near Staten Island to put the fire out. After being refloated, the *Capricorn* made it to Stanley where she was condemned and used as a storage hulk. During WWII she became part of a jetty, but today only some of the ribs and her bow and stern posts can be seen.

Built in Britain in 1945, the 23m steel fishing vessel *Philomel* came to the Falklands in 1948 and ran inter-island mail and passenger services for 20 years until replaced by the MV *Forrest*. She was beached across the harbour after a fire in 1971.

Jhelum   Map p84

Just west of the 1914 Battle of the Falklands memorial, the *Jhelum* was an East Indiaman,

KERRY LORIMER

Elephant seal pups (p42)

Antarctic fur seal (p42)

KERRY LORIMER

TONY WHEELER

Kelp goose (p55)

Striated caracara (p57)

TONY WHEELER

TONY WHEEL[ER]

Citroen 2CV in front of a traditional house, Stanley (p66)

TONY WHEELER

Whalebone Arch in front of Christ Church
Cathedral (p70), Stanley, East Falkland

Bodie Creek Bridge (p98), East
Falkland

TONY WHEEL[ER]

GLOBE TAVERN

CROZIER PLACE

TONY WHEELER

Globe Tavern (p81), Stanley, East
Falkland

ISAMBARD KINGDOM BRUNEL & THE SS GREAT BRITAIN

The Falkland Islands' most famous shipwreck lay near Stanley for over 80 years. The legendary Victorian engineer Isambard Kingdom Brunel (1806–59) built everything from suspension bridges, tunnels, railway lines and railway stations to docks, but it was his great ships for which he is most renowned. Brunel's *Great Western*, launched in 1837, was the first large steamship to cross the Atlantic without refuelling. He followed that with the even larger and more revolutionary *Great Britain* in 1843. The 98m-long vessel displaced 3600 tons, was the first ocean-going iron ship and the first to be driven by a screw propeller rather than by less efficient paddlewheels.

For the next 43 years the *Great Britain* operated as a passenger and cargo vessel, and probably transported more people between England and Australia than any other 19th-century vessel. She also carried troops to the Crimean War and to India during the Indian Mutiny. In 1861, back on the Australia route, the *Great Britain* carried the first English cricket team to tour Australia. She was laid up in Birkenhead in 1876, but in 1882 the now ageing vessel was converted to a sailing ship and carried coal from Wales to San Francisco, returning with cargoes of wheat.

In 1886 she was badly damaged while rounding Cape Horn and limped into the Falklands where it was determined the costs of repair were more than the ship's worth. Sold to FIC, the sturdy old ship was used to store coal and wool until it was abandoned and beached at Sparrow Cove in 1937. In 1970 the *Great Britain* was towed back to Britain on a pontoon and is now on display at the same dry dock in Bristol where she was originally constructed.

Over a metre in diameter, the great ship's mizzen mast returned to Britain with the ship, but after restoration was brought back to the Falklands as a reminder of the vessel's long sojourn in the South Atlantic. It's on display at Victory Green with a memorial plaque detailing the ship's history.

Brunel's final ship was probably too great a leap forward. The *Great Eastern*, launched in 1858, was not just big, it was monstrous. Stretching 211m in length, displacing 32,000 tons and carrying 4000 passengers it would be 50 years before a larger ship was constructed. Not all of Brunel's visionary projects were a dazzling success, and problems with this gigantic ship contributed to his early death a year after its launch.

---

used for trade between Britain and its great colony in the subcontinent. Launched in Liverpool in 1849, the 39m, 428 ton vessel was largely constructed of mahogany. In 1870, the *Jhelum* limped into Stanley en route for Dunkirk from Callao, carrying guano for use as fertiliser. She was leaking badly and her crew refused to risk their lives any further; carrying a boatload of bird shit was not a pleasant activity. Abandoned in 1871, she was purchased by the Packe Brothers of Sulivan House, the house right across the road from the wreck, for use as a storage facility.

Margaret   Map pp70-1

A 600 ton wooden barque, the *Margaret* was built in Halifax, Canada, in 1836. She made it into Stanley in 1950 heavily overloaded with a cargo of coal and cannonballs. She was over six months out from Liverpool en route to Valparaiso, Chile, and had spent no less than two months trying, unsuccessfully, to round Cape Horn. The leaky vessel was condemned and spent many years in

the harbour as a coal store. Today the upper decks have been cut away and the rickety government jetty extends over the ship, making it quite difficult to discern.

Charles Cooper & Actaeon   Map pp70-1

Packet ships dominated passenger, freight and mail services across the North Atlantic in the years before the American Civil War, and the square-rigged *Charles Cooper* was the last of the era. The 850 ton wooden vessel started her working life in 1856 and just 10 years later, leaking badly, limped into Stanley while carrying coal from Philadelphia to San Francisco. Like many others she would never leave. In 1968 the *Charles Cooper* was sold to the South St Seaport Museum in New York City, but it proved impossible to move her there for restoration and the project was abandoned in 1991. Her remains were directly behind the modern Capstan Gift Shop but, owing to continued deterioration, the ship was removed for display in 2003. It's hoped that the bow, at least, will be preserved and displayed by the Falkland Islands Museum (p71), where the ship's elegant transom can already be seen.

Inboard from the *Charles Cooper* is the *Actaeon*, a 560 ton barque built in New Brunswick, Canada, in 1838. In 1853 she was 154 days out from Liverpool en route to San Francisco with a cargo of coal when bad weather off Cape Horn drove her back to Stanley, where she was surveyed, condemned and scuttled.

William Shand, Snow Squall, Egeria & Fleetwing   Map pp70-1
The FIC's East Jetty incorporates a fleet of scuttled vessels. They're visible from the Public Jetty in front of the tourist office, from beyond the East Jetty or from the jetty itself. The *William Shand*'s story is a familiar one: cargo – coal; route – Liverpool to Valparaiso; Cape Horn – couldn't get round. She was a 432 ton barque built in Greenock, Scotland, in 1839. Alongside her is the *Snow Squall*, which limped into this final resting place in 1864.

The *Egeria*'s stern, dipping terminally into the harbour waters, has been roofed over with corrugated iron. Built in St John, New Brunswick, Canada, in 1859 and carrying coal and cement, the 1066 ton barque ended up in Stanley in 1872.

The remains of the 33m, 242 ton *Fleetwing* are located just east of the jetty. The brig's voyages started in 1874 and ended in Stanley in 1911.

Afterglow   Map p84
Fragments of the wreck of the *Afterglow* lie beached just to the west of the FIPASS floating dock. Built in Lowestoft in 1918 as a North Sea herring drifter, she came to the Falklands in the 1920s as a sealing protection vessel stationed at Elephant Jason. This role required mounting a small gun on her bow. From 1922 to 1926 she carried mail between the island settlements until, renamed the *Port Richards*, she made a complete reversal of her original Falklands role by becoming a sealer. During WWII she was requisitioned by the Royal Navy, renamed the *Afterglow* again, and spent the war years patrolling Falklands' waters. She broke her moorings and drifted ashore in 1945.

Golden Chance & Gentoo   Map p84
Beside Boxer Bridge, which is the military construction bridging the entrance to the inlet known as the Canache, lies a jumble of wrecks, piers, jetties and modern boats. Like the *Afterglow*, the *Golden Chance* and *Gentoo* were built as wooden steam drifters, constructed to pull huge drift nets for catching herring in the North Sea. The 26m, 90 ton *Golden Chance* was built at Lowestoft in 1914 and came to the Falklands in 1949 to work as a sealer out of the short-lived Port Albemarle sealing operation.

The *Gentoo* came to the Falklands in 1927, was converted to diesel power, carried cargo around the islands for the next 38 years, enjoyed a brief, unsuccessful spell of treasure hunting from Falklands wrecks and was bought in 1980 to be used as a houseboat. The Falklands War intervened before its new owner could move in and during the Argentine occupation it mysteriously sank.

The *Golden Chance* is on the beach, while the *Gentoo* is further out in the inlet.

Lady Elizabeth   Map p84
Stanley's most dramatic wreck is the magnificent 68m, 1200 ton iron barque *Lady Elizabeth*. Launched in Sunderland in 1879, she's a fine example of the last generation of deep sea sailing ships, built as bulk carriers for low cost cargoes such as coal, grain or wood. She visited Stanley 10 years later, carrying building material for the new cathedral. Her final visit in 1913 wasn't so happy. While rounding the Horn with a cargo of timber en route from Vancouver to Delagoa Bay, Mozambique, four men, two boats and part of the deck cargo were lost overboard. Limping into the Falklands with damaged steering, rigging and deck fittings, she ran onto Uranie Rock and would have sunk were it not for 200 tons of concrete she was carrying as permanent ballast. She was towed into harbour by the *Samson* (opposite), which was itself cast up on shore a short distance from the *Lady Elizabeth*'s final resting place.

Repairs proved too expensive and her cargo of £7000 worth of the finest Oregon timber was sold off for £2250, while the ship itself fetched just £1000. For a time she was moored next to the *Great Britain* and used as an overflow storage when that ship was filled to capacity with 3000 bales of wool awaiting trans-shipment. Later she was tied up next to the *Egeria* and finally anchored offshore in Stanley Harbour. In 1936 she broke her moorings in a gale and was blown across the harbour to lodge in Whalebone Cove. A sand spit runs out to the ship, making it easy to walk out for a closer inspection, but trying to board the rusting wreck is very dangerous.

Plym   Map p84
Just west of *Lady Elizabeth* on Whalebone Cove lies the wreck of the small 15m iron steam tug *Plym*. Built in Plymouth 1903 she worked in the Falklands until she ran aground in the 1930s.

Samson   Map p84
In 1896 the 1384 ton wooden American ship *City of Philadelphia* foundered on the Billy Rock, not far offshore from Cape Pembroke, and went down with all hands. Heavy seas prevented any rescue attempt although cries for help could be heard from the shore. As a result it was decided to station a powerful tug in Stanley and the 29m, 96 ton steam tug *Samson*, built in Hull in 1888, was brought out to the Falklands in 1900. In 1912, with help from the *Plym* and the government launch *Penguin*, the *Samson* rescued the passengers, more than 150 of them, and crew of the liner *Oravia* after it hit the Billy Rock; it was not able to save the ship itself. In 1945 the *Samson* broke adrift from its moorings in a gale and washed up on the coast just west of Whalebone Cove. It remains in relatively complete condition.

ACTIVITIES
Darts
In winter Stanley pubs sponsor a popular darts league, and darts tournaments take place in the Town Hall auditorium. For more information on such events, contact the **Darts Club** (☎ 21199).

Fishing
Fishing for sea trout, mullet and smelt is quite a popular pastime; the nearest site is the Murrell River, within walking distance of Stanley. There are many other suitable places in camp (p95), some easily accessible from the Mt Pleasant Hwy.

The season runs 1 September to 30 April. See p163 for more information.

Golf
There are a surprising number of 9-hole golf courses around the Falklands. **Stanley Golf Course** (Map p84; www.horizon.co.fk/golf/index.html) is on the west side of town and has regular Sunday fixtures. Its website has a home page featuring golfing rockhopper penguins.

Horse Riding
Check with Gardner Fiddes' **Tumbledown Trekking** (☎ 21494), which may be starting up horse riding excursions.

Running
Contact Sarah Allan of the **Stanley Running Club** (☎ 22119) for information. The club has a regular Wednesday training session at 5.30pm, plus cross-country sessions, 10km runs, 10-mile road races and orienteering. The annual winter race to Surf Bay finishes at the Midwinter Dip – combining running with a chilly swim.

Swimming
Stanley's popular **public swimming pool** (Map pp70-1; ☎ 27291; Reservoir Rd; ½hr visitor/normal sessions £1.55/2.90) is in the Community School building on the west side of town. The rather variable opening hours are posted at the reception area and are available from the Tourist Centre.

WALKING TOUR
Start this walk from the Jetty Centre tourist office; many of these sights are part of the Stanley Historic Trail, for which a free booklet is available from the tourist office.

The Falklands' prolific bird and mammal life is the major attraction for many visitors, and some of that wildlife can be seen right in the town. Commerson's dolphins are often seen in the harbour and will escort Zodiacs ashore from cruise ships. Southern giant petrels can be seen flying over the harbour or along the shoreline, where the endemic flightless steamer duck may also be encountered. Upland geese may make an appearance on Victory Green, across from the Upland Goose Hotel. The shipwrecks are often home to rock cormorants, while smaller birds flit into Stanley gardens, particularly the fine gardens of Government House.

Start the walk at a **plaque (1)** on the Public Jetty that notes the Duke of Edinburgh visited Stanley in 1871 during the first royal visit to the Falklands; the current Duke of Edinburgh dropped by in 1993. Turn right on Ross Rd to the highly incongruous sight of **Jubilee Villas (2)**, a quartet of authentic English late 19th-century terraced townhouses. The only giveaway is the corrugated iron roof; freighting heavy and fragile slate tiles out from England was deemed too risky and expensive, but everything else came out from the old country. The houses were built for the Dean Brothers, local traders who owned a number of islands around the Falklands and were engaged in almost every facet of Falklands business. Built in 1887, the name commemorates the Golden Jubilee of Queen Victoria.

Christ Church Cathedral (3) and Stanley's most famous icon, the **Whalebone Arch (4)**, are a few steps west. Across the road is the **Capstan Gift Shop (5)**, a very flashy gift and duty-free shop (p82). Behind the shop fragments of a decaying pier dribble out to the former site of the *Charles Cooper* **(6)**; see p72

for information on this and other Stanley shipwrecks.

Like so much else of Stanley's business activity, the Capstan is operated by FIC whose main outlet, the **West Store (7)**, faces it across Ross Rd. The West Store (p82) was originally the headquarters of JM Dean, the family firm we've already met at Jubilee Villas. Their carpentry and ship-repair business stood on this site while above the West Store was their bakery with a sail loft above it.

Cross back over Ross Rd to **Victory Green (8)**, which has four old cannons retrieved from Port Louis and a more modern Hotchkiss gun that is still fired on important holidays. The huge mizzen mast on the green comes from the *Great Britain*, Stanley's most important shipwreck (p73). From Victory Green gaze across Stanley Harbour to the names of four ships marked on the hillside of the Camber with white stones. The *Beagle* and *Barracouta* were naval cruisers patrolling the Falklands' waters in the 19th century to keep the notoriously argumentative sealers in line. HMS *Protector* patrolled Antarctic and Falklands' waters between 1955 and 1968 when

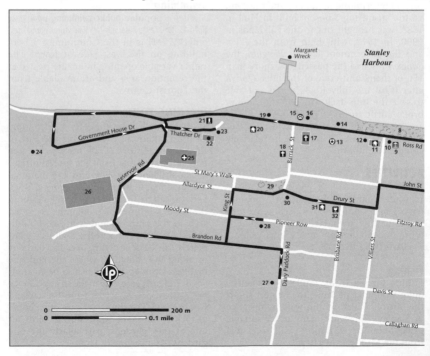

she was replaced by HMS *Endurance*, the fourth name on the hillside. The *Endurance* was about to finish her South Atlantic duties when the Falklands War broke out in 1982. She was replaced by a new vessel bearing the same name in 1991.

Stanley House (9) is a large brick building constructed for the FIC colonial manager in 1878. Bricks are expensive to ship and have proven difficult to manufacture locally so buildings like Stanley House and Jubilee Villas are very unusual. Today Stanley House is the boarding hostel for schoolchildren from camp. Next door is **Stanley Cottage (10)**, one of the first houses in Stanley; it occupied plot No 1 on the town's original plan. It was built by the first colonial surgeon as his own residence in 1844 and sold to George Markham Dean of the Dean family in 1866. After his death in 1890 his 'formidable' widow continued to live in 'Mrs Dean's Cottage' until 1920. In the 1950s it was Hardy's Tea Rooms and today it's used by the director of education. Note the stained glass window and the monkey puzzle tree in the front garden, then cross Villiers St to another Stanley landmark.

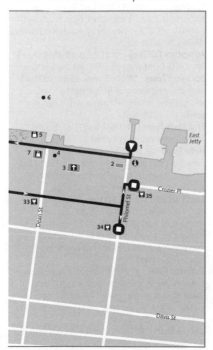

Marmont Row was built in 1854 and housed five cottages and the Eagle Inn. The well-known Dean family took over in 1875 and changed the name to the Ship Inn; they passed it on to the FIC when the businesses amalgamated. In 1969 it was renamed the **Upland Goose Hotel (11)**. The original Eagle Inn was principally patronised by sailors who had a dormitory fitted out like a ship's forecastle. For a half century until the 1990s the Colony Club – the principal meeting point of the Falklands' sheepocracy – convened here.

Past the Upland Goose, where the **British Antarctic Survey (12)** also has its office, is the early 1870s **police station (13)**. It's a classic example of a Victorian police station, complete with narrow cells and a walled-in exercise yard. Buttresses and S-ties on the north side show that it faced some construction problems right at the start, but that was nothing compared to the British missile that hit the station during the retaking of Stanley in 1982. The whale harpoon gun mounted in front of the station might indicate the Falklands' approach to crime, although the court reports in the *Penguin News* are distinctly low key. Across the road is the **Explosive Ordnance Disposal (EOD) Office (14)**, where you can find out all about the minefields and acquire a mine warning sign.

The bright red post box and traditional phone boxes add a distinctly British touch to the **Post Office (15)**. But Stanley's **Town Hall (16)** is solidly nondescript and not a patch on its more exotic predecessor, which was gutted by a fire in 1944. Behind the rather dull Town Hall there's not much to see of the *Margaret*, which is built into the Government Jetty.

Next door to the police station **St Mary's Catholic Church (17)** dates from 1899. It is an early example of a 'kit' building of weatherboard cladding topped by a corrugated iron roof. The church hall behind it is, in fact, an earlier St Mary's that was shifted from its original site in 1886. On Barrack St, the next junction is the **Tabernacle Free Church (18)**. This one was assembled here in 1891 from another kit, all of corrugated iron.

Back on Ross Rd continue west past the *Penguin News* **office (19)** on the coast side and the **Malvina House Hotel (20)** on the inland side to the **1982 Falklands War Memorial (21)**. The 'Thatcher Drive' signs are reminders that this is one place where the Iron Lady is always in favour (Liberation Day is an important Falklands public holiday). Public subscriptions and volunteer labour built the War Memorial, which was unveiled on 14 June 1984 – just two years after the conflict ended. The monument wall carries the name of all 252 military deaths on the British side and the three Falklands civilians who died. The retired Margaret Thatcher turned up to lay a wreath 10 years after the war ended.

Behind the memorial, the **Secretariat (22)** houses government administrative buildings. **Cable Cottage (23)** next door used to house the telegraph cable that linked Montevideo with the Falklands during WWI; it now houses the attorney general.

Continuing along the waterfront will bring you to **Government House (24)**, the 1914 Battle of the Falklands Memorial (p71), the wreck of the *Jhelum* (p72) and the Falkland Islands Museum (p71), but this stroll turns uphill. Take Reservoir Rd past **King Edward VII Memorial Hospital (25)** and the **Community School (26)**, opened in 1992, which houses Stanley's library and swimming pool (p75).

Turn left onto Brandon St and right on Dairy Paddock Row to see the **Whaling Display (27)**, or more correctly anti-whaling display, in the local metalworker's front garden. There's a variety of skeletons, a whaling harpoon gun and one of the 'No Whaling' signs that you'll see all over the Falklands.

Backtrack to the junction of King St and Brandon Rd and descend a block to **Pioneer Row (28)**. The cottages along this narrow street were brought out in kit form in the late 1840s to house the Chelsea and Greenwich pensioners, early settlers who were actually in their 30s and 40s. The brightly painted houses have all sorts of interesting architectural details. Look out for Cartmell Cottage at 7 Pioneer Row. It was built in 1849 and is now operated by the Falkland Islands Museum. Admission costs £1.

Descend another block to Drury St. The **children's playground (29)** sandwiched between Drury St and St Mary's Walk was originally an allotment garden for these early settlers to grow vegetables. They were housed in the **Marine Barracks (30)** on Drury St until their cottages were completed. Later it was used as barracks for the colony's Royal Marine detachment. It was subsequently a primary school, a library and a museum, but today has been divided up into three private homes.

Continue along Drury St past **Kay Mc-Callum's B&B (31)**, instantly recognisable by its neat garden crowded with gnomes and other creatures including, of course, penguins. At the junction with Brisbane Rd, named after Matthew Brisbane who was murdered by gauchos at Port Louis in 1833, is the **Rose Hotel (32)**. Originally built as two settlers' cottages, it was opened as the Rose public house in 1860, making it Stanley's oldest pub still operating under its original name.

Continue along Drury St to Villiers St and go downhill again to the corner of John St. On your left there's one of the town's curious and colourful fire hydrants. Turn right along John St past **Deano's Bar (33)** to Philomel St, where you can turn right to the **Victory Bar (34)** or left to the **Globe Tavern (35)** if you feel you need a drink to celebrate the end of this little stroll.

TOURS

There are a number of tour operators in Stanley, each with some degree of specialisation. Options include exploring Stanley, visiting settlements around West Falkland, making trips to Volunteer Beach and other popular wildlife sites, or specialised fishing, diving or boat trips.

Adventure Falkland (☎ 21383; pwatts@horizon.co.fk) Operated by Patrick Watts; specialises in battlefield tours.

Discovery Tours (☎ 21027; www.discoveryfalklands .com; discovery@horizon.co.fk) Operated by Tony Smith, who specialises in battlefield trips as well as operating general and wildlife trips.

Fred Clark Tours (☎ 31013; fax 21156) Operates tours around Stanley including two-hour walking tours.

Hebe Tours (☎ 21561; www.tourism.org.fk/pages /hebe-tours.htm; nrowlands@horizon.co.fk) Run by Neil Rowlands. It operates general tours and specialises in wildlife, fishing and general outdoor activities.

South Atlantic Marine Services (Map pp70-1; ☎ 21145; www.falklands-underwater.com; sams@ horizon.co.fk) Run by Dave and Carol Eynon. Boat excursions and, particularly, diving are its real specialities; and it does wildlife and 4WD trips, and may be able to help with trips to Kidney Island.

Tenacres Tours (☎ 21155; www.tourism.org.fk/pages /tenacres-tours.htm; tenacres@horizon.co.fk) Run by Sharon Halford; operates general and wildlife tours. Sharon probably makes the cross-camp trip to Volunteers Beach more than any other operator.

Ubique Tours (☎ 21654) Operated by Frank Leyland; does battlefield and wildlife tours.

FESTIVALS & EVENTS

The capital's most noteworthy public event is the annual **Stanley Sports**, between Christmas and New Year's, which features horse racing (betting is legal), bull riding and other competitions.

Every March, the Falkland Islands Horticultural Society presents a competitive **Horticultural Show**, displaying the produce of kitchen gardens in Stanley and camp, plus a wide variety of baked goods. At the end of the day, the produce is sold in a spirited auction.

In August, the annual **Crafts Fair** in the gymnasium displays the work of local weavers, leather workers, photographers and other artists (there are many talented illustrators and painters). Particularly interesting is the horse gear, whose origins lie in 19th-century gaucho traditions.

SLEEPING

Stanley has a good choice of accommodation but the number of rooms is limited. If you arrive without a reservation the arrivals officials will phone around until they find one for you. Several B&Bs also offer full board, and Kay McCallum and Celia Stewart at Scotia House B&B let backpackers camp in their back garden (with the gnomes in Kay's case). Central heating is a feature of nearly all B&Bs, guesthouses and hotels. All room prices that follow include breakfast.

B&Bs

Kay McCallum's B&B (Map pp70-1; ☎ 21071; kay@ horizon.co.fk; 14 Drury St; per person/tent £18/5) Certainly Stanley's favourite backpacker, this is a very pleasant and well-kept place to stay. There are just two rooms, one twin and one double, sharing a bathroom. An additional charge of £2.50 per camper covers breakfast and a shower. Kay's meals are rightly praised and her guest book is full of comments about trying to lose weight after a spell here. Dinner costs £6. Kay is also remarkably good at sorting out flights, making bookings, suggesting places to go and generally acting as an unofficial tourist office and travel agent. Her garden is also a Stanley landmark, and is dotted with a world-class collection of garden gnomes; some of her visitors have sent garden creatures to add to the assembly after they've returned home.

Scotia House B&B (Map pp70-1; ☎ 21191; bob stewart@horizon.co.fk; 12 St Mary's Walk; per person £20) There are two well-equipped family rooms sharing a bathroom. Bob and Celia Stewart's economically priced B&B is centrally located and has a guest lounge with TV. Backpackers can arrange to camp on the back lawn and have breakfast in the house.

Sue Binnie's B&B (Map pp70-1; ☎ 21051; 3 Brandon Rd; per person £25) There is just one double room with shared bathroom. It's centrally located and Spanish is spoken here.

Lafone House B&B (Map pp70-1; ☎ 22891; Ross Rd E; s/d £45/70) On the east side of Stanley, but within easy walking distance of town. Upstairs there are panoramic views over the harbour and two en suite doubles and another double and two singles with shared facilities at slightly lower prices. Downstairs there's a spacious dining room and lounge area. Arlett Betts insists that guests have the run of the house.

Tenacres B&B (Map p84; ☎ 21155; tenacres@horiz on.co.fk; Mt Pleasant Hwy; per person £28) Slightly out of the centre on the road in from Mt Pleasant International Airport. There are fine views over Stanley Common and the surrounding hills from this very comfortable house. There are two twin rooms with TVs and shared bathroom; and there's a washing machine that guests can use. Meals are available 'country house' style.

Guesthouses

Dolphin Guesthouse (Map pp70-1; ☎ 22950; fprintz@ horizon.co.fk; 46 John St; per person £28) Run by June and Norman Clark, this guesthouse has eight rooms in all: two singles, two doubles, four twins and two family rooms. None of the rooms have attached bathrooms, but four have wash basins. There's a lounge area with Internet access; laundry service, dinner and packed lunches are available.

Waterfront Guesthouse (Map pp70-1; ☎ 22331; thewaterfront@horizon.co.fk; 36 Ross Rd; per person £33) On the waterfront road close to the Public Jetty, Paul and Shula Phillips' guesthouse has eight rooms: four singles, one double, one twin, one triple and one family room. Two of the singles have a toilet and wash basin but share a bath; all the other rooms have attached shower, wash basin and toilet. The Waterfront has a licensed restaurant, lounge, Internet access and fine views over Stanley's harbour.

Hotels

Malvina House Hotel (Map pp70-1; ☎ 21355; malv ina@horizon.co.fk; 3 Ross Rd; s/d low season from £75/80, high season £85/115) The hotel has 18 rooms, all with attached bathroom, direct dial phone, satellite TV and other mod cons. Two of the rooms are larger harbour-view suites costing an additional 15%. Credit cards are accepted. The old Malvina House, which predates the current hotel, was demolished in the 1960s and the Conservatory Restaurant (right) is the only part that survives from that era. Most of the rooms are in a new extension added in 1997.

Upland Goose Hotel (Map pp70-1; ☎ 21455; www .the-falkland-islands-co.com; fic@horizon.co.fk; 20-22 Ross Rd; economy s/d from £50/70, with attached bathroom £50/95, full board £75/140) The best-known hotel in the Falklands is a venerable establishment in a mid-19th-century building on the waterfront road. There are 18 rooms with phones and TVs, but only one room has a double bed. The hotel also has one of Stanley's better-known restaurants (opposite). Credit cards are accepted.

Shorty's Motel (Map pp70-1; ☎ 22855; www.shortys -diner.com; West Hillside, Snake Hill; s/d £28/50) This motel has two doubles and four twins, all en suite and with TVs.

EATING

Stanley's modest and inexpensive snack bars have been joined by some fine dining opportunities. Most of the B&Bs offer meals to their guests and they can be better than the restaurants. Kay McCallum's and Tenacres (both p79) are particularly praised.

Snack Bars & Cafés

Bread Shop (Map pp70-1; ☎ 21273; Dean St; junction with Fitzroy Rd & Philomel Hill; opposite Globe Tavern; ☻ 7.30am-1.30pm Mon-Sun) Serves bread and snacks. You can get packaged lunches here if you're going out for the day. The Philomel Hill branch has a café open from very early morning until about noon.

Michelle's Cafe (Map pp70-1; ☎ 21123; Philomel Hill; ☻ noon-8pm Mon-Thu, noon-10.30pm Fri & Sat, 11.30am-5pm Sun) Serves tea, coffee, cakes, burgers and daily specials. It's opposite the Falklands Brasserie.

Leif's Deli (Map pp70-1; ☎ 22721; 23 John St; ☻ 7.30am-5pm Mon-Fri, 9.30am-noon & 1-4pm Sat) Has vegetarian specialities and good sandwiches, snacks and coffee.

Dolphin Café (Map pp70-1; ☎ 22950; 46 John St; ☻ noon-5pm Mon, 10am-5.30pm Tue-Fri, 10am-4.30pm Sat; meals £1.75-4.65) This popular café has sandwiches and rolls, salads, and fish or chicken and chips, all washed down by tea, coffee or soft drinks. The menu also prices everything in US dollars for cruise ship visitors.

Woodbine Café (Map pp70-1; ☎ 21002; 29 Fitzroy Rd; ☻ 10am-2pm Tue-Sat, 6.30-8.30pm Mon, Wed & Fri; meals £2.50-3.80) Stanley's standard locale for anything that can be served with chips to eat there or take away. That can include a Cornish pasty, sausage roll or pie with chips, fish and chips, chicken and chips, and an assortment of burgers, sandwiches or hot dogs.

Shorty's Diner (Map pp70-1; ☎ 22855; West Hillside, Snake Hill; ☻ 11am-8.30pm Tue-Sun; breakfast/snacks & meals £5.60/2.20-9.50) This diner is east of the town centre, en route to FIPASS. It has some straightforward, anywhere-in-the-world diner-style food like burgers (including the traditional Chilean sandwich known as a *chacarero*), baguettes and paninis, complete meals and breakfast (eggs, bacon, the whole deal); drinks are 65p to £1, beer £1.20 and wine £1.60.

Waterfront (Map pp70-1; ☎ 22331; Ross Rd; snacks & meals £2-4.50) On the waterfront (as the name indicates); does sandwiches and meals.

Lighthouse Seamen's Centre (Map p84; ☎ 22780; beside FIPASS entrance; ☻ 10am-5pm Tue-Sun, until 9pm if fishing boats in port; snacks & meals under £5) Here you can get burgers, an omelette, sandwiches and breakfasts large and small. Although it's aimed at visiting seamen you won't feel out of place and there's also a pool table, table tennis, a twiddly football game, TV, video and lots of books.

Vans dispensing hamburgers, hot dogs and other snacks set up around the pubs (opposite) in the evening; find them behind the Globe and the Victory. In summer months an **ice cream van** can often be found opposite the Pink Shop (p82). On summer weekends and when cruise ships are in port there's a bus selling snacks and drinks at Gypsy Cove (p84) for penguin watchers and walkers.

Restaurants

Malvina House Conservatory Restaurant (Map pp70-1; ☎ 21355; 3 Ross Rd; starters £2.95-3.75, mains £12-15) Located in the glassed-in conservatory at the front of the hotel. Starters include

Falkland-connected dishes like wok-fried squid or upland goose pâté. Main courses also feature a couple of Falklands inspired dishes including, inevitably, rack of lamb. There's a good selection of wines, particularly from Chile, and you can have a predinner drink in the Beagle Bar.

Upland Goose Restaurant (Map pp70-1; ☎ 21455; Ross Rd; buffet dinner £13) Situated in the hotel's pleasant conservatory dining area, but the three-course, serve yourself dinner-time buffet can be very uninspiring. Some nights there are food theme nights, which may raise the standards. The adjoining bar does have some Falklands style and is a good place for a drink.

Falklands Brasserie (Map pp70-1; ☎ 21159; brasserie@horizon.co.fk; ☒ noon-2pm Tue-Sun, 6-9pm Mon, Wed, Thu & Sun, 6-10pm Fri & Sat; starters £2.95-4.95, mains £11-15) A contender for the fine dining in Stanley crown. You can start with soup or a choice of starters with a Falklands flavour like Falklands calamari or Upland goose terrine. Main courses also feature a local accent, such as grilled Falklands lamb cutlets or escalopes of *mero mero* (sea bass). Desserts are £3.25 to £3.95, house wine by the glass is £2.25 or £9 for a bottle. Other bottles of wine are mostly in the £13 to £15 bracket.

DRINKING

Stanley does have several pubs but, remarkably, only one of them has beer on tap; otherwise it's down to bottles of Beck's, Heineken, Foster's, Carlsberg and even, would you believe, Budweiser. Opening hours are 10am to 2pm Monday to Saturday, 5.30pm to 11pm Monday to Thursday, 5.30pm to 11.30pm Friday to Saturday, noon to 2pm and 7pm to 10pm Sunday; open all day when cruise ships in port.

Globe Tavern (Map pp70-1; ☎ 22703; cnr Crozier Pl & Philomel St) The best-known pub in town. It serves bar meals including that peren-

nial English favourite, curry and chips. Of course, there's also fish and chips and it's the only pub in town with draught beer. Disappointingly, though, it's a German lager called Isenbeck, not British bitter, and anyway it can run out. There's a beer garden out back, just in case the sun is shining.

Victory Bar (Map pp70-1; ☎ 21199; cnr Philomel St & Fitzroy Rd) Only a stone's throw uphill from the Globe Tavern and is probably the most popular local pub; it's said to be the place where most Stanley gossip gets reviewed over a beer.

Rose Hotel (Map pp70-1; ☎ 21067; Brisbane Rd) Opened as the Rose Public House back in the 1860s.

Deano's Bar (Map pp70-1; ☎ 21292; John St) Also known as Monty's bar, it offers the usual worldwide selection of beers along with hamburgers, fish and chips and other snacks.

Stanley Arms (Map p84; ☎ 22258; John Biscoe Rd) A relatively new addition, just off Ross Rd West beyond the museum at the western end of town.

Narrows Bar (Map p84; ☎ 22272; 39 Ross Rd E) This is a new pub (an indicator of Stanley's expansion in recent years) on the eastern end of town. It looks straight across to the Narrows and puts on buffet meals.

The two Stanley hotels also have bars open to the public. The Upland Goose has the **Ship Bar** (Map pp70-1) and a rather more atmospheric lounge bar with nautical prints and pictures. At Malvina House Hotel it's the **Beagle Bar** (Map pp70-1).

ENTERTAINMENT

Stanley is no nightlife hotspot, but many discos and dances with live music take place throughout the year, usually at the town hall. Listen to the nightly FIBS (Falkland Islands Broadcasting Station) announcements for dates and times. There are no cinemas apart from the Phoenix at Mt Pleasant, but most

---

WHERE'S THE BREWERY?

Why hasn't anybody set up a boutique brewery, surely a much better investment than putting £4 million into the soon-to-go-bankrupt abattoir? In fact, there was a local brew launched soon after the Falklands War, but with tourism yet to take off and the cruise ship business still in its infancy there wasn't enough demand to support it. These days Stanley's pubs clearly need something on tap, and what cruise ship visitor wouldn't take a six pack of Rockhopper Bitter or King Penguin Lager back aboard? With all that peaty water, just like the Scottish Highlands, a Falklands distillery could probably do good business as well.

STANLEY

hotels and guesthouses have video lounges. Appearances of the Fighting Pig Band, the Falklands' own rock band, are publicised in the *Penguin News*. The band even has its own venue, the **Trough** (☎ 22751), near the petrol station (Map p84) on the Stanley bypass on the FIPASS side of town.

SHOPPING
You won't mistake Stanley for a main street shopping experience, but most things you might need can be found and there are certainly plenty of outlets catering to visitors. In shops aimed at the visitor market, Falklands knitwear is probably the most typical local product. Apart from the shops around Stanley, the Jetty Centre also sells local crafts, including painted silk cards and pictures by Sarah Baker of Wriggly Tin Designs. Jewellery incorporating highly polished Falklands pebbles are another nice local product. Stanley opening hours will almost always include the subtext 'open when there's a cruise ship in port'.

FIC West Store (Map pp70-1; Ross Rd) For day-to-day shopping, this could pass for a sizable supermarket almost anywhere in the world, and also offers video rentals, a newsagent, bookshop and stationery section, and a travel agent handling Royal Air Force (RAF) TriStar flights (opposite).

Beauchêne Shopping Centre (Map pp70-1; John St) There's also the the Kelper supermarkets and a number of other shops around town.

Tourist Outlets
Capstan Gift Shop (Map pp70-1; ☎ 27654; capstan .gifts@horizon.co.fk; Ross Rd) Often full to capacity when there's a cruise ship in town, but it has also proved popular with Falkland Islanders. This souvenir-packed emporium has a terrific selection of postcards, books and locally produced souvenirs, including woollen goods, craftwork and the like (but it has also got lots of goodies with absolutely no Falklands connection).

Pink Shop (Map pp70-1; ☎ 21399; pink.shop@hor izon.co.fk; 33 Fitzroy Rd) Sells gifts and souvenirs, Falklands and general-interest books, excellent wildlife prints by owner–artist Tony Chater, and work by other Falklands artists. It's said the original building was constructed by Andrez Pitaluga, whose family, four generations later, still run Gibraltar Station at Salvador.

Penguin Express (Map pp70-1; ☎ 21802; penguin .express@horizon.co.fk; cnr Philomel St & Fitzroy Rd) Has a variety of gifts and collectables related to the Falklands and Antarctic.

Falkland Wool Centre (Map pp70-1; ☎ 21595; www.falklandknitwear.com; Philomel St) Also known as A&E Knitwear, it has an interesting collection of attractive knitwear with some uniquely Falklands designs. It also sells wool if you'd care to knit your own.

Falkland Collectibles (Map pp70-1; ☎ 21174; www.falklandcollectibles.com; Fitzroy Rd) This shop has collectibles ranging from stamps to banknotes to phonecards.

Pod (Map pp70-1; ☎ 22655) In the old Philomel Store beside the Jetty Centre, the Pod is run by Pat Pratlett and Patrick Berntsen (they used to run a popular guesthouse named the Pod at Port San Carlos; Pat and Patrick were the two Ps in the Pod). They have local crafts and gifts.

Cat's Whiskers (Map pp70-1; ☎ 21673; Dean St) Has a variety of local crafts, including pottery made with Falklands clay and Falklands pebble jewellery.

James Peck Studio (Map pp70-1; ☎ 21896; east end of St Mary's Walk) This studio displays the work of the local artist in his studio, ranging from pen and ink drawings through watercolours to oils.

Uncle Tom's Cabin (☎ 21428; 15 Ross Rd W) Features belts, handbags, drink coasters and other small leather goods made to order.

Philatelic Bureau (Map pp70-1; ☎ 27159; Ross Rd; 🕑 9am-noon, 1.15-4pm Mon-Fri) Located at the post office; sells colourful Falklands postage stamps and first day covers, and also handles stamps from South Georgia and the British Antarctic Territory.

Treasury (Map pp70-1; ☎ 27141; Secretariat, Thatcher Dr) Sells commemorative Falklands coins.

Explosive Ordnance Disposal Office (Map pp70-1; EOD; ☎ 22229; Ross Rd) The place to acquire a minefield warning sign.

GETTING THERE & AWAY
Air
International flights to the Falklands are either with LanChile or on the RAF TriStar service.

Local flights within the Falklands are operated by FIGAS.

In Stanley, you can contact the following organisations for all necessary flight and travel information.

FIGAS

Contact **FIGAS** (☎ 27219; figas.fig@horizon.co.fk).
FIGAS agents include:
International Tours & Travel Ltd (Map pp70-1;
☎ 22041; se.itt@horizon.co.fk; Beauchêne Complex,
John St)
Mt Pleasant Travel Office (☎ 76691; 12 Facility
Reception, Mt Pleasant International Airport)
Stanley Services (☎ 22622; sslcab@horizon.co.fk;
Airport Rd)

LANCHILE

International Tours & Travel Ltd (above)

RAF TRISTAR

Falklands Island Company (FIC; Map pp70-1;
☎ 27633; West Store, Ross Rd)

Boat

For information on travelling between
Punta Arenas (Argentina) and Stanley on
the *Tamar*, or on cruise and expedition ships
see p177. The *Tamar* and some of the smaller
cruise ships tie up either at East Jetty in the
centre of Stanley or at the FIPASS dock, east
of the centre. Cruise ships simply drop anchor in Stanley Harbour and land their passengers at the Public Jetty by Zodiac. Larger
cruise ships are unable to enter the Narrows,
the aptly named narrow passage into Stanley
Harbour. Instead they anchor outside in Port
William and from Stanley they can often
be seen towering incongruously over the
Camber, the spit of land separating Stanley
Harbour from Port William.

GETTING AROUND
To/From the Airport

There are two main airports serving the
Falklands.

MT PLEASANT INTERNATIONAL AIRPORT

The international airport (known as MPA)
is 56km southwest of Stanley. LanChile and
RAF TriStar flights arrive and depart from
MPA, which is also the main British military
airport and definitely feels like it; there's a
Phantom interceptor on display just outside
the terminal. There is, however, a duty-free
shop in the departure area and the **Ro-No-Kes
Restaurant** (☎ 32114) across the road from the
terminal and 100m to the left.

Falkland Islands Tours & Travel (☎ 21775;
jastewart@horizon.co.fk) takes passengers to Mt
Pleasant for £13 single. It's wise to make res-

ervations before arrival because the size of
bus they bring out to the airport depends on
demand. A taxi to the airport costs £40, so
for three people it's virtually the same cost
as the bus and for four or more it's cheaper.
Stanley has some minibus-size taxis.

LanChile checks everybody in before the
flight arrives, so you need to arrive two
hours before departure time.

STANLEY AIRPORT

Stanley Airport (Map p84; ☎ 27303), for local
(FIGAS) flights, is about 5km east of town.
The standard taxi fare is £2.50 to £3.50;
there's a BK Cabs 'freefone' at the airport
and you'll be picked up in 10 minutes.

FIGAS flights also operate to and from
Mt Pleasant so it's possible, if pre-arranged,
to arrive at MPA and fly out immediately
rather than going to Stanley.

Bicycle

Celia Stewart (☎ 21191; Scotia House B&B, 12 St Mary's
Walk; rental per day £10) has a couple of bicy-
cles to rent (see also p79). The Falklands'
notoriously windy weather means cycling
may not always be great fun, but around
Stanley a bike could be a good way to get
out to Gypsy Cove (p84), Cape Pembroke
Lighthouse (p85) or just around town.

Car

The improving road network has made
this a more attractive alternative for getting around, but drivers without local experience often get stuck in the boggy soft
camp on off-road tracks. This problem is so
common, even for experienced drivers, that
locals often carry a 2m 'ham' radio to call
for help. Vehicle renters will probably specify
that their cars cannot be used off-road.

Vehicle hirers include:
FIC Vehicle Hire (Map pp70-1; ☎ 27678; fic.auto@
horizon.co.fk) Has Land-Rover Discoverys and Defenders,
and Suzuki 4WDs.
Ian Bury (☎ 21058; fax 22643) Has Land-Rovers for hire.
Stanley Self-drive (☎ 21574; tporter@horizon.co.fk;
5 Jeremy Moore Ave) Has a Suzuki 4WD and a Citroën
station wagon.

Taxi

Lowe's Taxis (☎ 21381) and **BK Cabs** (☎ 21344)
are the two Stanley taxi operators, and for
a small town there seems to be an amazing number of taxis, particularly on Friday

nights. The vehicles are an assortment of cars, 4WDs and minibuses and there are standard fares to most locations. One-way fares for up to four passengers are around town £2, Moody Brook £3.50, Mt Kent £25, Goose Green £80, North Arm £100 and Gypsy Cove (per passenger return) £6.

AROUND STANLEY

GYPSY COVE

The short drive to the beach at Gypsy Cove, just outside the Narrows, is a popular local excursion. Many cruise ship visitors zip out there for a quick penguin fix, although in recent years the number of Magellanic penguins that have their burrows here has been in steady decline. Whether it's due to too much tourist attention or the downturn in numbers that has hit a number of Falklands penguin colonies is uncertain – although efforts to discourage visitor encroachment may help. It has also been suggested that sea lions have been finding this particular colony of penguins altogether too tasty.

Even if you don't encounter penguins, Gypsy Cove makes a pleasant excursion by vehicle or even on foot. It's about a 1½-hour stroll from the centre of Stanley, past the cemetery and FIPASS dock and across the bridge over the inlet known as the Canache. Back in the sailing era ships were careened here – deliberately run aground to lie on their side at low tide for repairs to be done. After the Falklands War and until the Mt Pleasant base was opened in 1985, many of the British troops in the Falklands were housed in floating 'coastels'. Two of them were moored at the entrance to the Canache; both later ended up in the USA, one as a floating jail in New York and the other as a holding centre for immigrants.

The route continues past Whalebone Cove, with the impressive wreck of the *Lady Elizabeth* (p74) and the much smaller one of the *Plym* (p75), and on to Yorke Bay. This beautiful long sweep of sand, just west of Stanley Airport, was mined by the Argentines, who expected a British frontal assault on the town. It's still suspected to be riddled with plastic mines and fenced off, but the

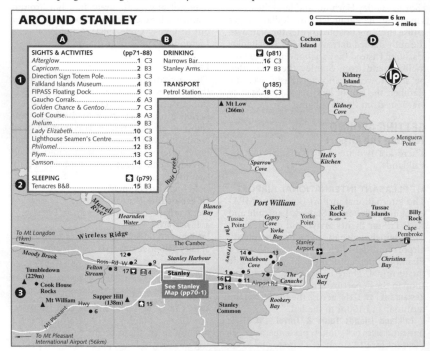

AROUND STANLEY

| | | 0 ————— 6 km |
| 0 ————— 4 miles |

SIGHTS & ACTIVITIES	(pp71-88)
Afterglow	1 C3
Capricorn	2 B3
Direction Sign Totem Pole	3 C3
Falkland Islands Museum	4 B3
FIPASS Floating Dock	5 C3
Gaucho Corrals	6 A3
Golden Chance & Gentoo	7 C3
Golf Course	8 A3
Jhelum	9 B3
Lady Elizabeth	10 C3
Lighthouse Seamen's Centre	11 C3
Philomel	12 B3
Plym	13 C3
Samson	14 C3

SLEEPING	(p79)
Tenacres B&B	15 B3

DRINKING	(p81)
Narrows Bar	16 C3
Stanley Arms	17 B3

TRANSPORT	(p185)
Petrol Station	18 C3

exclusion of human visitors has helped the bay's population of gentoo penguins.

At the cove there may be a warden on-site on busy summer weekends or when there's a cruise ship in port. A bus-borne snack bar also sets up at Gypsy Cove on those active occasions.

Rock cormorants and black-crowned night herons are also often seen on the northern headlands beyond the cove, while Commerson's dolphins often appear offshore. Looking across Port William from Gypsy Cove, Sparrow Cove lies directly to the north. For many years this was the resting place of Brunel's pioneering *Great Britain* (see the boxed text p73). Instead of retracing your route to Stanley, you can leave the road and follow the coastline around to Tussac Point, passing a rusting WWII Vickers naval gun on the way. From there the coastline curves round to overlook the Narrows, which is a good point from which to watch ships. The walk passes the wreck of the *Samson* before arriving back at Whalebone Cove.

CAPE PEMBROKE

The trip out to Cape Pembroke, the most easterly point on the Falklands with its dramatically sited lighthouse, starts out towards Stanley Airport. En route you pass the tall **totem pole** post studded with signs to locations all over the world. It started courtesy of visiting soldiers after the Falklands War. Nearby are the greenhouses that supply fresh vegetables to locals.

Just before the airport, the route to Cape Pembroke branches off east and deteriorates to a sandy, muddy 4WD track. (Or series of tracks, since every lighthouse visitor has endeavoured to find a new route, resulting in a spiderweb tangle of conflicting lines.) On the south side of the cape is Christina Bay, which is home to a variety of shorebirds and visited on occasion by sea lions.

It was quickly realised that the string of rocks and reefs running parallel to the north side of the cape was a major danger for shipping. The Billy Rock, which barely breaks the surface most of the time, has claimed 15 ships and many lives over the years. Unlit markers were constructed soon after Stanley was settled and in 1855 the present 18m-high, cast-iron **Cape Pembroke Lighthouse** was shipped out from Britain and

lit for the first time. Powered by rape seed oil, the light could be seen up to 22km out to sea. The lighthouse got through more than a thousand gallons of oil a year and for a time sea lion oil was tried in an attempt to reduce the operating costs.

The lighthouse was rebuilt in 1906 with a paraffin light turned by a clockwork mechanism which, with hourly windings, continued to operate until the Falklands War. After the war it was replaced by a much less romantic automatic lighthouse, which is the featureless structure just to the east of the old black-and-white lighthouse.

In the early days, the light keepers and their families lived in a cottage that used to stand at the base of the lighthouse. They were supplied by ship from Stanley because presumably the 11km land route was even more difficult than it is today. In the late 19th century the entire Cape Pembroke peninsula constituted one of the few small farms on the islands. It was leased by the government to Stanley resident James Smith, a vocal advocate of agrarian reform, which did not finally come about until a century later.

The lighthouse has been restored and visitors can borrow the key to get inside from the Falkland Islands Museum (p71) for £5. On the west side of the lighthouse a plaque identifies the view in that direction. On the other side the lighthouse's latitude and longitude is numerated, but don't try navigating by the figures – Cape Pembroke is a full degree further west.

Parts of the headland have been fenced off and efforts are being made to regrow the tussock grass that once cloaked the cape. The cape can be an excellent place for birdwatching.

Surf Bay

The long sweep of sand at the western end of Cape Pembroke peninsula is a popular beach outing for Stanley residents. Fortunately this one wasn't mined by the Argentines. The water temperature is enough to dissuade most would-be swimmers, but some locals take an occasional summer dip. And a lot do so in the annual midwinter swim, which takes place on the nearest Saturday to 21 June (the shortest day of the year). Boogie board enthusiasts with a good wet suit report that Surf Bay does indeed have good surf.

STANLEY

BATTLEFIELDS & HIGH POINTS

The British advance on Stanley in the final days of the Falklands War was based on securing the high ground overlooking the town. Once this had been achieved the end was inevitable, even though the Argentine forces in Stanley considerably outnumbered the British. Mt Kent (458m) fell on 31 May 1982 to a party brought in by helicopter well ahead of the general British advance. From Stanley, Mt Kent stands on the horizon, about 20km away to the east.

The battle for Stanley began with the taking of Mt Longdon, Mt Harriet and the Two Sisters Mountains on 11 June. Mt Longdon involved some of the heaviest fighting of the war, with 23 British and more than 30 Argentines killed. Two days later, on 13 June, the British took Tumbledown and Wireless Ridge, directly across Stanley Harbour from the town. The following day the Argentines surrendered.

See p78 for information on local tour operators that conduct battlefield tours; the highpoints around the town are also popular walks. It takes less than an hour to walk from the centre of Stanley to **Sapper Hill** (138m), named after the Regiment of Royal Sappers and Miners who accompanied Governor Moody during his period as governor from 1842 to 1843. The hilltop, marked by communication aerials, lies north of the Mt Pleasant Hwy just to the west of the town. It's a 1½- to two-hour walk from Stanley, perhaps half an hour less from Sapper Hill, to the summit of Mt Harriet (442m). The peak was taken by 42 Commando Royal Marines and a memorial cross marks the summit.

Moody Brook, at the western end of Stanley Harbour, makes a good jumping-

---

MT WILLIAM & TUMBLEDOWN WALK *David Burnett*

Climbing the hills overlooking Stanley offers spectacular views of Stanley Harbour; and the chance to immerse yourself, perhaps literally, in some typical camp bog. A mid-morning start, a leisurely pace and lunch on Tumbledown's summit will have the sun behind you all the way, and leave time to enjoy the views on a half-day walk.

Bring water, warm windproof clothing and sunscreen; you'll burn quickly in this treeless landscape. Although the area is believed to be free from mines you should follow existing tracks and report anything suspicious to the EOD (p82).

Follow Ross Rd West out of Stanley. The sealed road deteriorates to a potholed, gravel track, which narrows as it approaches Moody Brook. Along the way you'll pass an unstaffed meteorological station with a distinctive, tall boom and, in the fields to the left, the rusted stump of a 1960s-era European space-tracking tower.

Half an hour from town, a concrete ford marks where Moody Brook enters Stanley Harbour. The Moody Brook Track continues in the lee of Wireless Ridge towards the settlement at Estancia, but head left to the ruins of the old wireless station (1918), a collection of whitewashed buildings with a yard full of machinery. Following the track left past these buildings brings you to a pleasant, modern farmhouse, nestled at the foot of the rise. This marks the beginning of the Tumbledown climb.

Just past the farm, directly ahead, is a large concrete foundation. The track leading directly to Tumbledown, which you follow on the way down, starts from just right of this structure, over a small brook. Following the vehicle tracks, you could reach Tumbledown's summit in half an hour to an hour.

Instead, take the major tangle of vehicle tracks up to the left and follow them as they swing gradually right to strike directly towards Mt William. If this is your first experience of typical camp bog, watch your step – between the clumps of tussock grass lurk water-filled holes up to a metre deep!

The vehicle tracks slowly climb across a sweeping amphitheatre with impressive views back to Stanley Harbour. To your right are small examples of the famous Falklands 'stone runs' (see p37), the rivers of jumbled rocks and boulders slicing across the tussock grass. After 20 minutes or so, a set of fresh wheel ruts may branch off to the right, heading for the prominent radio mast on the saddle between Mt William and Tumbledown. Closer to Mt William, the overturned wreck of a Land-Rover testifies to the hazards of camp travel.

off point for other hill walks. From here you can look down the length of Stanley Harbour to the wreck of the *Lady Eliza-beth* in Whalebone Cove. It takes about 40 minutes to climb to the top of **Tumble-down** (229m). If the ground is reasonably dry this can also be a good trip to make by mountain bike. Tumbledown prob-ably takes its name from a gaucho horse round-up that went wrong – the horses fell over the edge of rock face and tum-bled down.

It's only a 20-minute walk from Moody Brook to **Wireless Ridge** (171m), which is also topped by a war memorial. Another hour will take you from Wireless Ridge to the top of Mt Longdon (198m), again topped by a Falklands War memorial. It takes a similar time to reach the Two Sisters (just over 305m at the West Peak), which can be combined to make a Wireless Ridge–Mt Longdon Two Sisters–Goat Ridge round trip.

GAUCHO CORRALS

Just to the south of the Mt Pleasant Hwy, a couple of kilometres west of Stanley, is a circular, stone-walled enclosure. You can't walk over to inspect it more closely because it's in a minefield, but this is one of the Falk-lands' many stone corrals – a reminder of the era when gauchos crossed the landscape and when cattle had not yet been pushed to one side by sheep. Although many of the gauchos were indeed from South America, it was as much a job description as a record of nationality; one early account writes of a man who was a 'Scottish gaucho'.

Some of the earliest corrals were built of turf, sometimes topped with gorse bushes. Many of these constructions have faded or

A hundred metres beyond the wreck the track steepens to meet the rocky, lower slopes of Mt William, perhaps 40 minutes from Moody Brook Farm. From here a scramble among the steep and broken slabs could take you to the summit; a low radio mast nestles just below. This is hazardous country, so it might be better to take an easier ramble to the nearest vantage-point on the summit ridge's lower slopes, from where the views over the Mt Pleasant Hwy to the southern coast are ample reward. To the east the entire length of the ridge from Mt William to the telecommunications masts on Sapper Hill is visible, with the distant houses of Stanley dot-ting the harbour's southern shore. It is possible to traverse this ridge, or an indistinct vehicle track to its left, back to Stanley, but the going can be boggy and the views are no better than those you have already taken in.

Return to the slightly flatter ground below the rocks, and follow the wheel ruts that continue left towards the tall radio mast that has graced the western horizon during the climb to Mt William, passing to the right of some black peat-hillocks. The tracks may come and go, but the way forward is obvious – across the broad saddle with the summit cross on Tumbledown directly ahead.

Another 15 minutes brings you to Tumbledown's lower slopes, and some conspicuous vehicle tracks that wind among the rocks towards the peak. The tiny, poignant stone circles – perhaps adorned with a clump of plastic poppies – mark the exact places where British soldiers fell during the pitched night-time battle for this strategic high-point in the last hours of the 1982 conflict.

The views from Tumbledown's summit are superb. To the west, craggy Goat Ridge runs to-wards the (partly obscured) Two Sisters; just left of this Mt Harriet broods on the horizon. To the north Moody Brook trickles eastward to Stanley Harbour. On the valley's far flank Mt Longdon and Wireless Ridge is another significant battlefield with some excellent walking. Tumbledown's summit cross is usually festooned with tributes to the soldiers who fell while fighting their way up this intimidating slope – you'll better appreciate the dramatic painting of the scene in the Stanley museum after you've clambered over these crags.

From the top descend through the outcrops to a prominent vehicle track, which heads down and left. Just before leaving Tumbledown and striking out for Cook House Rocks – the low crags clearly visible in the direction of Stanley Harbour – the track passes some rusty military vehicles and debris bearing Argentine military insignia. The steel tubes and openings suggest fearsome weapons of war, but they're actually the ovens and stovepipes of abandoned mess trailers.

The route back to the Moody Brook Farm follows intertwined, boggy vehicle tracks to the right of Cook House Rocks, with magnificent views of Stanley Harbour the whole way.

disappeared at ground level, although they can often be discerned from the air. The stone corrals, sometimes beautifully constructed from finely chosen stones, have lasted much better. They've become an important symbol of the islands' history and farmers often go to great trouble to restore and conserve them. The corrals were built to pen cattle before they were sorted, castrated or culled. Stanley's Sapper Hill corral was mentioned in some of the earliest reports on Stanley, but it's unknown who built it or when. There are far more corrals on East Falkland (p99) than on West.

KIDNEY COVE & KIDNEY ISLAND

Just north of Port William, Kidney Cove and Kidney Island make a good day trip from Stanley, although an overnight stay is really required to properly appreciate the island. Kidney Cove can be reached by road around Port William, although it's more interesting and convenient to take a boat out through the Narrows from Stanley and across to Sparrow Cove, from where you will be picked up and taken by Land-Rover to Kidney Cove. Unfortunately, all the land east of the imaginary line between Sparrow Cove and the southern end of Kidney Cove, down to the end of Menguera Point, has been marked off as a minefield.

Kidney Cove

Tours to the cove are run by Adrian and Lisa Lowe of **Kidney Cove Safari Tours** (☎ 31001; allowe@horizon.co.fk; £60 per day, £35 per half day). Kidney Cove is partly owned by the Lowes, whose Murrell Farm is about 15km west of the cove. It's only about half an hour by boat from Stanley to Sparrow Cove, the long term resting place of Brunel's flagship the *Great Britain* (see the boxed text p73). From there the route to Kidney Cove traverses the slopes of Mt Low (266m), from where there are fine views back across Stanley 10km to the south; and north to tussock-covered Cochon Island or east

down to Kidney Cove and Kidney Island. There's a cabin on the slopes of Mt Low where it may be possible to stay.

Kidney Cove has breeding colonies of gentoo, Magellanic and king penguins. The only other breeding colonies of king penguins in the Falklands are on Saunders Island and the much larger colony at Volunteer Beach (p92). There's also a rockhopper penguin colony, mixed in with king cormorants, on the Berkeley Sound coast, further to the west and due north of Mt Low. Other birds encountered here include turkey vultures, skuas and occasional red-backed hawks.

Kidney Island

Totally covered in tussock grass, the small island (33 hectares) is maintained as a nature reserve. It is a fine example of a Falklands environment, untouched by the introduced animals that have devastated the tussock growth on the main island and killed off many small bird species. The grass is so tall on the island that it can be very easy to get lost – and since sea lions sometimes laze in the grass it's wise to walk with caution. Small birds like Cobb's wren and tussock birds are common on the island; rockhopper penguins and king cormorants can be found on the rocky outcrops on the north coast; and sooty shearwaters migrate here in great numbers from late spring. Visitors need to stay overnight to see them since they congregate offshore in the evening, waiting for darkness to fall before they come ashore to their burrows. In daylight they'd be easy prey for the skuas and other predators. Overnight visitors are sometimes lucky enough to see short-eared owls.

Kidney Island is reached by boat from Stanley, landing on the beach on the southwest side of the island. There's a hut in the centre of the island where visitors can stay.

Contact **Seaview** (☎ 22669; seaview.sawle@horizon.co.fk) for information on getting to Kidney Island; the round trip costs £30 per person. See also p78.

East Falkland

CONTENTS

EAST FALKLAND

The area of East Falkland is only slightly larger than that of West Falkland, but the population is much greater. This does not mean East Falkland feels crowded; get outside Stanley or Mt Pleasant and, like most of the Falklands, it's almost empty. Almost all visitors will include Stanley on their itinerary, but it's in camp (anywhere in the Falklands outside Stanley) where the real interest lies. For Falklands visitors the 4WD trek across camp to Volunteer Beach, with the most photographed penguin colony on the islands, is probably the most popular excursion outside Stanley.

East Falkland was the site for much of the historic development of the Falklands. It was here where the French established the first settlement at Port Louis, later to be handed over to the Spanish who renamed it Puerto de la Soledad, and later to be handed on again to the Argentines. The British took it over briefly before moving their capital to Stanley. It was also on East Falkland that the Falklands' sheep industry initially developed and where nearly all the land-based fighting of the Falklands War took place. There's Falklands War history at San Carlos and Port San Carlos, where the British landings took place, and at Darwin and Goose Green, where some of the fiercest fighting of the war took place and where many of the Argentine dead are buried. San Carlos has a Falklands War Museum and the British War Cemetery, although most of the British dead were returned to Britain for burial. The San Carlos River is also the prime trout fishing river in East Falkland.

East Falkland divides into two distinctly different regions. The northern part of the island is rolling and often mountainous, in fact, very much like West Falkland. The highest point is Mt Usborne at 705m, only a little higher than Mt Adam, the highest point in West Falkland. A narrow isthmus joins this northern part of the island to the southern part. Known as Lafonia, the southern half of East Falkland is monotonously flat, and dotted with innumerable lakes and ponds.

HIGHLIGHTS

- Studying three species of penguin, including the regal king, at **Volunteer Beach** (p92)

- Admiring the islands' best gaucho corral on the forgotten plains of **Lafonia** (p99)

- Fishing for sea trout along the bends of the **San Carlos River** (p94)

- Strolling across the world's southernmost suspension bridge at **Bodie Creek** (p98)

- Visiting the sites of the fiercest Falklands War fighting at **Goose Green** (p98)

CAMP

Anywhere in the Falklands outside Stanley is 'camp' and nearly everyone in camp is engaged in sheep ranching, though a few work in tourism and minor cottage industries. Since the advent of large sheep stations in the late 19th century, rural settlement in the Falklands has consisted of tiny hamlets, really company towns, near sheltered harbours where coastal shipping could collect the wool clip. In fact, these settlements were the models for the sheep *estancias* of Patagonia, many of which were founded by Falklands emigrants. On nearly all of these stations, shepherds lived in 'outside houses' that still dot the countryside. Since the agrarian reform of the late 1970s and 1980s, this pattern of residence has not changed greatly despite the creation of many new farms, but the population has dropped precipitously. Many camp settlements have closed completely; others are run with much smaller work forces and many outside houses stand empty.

GETTING AROUND

East Falkland has the islands' most extensive road network. Almost anywhere in East Falkland where these new roads run can be reached within a two- or three-hour drive of Stanley. Stretches between Stanley and Mt Pleasant International Airport (MPA) are surfaced; otherwise the roads are gravelled, but of a good standard and well maintained. The road network is still being extended, but for now the Mt Pleasant Hwy is the principal road from Stanley via Mt Pleasant to Darwin-Goose Green and on to North Arm at the southern end of Lafonia; a spur runs from just before Darwin north to San Carlos.

From Pony's Pass on the Mt Pleasant Hwy, an excellent road runs northwest via the Estancia (a farm west of Stanley) and the Teal Inlet settlement to Port San Carlos. Along the way spurs turn off to Port Louis and Rincon Grande, to Salvador, most of the way to Cape Dolphin and finally, shortly before Port San Carlos, to Green Field Farm.

Most other tracks require 4WD. The before and after trip between Stanley and Port San Carlos gives a good idea of what travel across camp used to be like. Today you can do the 115km trip in less than two hours; 1

hour 40 minutes is a good average time; a bit slower when the road is wet. Before the new road was built in the 1990s the trip typically took 10 or 11 hours in the summer when the surface was dry. In winter, when it was wet, it took 17 or 18 hours – so long as you did not get seriously bogged. That's a best conditions average of less than 12km/h and a worst case of less than 7km/h.

Despite the curious road signs telling you to put your seat belt on as you leave Stanley towards Mt Pleasant and then insisting you should take them off once you leave that road or continue beyond MPA, wear your seat belt. It's out on the 'nondesignated' roads where single vehicle accidents are much more likely.

Several Stanley tour operators (p78) run day trips to East Falkland settlements.

NORTHEAST EAST FALKLAND

PORT LOUIS

Port Louis is the Falklands' oldest settlement, dating from the French foundation of the colony by Louis de Bougainville in 1764. One of the oldest buildings is the ivy-covered 19th-century **farmhouse**, still occupied by farm employees. There are also **ruins** of the French governor's house and fortress, and Louis Vernet's settlement scattered nearby. The settlement also has the **grave** of Matthew Brisbane, Vernet's lieutenant, who was murdered by gauchos after British naval officer John James Onslow left him in charge of the settlement in early 1833. Port Louis' period as the capital ended in 1845 with the shift to Stanley.

Peter and Melanie Gilding's recently renovated **Garden House** (☎ 31060; fax 31061; plouis@horizon.co.fk; per person £25) overlooks the harbour and has a double bedroom and two twins. It has central heating, a gas cooker, fridge, TV and music centre.

Port Louis is just off the route to Volunteer Point; the graded road continues beyond Port Louis to Johnsons Harbour.

SEAL BAY

It's a difficult drive north across camp from Port Louis to Seal Bay. There are **colonies** of rockhopper and gentoo penguins and of

EAST FALKLAND

THE RISE & RUIN OF PORT LOUIS

The Falklands' history often seems to be convoluted, but it would be hard to find a more complicated timeline than that of Port Louis:

1764 French explorer Louis Antoine de Bougainville sets up a French settlement.

1765 British explorer John Byron sets up a British settlement at Port Egmont on Saunders Island, unaware that the French have laid claim to the Falklands.

1766 British and French bump into each other.

1767 Before the British and French can sort out who the place belongs to the French sell out to the Spanish, who rename the settlement Puerto de la Soledad.

1770 Spanish kick the British out of the Falklands.

1771 After threats and counter-threats between Britain and Spain, the British return to the Falklands at their Port Egmont settlement.

1774 British abandon Port Egmont.

1806 Spanish abandon Puerto de la Soledad, and five years later abandon Falklands/Islas Malvinas completely.

1820 United Provinces of the River Plate, later to become Argentina, takes over Puerto de la Soledad.

1823 Louis Vernet, born in France but naturalised as an Argentine citizen, assumes command, but stays for only a year.

1826 Vernet returns.

1828 Vernet granted fishing and sealing rights to the islands and becomes governor.

1829 Vernet arrests three American sealing ships for sealing illegally.

1831 America refuses to recognise Argentine sovereignty and despatches Silas Duncan on board the USS *Lexington* to sort things out. Duncan wrecks Puerto de la Soledad and proclaims that there is no government in the Falklands and it's open season on seals. Vernet's governor, Matthew Brisbane, is arrested and shipped out to Montevideo.

1832 A temporary new governor is sent from Argentina only to be murdered by mutinous gauchos. The British, after an absence of nearly half a century, pop up with Captain John James Onslow on board HMS *Clio*.

1833 Onslow informs the replacement governor, Jose Maria Pinedo, that Islas Malvinas are now, once again, the Falklands and he should head home to Buenos Aires, which he does. Vernet pursues his claims for property damages in British courts for nearly 30 years, with little success. Matthew Brisbane returns from South America and takes over command again, only to be murdered by more mutinous gauchos, this time led by Antonio Rivero.

1834 The British really take over.

1842 Richard Moody arrives on board the *Hebe* to become lieutenant governor.

1843 Moody appointed governor and decides to shift his capital to Stanley.

1845 Stanley officially replaces Port Louis as the capital.

1982 Argentina invades the Falklands and renames Stanley as Puerto Rivero. This does not go down well with the islanders, who already have a Brisbane St, so it's quickly renamed Puerto Argentina.

cormorants along this coast. At one time it was possible to walk from Port Louis to Seal Bay, stay at Seal Bay House and then walk along the north coast, with its dramatic headlands, fine beaches and sea lion colony near MacBride Head, to a Portakabin shelter near Dutchman's Brook. From there walkers could continue past Cape Carysfort and Cow Bay to Volunteer Beach. This is no longer possible, although there has been talk of organising guided walks on this route.

VOLUNTEER BEACH

The popular excursion from Stanley to Volunteer Beach takes visitors to by far the largest **king penguin colony** in the Falklands. The photogenic kings are at the northern limit of their range in the Falklands. One or two turn up at a number of other sites around the islands and there's a small but growing colony on Saunders Island. King penguins were reported at Volunteer Beach in the early 18th century, but by the late 1800s these majestic birds had been virtually wiped out in the relentless exploitation of the Falklands' wildlife. The first return of king penguins to the beach was recorded in 1933, but by 1967 there were just 15 breeding pairs. Since then the numbers have steadily grown, topping 400 pairs in 2001 and more than 750 in 2003.

Volunteer Beach also has large colonies of gentoo and Magellanic penguins. These colonies did not appear to be hit by the drastic fall in numbers that has recently hit other Falklands colonies, but the 2002–03 season included a flash flood that killed many penguin chicks. The colonies are on the grassy isthmus between the open sea on the north side and the sheltered bay on the south. The penguins usually arrive and depart by the north beach, but they also play around in the water off the south beach. Upland geese and the usual predators are also common around the colonies.

During the summer months Falklands Conservation (FC) has a warden stationed at the beach. The warden can answer questions and has an information kiosk at the carpark, where there are also some informative display boards. Outside of these months a visit may be difficult to arrange.

From Volunteer Beach it's a couple of hours' walk to **Volunteer Point** at the end of the promontory. An offshore breeding colony of **southern fur seals** can be seen through binoculars and elephant seals are sometimes found on the beaches. It may be possible to stay in the well-kept outside house at Volunteer Beach. Contact **Falklands Conservation** (Map p84; ☎ 22247; fax 22288; conservation@horizon.co .fk; Jetty Centre, Stanley).

Getting There & Away

Tenacres Tours, Discovery Tours and Hebe Tours (p78) run day trips to Volunteer Beach for around £55 to £65 per person, with a minimum of three people. The cost includes lunch and the £12 per person charge to enter the landowner's property.

It takes about 2½ hours to drive to Volunteer Beach. The first 56km is along a good graded road past Port Louis and Johnsons Harbour, but the final 17km skirts Mt Brisbane (176m) across often challenging stretches of camp; finding the route really requires local knowledge. There is no intention to continue the graded road all the way to the beach, but in recent years it has been extended further from Stanley, reducing the travel time from as much as four hours.

Cruise ships sometimes come to Volunteer Beach although big swells on the beach often prevent landings.

RINCON GRANDE

On the east side of Salvador Water it's possible to camp at Arthur and Elaine Turner's **Rincon Grande Farm** (☎ 31119; fax 31149). Near the settlement there are penguins, including Magellanics and kings, sea lions and a variety of birdlife. Armantine Beach on the north coast takes its name from the wreck

of the French ship *Armantine*. Although little is known about the vessel, Wreck Mountain also refers to the incident.

SALVADOR & CAPE BOUGAINVILLE

The settlement at Salvador makes an interesting base to explore the northwest of East Falkland and is also an interesting settlement to visit in its own right. From Salvador it's an easy trip across camp to Cape Bougainville.

Salvador

Originally founded by Andrez Pitaluga, a Gibraltarian who arrived in the islands via South America in the 1830s, the settlement at Salvador, correctly known as Gibraltar Station, is East Falkland's oldest owner-occupied sheep farm. Five generations of Pitalugas have run the farm, which still covers 21,000 hectares but at one time was 120,000 hectares – most of the northern part of East Falkland. Today they raise sheep from a stud of Tasmanian origin, but accommodation is no longer available. On the station's north coast are **penguin colonies** made up of five different species, and many other shorebirds and waterfowl, while Centre Island in Port Salvador (also known as Salvador Water) has breeding populations of elephant seals and sea lions. Trekking along the north coast is possible with permission. The well spread out settlement also has a **graveyard** and the remains of an old Wessex **helicopter**, brought here after it ditched in the sea as a result of a peacetime incident before the 1982 conflict. There's a small gentoo colony within walking distance of the settlement and mullet fishing in the creek.

Cape Bougainville

The turn-off to Cape Bougainville is 11km before Salvador, and from there to the point is about 8km across typically tricky camp territory. There's a Portakabin at the cape, which the rocky point's large **rockhopper penguin colony** shares with king cormorants. The odd macaroni penguin is also seen here. Sea lions come ashore between the two rockhopper colonies and can often be seen either on the rocks or in the tussock grass. Further along the coast at **Mare Rincon** there are gentoos, Magellanic and some king penguins.

West of Cape Bougainville is Concordia Bay, named after a German barquentine,

ROSE DE FREYCINET & THE WRECK OF L'URANIE

Although there's nothing to see of the shipwreck, the story of *l'Uranie* is one of the most interesting and best documented of the many Falklands founderings. In 1817 the aristocratic Captain Louis de Freycinet departed France on a three-year scientific voyage around the world. He made numerous observations and scientific studies; wrote a host of journals and reports that still make fascinating reading today; and left reminders of his visits in the names of many geographic features, including the beautiful Freycinet Peninsula in the Australian state of Tasmania.

In February 1820 the voyage almost came to a disastrous conclusion when the ship hit a rock and the crew were forced to beach it in French Bay, now Uranie Bay, just south of Long Island towards the western end of Berkeley Sound. After a great deal of intrigue and double-dealing the unfortunate Freycinet managed to first charter and then purchase an American sealing ship, which was renamed *La Physicienne*, and brought the party safely home to France.

The subsequent court martial to examine the shipwreck exonerated de Freycinet, but the explorer must have been concerned that losing his ship was not the only slip-up. Against all regulations he had taken his wife along for the trip. Rose de Freycinet was only 22 years old when, dressed as a man, she managed to sneak onto the ship just before departure. As it turned out she had a remarkable voyage, earned the admiration and respect of the crew and kept a journal of her adventures that was not published in French until 1927; and not in English until 1996, when it appeared as *A Woman of Courage: the journal of Rose de Freycinet on her voyage around the world, 1817–1820*. Of course, she had also become one of the first women to circumnavigate the world.

The Western Australian Maritime Museum, recognising de Freycinet's important connections with Australia, organised an expedition to the Falklands to search for remains of his ship in 2001. In fact, the ship had been discovered by Falklands diver David Eynon back in 1971 and he helped the university team on their recent investigations.

Concordia, shipwrecked here in 1891. Much of the wreckage is covered by sand; markers indicate its location and the sand sometimes shifts to reveal the wreckage.

Sleeping

Unfortunately the cosy Salvador Lodge is no longer operating. The road to Salvador passes close to the settlement at Douglas, where there has been accommodation in the past, although it is also not currently available. There are some good coastal walks and mullet fishing possibilities in the Douglas area. At Estancia it's possible to camp with permission from Tony and Ailsa Heathman of **Estancia Farm** (☎ 31042).

Getting There & Away

From Stanley the road to Salvador, Port San Carlos and other settlements turns off the Mt Pleasant Hwy and skirts around Mt Kent (459m), which is topped by military communications equipment. On the north side of the road is the wreckage of an Argentine Puma helicopter and, closer to the road, a twin-rotor Chinook; both were destroyed while on the ground. The road passes by the

Estancia settlement and continues to Teal Inlet, where the settlement has a surprising number of trees (by Falklands standards).

Further along, the road turns off to the Douglas settlement and skirts around Port Salvador before ending at Salvador, 104km from Stanley. It's also possible to fly to Salvador with Falkland Islands Government Air Service (FIGAS; £25, 20 minutes).

WEST OF STANLEY

PORT SAN CARLOS

San Carlos and Port San Carlos take their name from the visit to East Falkland by the Spanish ship *San Carlos* in 1768. A number of Falklands settlements like Darwin-Goose Green or Fox Bay East-Fox Bay West are in two parts, often only a short distance apart. But confusingly, Port San Carlos and San Carlos are far apart on the two separate arms of San Carlos Water. Both settlements are accessible by a good road from Stanley but the road that runs to each of them splits just a short distance out of Stanley. The San Carlos settlement has a population of 10 people.

Port San Carlos is an excellent base for wildlife trips to Cape Dolphin and Fanning Head, and is close to the fishing delights of the San Carlos River. San Carlos Water was dubbed Bomb Alley after the concentrated Argentine attacks on the British fleet during the major landing of the Falklands War.

War Relics

There's virtually no sign of the British landing at Green Beach at Port San Carlos – the only one of the three landings that was opposed by Argentine troops. If you walk from the settlement towards the airstrip you can find some old Argentine **foxholes** inland of the runway, including one roofed-in dugout complete with bench seats. Continue past the airstrip to the coast and past two smaller bays before you reach the third bay with the wide sweep of Green Beach. The airstrip was used as a refuelling point for the British Harriers during the closing stages of the conflict.

There are reminders of wartime activity further upriver. Walk down to Smylies Farm and ask permission to walk across their land up the San Carlos River. Beside their jetty look for the **pontoon**, formerly used to float vehicles across the river; flotation is provided by a gaggle of Argentine aircraft fuel drop tanks. For weeks after the war ended drop tanks floated ashore on Falklands' beaches. There are more traces of foxholes just beyond the shearing shed. A 20-minute walk upstream along the inlet will take you to a **memorial** to three British airmen killed during the landing assault. As the Argentine troops retreated towards Stanley two Gazelle helicopters pursued them, only to be brought down by ground fire.

Fanning Head & North Coast

Fanning Head, at the entrance to San Carlos Water, is a relatively short distance from Port San Carlos. However, the route there is all off-road, so the 70km round trip really takes all day. It's possible to walk directly to Fanning Head in about six hard hours. En route to the head there's a **gentoo penguin colony** a good 2km to 3km back from the coast and high up on a hill. From the hilltop the penguins can see the whole length of Bomb Alley as well as both sides of Fanning Head. There's a large **rockhopper colony** at the head and a **gentoo colony** at Rookery Sands, with a **Magellanic colony** nearby. The round

trip continues back to Port San Carlos along the north coast of the peninsula, with a stop to collect Falklands pebbles. Past the pebble beach there are views across to Paloma Sand Beach where there's a gentoo colony and the odd visiting king penguin. You'll need a 4WD and a knowledgeable local guide.

Cape Dolphin

Commander Byron named this cape after his ship, HMS *Dolphin*, when he circumnavigated the Falklands and set up the settlement at Port Egmont in 1765. Although the round trip to Cape Dolphin is about 120km from Port San Carlos, much further than the Fanning Head trip, half of the circuit is on graded road so the travel time is about the same. **Penguin colonies** include gentoos (with 1000 or more pairs) and Magellanic penguins (close to the head). There's also a **blowhole** with cormorant colonies nearby. In season, up to 100 sea lions can be seen. They're remarkably unconcerned by visitors on the beach except during the mating season, when the bulls can get a little heated. Peregrine falcons are also observed here and giant petrels are common around the point. On Swan Pond, black-necked swans, grebes and lots of yellow-billed teal are often seen. Finally, on the return trip along the southwest side of the cape, there's another large gentoo colony with more than 1000 pairs.

Fishing

Mullet can be caught near the settlement year-round, but the San Carlos River is the major attraction. In fact, the river is closer to Port San Carlos than to San Carlos. It was in the San Carlos that the Falklands' record sea trout was caught and San Carlos enthusiasts insist that it's a more interesting river than the Warrah (the principal West Falklands river) with more bends, curves and pools. Just before Port San Carlos, a branch turns left off the road, fords the river and continues to Green Field Farm and, across camp, to San Carlos. The ford is just above the tidal range of the river and is a good place to fish.

Sleeping

Smylies Farm (☎ /fax 41013, ☎ guests 41004; per person £12) Tony and Jenny Anderson have a four-bedroom, self-catering cottage with room for eight people. There's central heating and cooking equipment, but meals can also be taken in the farmhouse. Trips are made from the farm to the gentoo colony at Paloma Sand Beach.

Getting There & Away

The 115km drive to Port San Carlos from Stanley takes less than two hours. FIGAS (£37, 30 minutes) also flies from Stanley.

SAN CARLOS

British forces in the 1982 conflict first came ashore at San Carlos settlement at the south end of San Carlos Water. Until 1983, when it was subdivided and sold to half a dozen local families, San Carlos was a traditional large sheep station – the isolated 'big house', with its lengthy approach, will give you some idea of how farm owners and managers distanced themselves from labourers.

A fine **stone corral**, built in 1871, stands close to Ceritos Hill and Mt Usborne. The corral can be approached from Darwin or San Carlos.

The excellent small **museum** in San Carlos has three sections. One covers rural life in the Falklands; another, by FC, looks at the islands' natural history; and the third covers the Falklands War and, in particular, the landings from San Carlos Water. Many of the events of that epic period took place just a stone's throw from the museum.

Continue through San Carlos to the immaculately kept **British War Cemetery** close to the water's edge. A total of 252 British servicemen died during the conflict. Some remain entombed in their sunken ships, but most were returned to Britain where Falklands' combatants are commemorated at the Falkland Islands Memorial Chapel at Pangbourne, Berkshire. The San Carlos cemetery has just 14 graves from the 1982 conflict; among them is that of Lieutenant Colonel 'H' Jones, whose heroic death during the taking of Goose Green was rewarded with one of the conflict's two Victoria Crosses.

Across San Carlos Water are the ruins of the **Ajax Bay Refrigeration Plant**, a madcap 1950s Colonial Development Corporation (CDC) project that any idiot could have seen was doomed to failure from the start. Quite apart from the fact that the Falklands' sheep population was bred for wool, not mutton, there were minor problems like location – Ajax Bay was a long, long way from anywhere – and basic facilities – Ajax Bay had limited supplies of fresh water, essential for a meat-freezing operation.

Then the project budget and schedule blew out – the builders were paid way over the odds and construction was still dogged by industrial unrest. Eventually the plant opened in 1953, years behind schedule and way over

---

THE SAN CARLOS LANDINGS & THE BATTLE OF BOMB ALLEY

Where would the British make their Falklands landing? They could make a full frontal assault on Stanley; the minefields which remain, over 20 years later, show that the Argentines certainly considered that possibility. They could land on West Falkland and use that island as a base to move onto East Falkland and Stanley. Or they could land somewhere on East Falkland and advance from there to Stanley.

The decision was made to land at three points around San Carlos Water, code named Blue Beach (San Carlos), Red Beach (Ajax Bay) and Green Beach (Port San Carlos). The Argentine forces were overwhelmingly concentrated in Stanley, with major contingents in Port Howard and Fox Bay on West Falkland, and in Goose Green on East Falkland. But elsewhere, including Port San Carlos, there were only small numbers of men and only Green Beach was defended.

The real action did not take place on the beaches, but out on San Carlos Water, a narrow channel which would be dubbed 'Bomb Alley'. The museum in San Carlos shows just how tightly packed the British fleet was in San Carlos Water. A furious Argentine air assault commenced with Mirages and Skyhawks hurtling in close to sea level to attack the British fleet. 'Any nation which produces first-class Formula-One racing drivers is also likely to turn out some pretty good pilots', was one comment on the often suicidal bravery of the attackers. In the following days the frigates HMS *Ardent* and HMS *Antelope*, and the destroyer HMS *Coventry* were sunk, but the major blow to the British war plan was the destruction of the container ship *Atlantic Conveyor*. The ship's cargo of helicopters was intended to leapfrog the British troops forward from the San Carlos Water landing sites to Stanley. Now they would have to walk.

cost. In the first year just 14,000 sheep were brought in for processing and 39% of those were rejected for being of low quality. In the following year the numbers rose to just 16,000 and the year after that the shambolic disaster was shut down. The prefab houses that were imported for labourers were dismantled and moved to Stanley, where they can be seen on Ross Rd West. Gentoo penguins occasionally wander through the ruins, which served as a military field hospital during the 1982 conflict. Take a torch (flashlight) if you plan to explore the ruins, which are about a four-hour walk around the south end of San Carlos Water.

Sleeping
Although the building, complete with sign, is still there, the Blue Beach Lodge has closed down.

Getting There & Away
There's a good gravelled road all the way to San Carlos; take the Mt Pleasant Hwy and turn-off a few kilometres before Darwin. Alternatively you can get there from Port San Carlos, although the last 10km of the 36km trip are across camp.

There are fine views of Bomb Alley as you drop down from the ridge between Green Field Farm and San Carlos. If there was a way of crossing the river at Port San Carlos you could walk the 7km directly to San Carlos in a couple of hours.

PORT SUSSEX
There's an assortment of birdlife around the settlement and dolphins often appear in the inlet. South of San Carlos, towards Darwin-Goose Green, it's possible to camp at Richard and Toni Steven's **Port Sussex Farm** (☎ 32203, fax 32204; psussex@horizon.co.fk). There's a cabin if the weather proves too severe for camping.

SOUTHWEST OF STANLEY

FITZROY
Named after Robert FitzRoy, captain of HMS *Beagle*, who surveyed Falklands' waters between 1828 and 1836, Fitzroy is about halfway between Stanley and Mt Pleasant and a short distance off the road. Today

the farm is part of the Falkland Landholdings Corporation and grows a major part of Stanley's vegetable production.

Although the Mt Pleasant road now bypasses Fitzroy, a bridge built across the Fitzroy River in 1934 considerably speeded travel between Stanley and Fitzroy and onto Darwin-Goose Green. It was actually proposed to tow the SS *Great Britain* (see the boxed text p73) from its resting place in Sparrow Cove to the river and sink it as foundations at the deepest section of the crossing. Fortunately that scheme was abandoned and the 180m bridge was made of wood on concrete piles.

MT PLEASANT
After the Falklands War in 1982 British military personnel were housed in and around Stanley until the Mt Pleasant base was completed in 1986. At its post-1982 peak the military personnel numbered more than 2000 and even today there are probably more than 1000, making it easily the second biggest population centre in the islands.

A large proportion of Falklands' visitors will arrive and depart via the MPA, but otherwise few visitors bother to drop in. The public areas of the base are open to outsiders and include a bar, restaurant, cinema and shops. In the civilian area, across from the airport terminal, the **Ro-no-kes Restaurant** (☎ 32114) is a fast-food café during the day and operates as a restaurant in the evening.

Mt Pleasant is 56km from Stanley. See p83 for bus and taxi transport details.

About 10km south of Mt Pleasant, Mare Harbour, the shipping port for the military base, is not open to the public.

DARWIN-GOOSE GREEN
Situated at the narrow isthmus separating Lafonia from the northern half of East Falkland, Darwin is named after the young Charles Darwin, who visited the Falklands from 1833 to 1834 on HMS *Beagle* and spent a night ashore close to where the settlement is today. Darwin was the site of Samuel Lafone's *saladero* (a salting and slaughtering house for meat), where the local agents of Montevideo merchants slaughtered feral cattle and processed their hides. Later it became the centre of the Falkland Islands Company's (FIC) camp operations, but by

EAST FALKLAND

1920 the farm site had become too small for the thriving settlement and there were water shortages. Over a two-year period most of the population was shifted to nearby Goose Green. At that time Darwin-Goose Green was the largest Falklands settlement outside Stanley. The two settlements are just 2km apart, but Goose Green today is much larger than Darwin – which has a permanent population of only four.

Darwin

Today Darwin is little more than the big new lodge building (see Darwin House, right) and a smaller, older building housing two self-catering cottages. Close to the lodge is a fine and recently restored **stone corral** built in 1874, back in the gaucho days. It's unusual for having a smaller circle appended to the larger one, and for the square holes around the base of the wall. Quite what they were for is not known; perhaps they were for drainage if the corral collected water, or perhaps they were for dogs to enter and leave the enclosure. Two more stone corrals, one of them said to be the best example in the Falklands, lie further south in Lafonia (opposite).

Falklands War Sites

As you approach Goose Green from Stanley the well-kept **Argentine cemetery** from the 1982 conflict is just off the road to the left (south). There's something very moving about this simple memorial to the sad loss of life from this futile conflict. Simple white crosses mark the 234 graves; a large proportion of them unmarked because many of the conscripts did not wear identification tags, or else their comrades took them to return to relatives. Other graves carry moving memorials to young men who would not be returning to their 'mama, papa' or their *hermanos* (brothers) or *hermanas* (sisters).

A little further down the road there's a small **memorial** to three British soldiers close to the road, and a little further back another one marking where 'H' Jones, the British hero of the assault on Goose Green, was killed. Close to the Darwin lodge a larger **memorial** honours the British troops of 2 Para Battalion who died in the attack. The heaviest ground fighting of the Falklands War took place here. There's a fine view down to Goose Green from the memorial.

Goose Green

A couple of kilometres from Darwin is Goose Green, which with 30-odd residents is the largest settlement in camp. At one time Goose Green had a population of as many as 250, but today many of the houses are empty, although the shop and the school still operate. In the middle of the settlement is the community hall where more than 110 of the residents, ranging in age from three months to over 80, were crammed in by the Argentines and held for nearly a month until they were released by victorious British troops in 1982. Goose Green is one of the farms owned by the government-operated Falkland Landholdings Corporation; it runs 75,000 sheep.

Goose Green's jetty is built over the hulk of the **Vicar of Bray**, the last survivor of the 700-odd ships that were used during the 1849 California Gold Rush. The *Vicar of Bray* was built in Britain in 1841 and altogether made 20 round trips to California before ending its sailing career in the traditional Falklands fashion in 1870. It ended up as a piece of jetty 10 years later. Across the bay on the east coast of Darwin Harbour you can see the wreck of the *Garland*, an iron, 580-ton British barque that was condemned in Stanley in 1900.

Bodie Creek Bridge

Head out of town on the North Arm road past the Goose Green golf course and turn off east to Bodie Creek. About 5km along a track is the unusual sight of a 120m suspension bridge across the deep waters of Bodie Creek. The bride was built between 1924 and 1925. It considerably shortened the trip for sheep being driven from the Walker Creek settlement to Goose Green. This surprisingly serious-looking steel construction is the world's southernmost suspension bridge. It was fabricated in London at a cost of £2290 and shipped out to the Falklands. Today it's rusting badly, and looks likely to deteriorate if it doesn't get some care and attention quite soon.

Sleeping & Eating

Either Darwin or Goose Green can be a good base for exploring the western part of East Falkland or south into Lafonia.

In Darwin, Ken and Bonita Greenland's **Darwin House** (☎ 32255, ☎ guests 25248; fax 32253; darwin.h@horizon.co.fk; per person £60) sits beside the

THE BATTLE OF GOOSE GREEN

The most fiercely fought land battle of the Falklands War took place on 28 May 1982 at Goose Green. The landings at Port San Carlos, San Carlos and Ajax Bay a week earlier had been relatively casualty free although the Argentine raids on the British fleet in San Carlos Water had involved some of the most dramatic and bloody fighting of the whole conflict.

The decision to take Goose Green remains a mystery. All of West Falkland was bypassed after the landing on East Falkland and Goose Green could probably have been left to one side as well. Whatever the reason, the 2 Para Battalion fought a pitched battle with the Argentine defenders across the rolling hills of Goose Green. The heroic death of the battalion's commanding officer, Lieutenant Colonel 'H' Jones, was rewarded with one of the Falklands War's two Victoria Crosses – Britain's highest military award. Eventually 1400 Argentines surrendered to the much smaller British force. Over 250 men were killed in the battle for Goose Green. Today, Ken Greenland from Darwin House (opposite) conducts battlefield tours of the area.

sheltered waters of Choiseul Sound, back-dropped by the rolling hills over which the pitched battle for Goose Green was slugged out in 1982. The recently built lodge has one double, one twin and three family rooms, each with one double and one single bed. It's very comfortable and well equipped, with a dining room, lounge and bar. Nightly costs per person include all meals.

Commerson and Peale Cottages, the adjacent cottages dating from 1911, were rented out as self-catering accommodation, but have recently been sold and are currently not available.

Stone Cottage (☎ 32270, 32292; self-catering per person £15) at Goose Green has one double and two single rooms. One of the oldest buildings in the settlement, the cottage is unusual for being built of stone. It has been extensively renovated and is well-equipped with a fridge, microwave, stove, heating, bathroom with shower, TV and so on.

Food is available from the Goose Green **shop**.

Getting There & Away

The 112km from Stanley to Darwin takes about 1½ hours. Stanley taxi operators charge £80 for up to four passengers. It's not much over half an hour from MPA to Darwin, so an airport pickup can be arranged or Darwin-Goose Green can be used as your final Falklands stop before flying out.

FIGAS (£36, 20 minutes) flies to Darwin's airstrip from Stanley.

LAFONIA

A narrow isthmus at Darwin-Goose Green separates the northern part of East Falkland from the southern Lafonia region. Lafonia was named after Samuel Lafone, an English merchant from Montevideo who bought the land in 1846 with the intention of rounding up the wild cattle that roamed the region. By 1849 he'd made a pretty good job of wiping out the cattle, but by 1851 he was heavily in debt and was taken over by the FIC, which soon became the islands' largest landholder.

The flat, pond-freckled expanses of Lafonia are quite unlike the rest of East or West Falkland. It's probably the least-visited part of the Falklands; few visitors venture beyond Darwin-Goose Green, although a good road now extends all the way to North Arm, the remote settlement at the northern end of the Bay of Harbours. North Arm is one of the largest sheep farms in the Falklands, with 75,000 sheep on 110,000 hectares; a visit here is a real opportunity to experience remote Falklands life. There's excellent mullet fishing in the creeks around the settlement.

From North Arm it takes about two hours to drive across camp to Bull Point, as far south as you can get on the main islands. Gentoo penguins and sea lions can be seen on the sandy beaches around the point; Magellanic penguins, black-necked swans and the usual selection of geese may also be encountered, while dolphins are often seen offshore.

Lafonia also has two of East Falkland's finest **stone corrals**; both of which are close to the Falkland Sound coast, due west of Goose Green. The Egg Harbour corral was built in the late 1860s or early 1870s and features small square openings in the walls, like the Darwin corral (p98). The 1.5m-high Kelp Creek corral in Hope Cottage Rincon is generally acknowledged to be the finest corral in the islands. It was beautifully built by stonemason James Smith in 1852, who was paid £26 and seven shillings for his labours.

You'll need a 4WD to reach these rarely visited corrals.

Sleeping & Eating

Ian and Eileen Jaffray run the **North Arm Farm** (☎ 32080; fax 32081; per person for 2/extra person £10/3), where there are two houses with four bedrooms each; one has 10 single beds and the other seven singles and one double. There are gas cookers and oil-fired central heating, but visitors must supply their own sleeping bags or bedding, towels and food supplies; a small selection of cooking equipment is provided.

There is a **store** at the settlement.

North Arm and Walker Creek are part of the government-owned Falkland Landholdings Corporation and there are several **outside houses** (☎ 22698; fax 22699; fhl@horizon.co.fk) on its land. The **Walker Creek cottage** can also be booked on the same numbers as Stone Cottage (p99), which it also operates.

It's less than an hour from North Arm, en route to Bull Point, to reach the **Northwest Arm House** (cottage per night £15), which has 14 beds and a peat-fired cooking stove. You will need sleeping bags, although some dishes and pans are provided.

There are other fairly basic **outside houses** at Danson Harbour and Fanny Cove, the latter between the Northwest Arm House and Bull Point. These places have peat-fired stoves for cooking and heating, and a diesel-powered generator for electricity.

At Walker Creek, on the southern side of Choiseul Sound in Lafonia, there's a **self-catering cottage**; **camping** is also permitted but permission should be requested from the farm manager.

Getting There & Away

There are no regular tours into this least visited region of the Falklands. You'll need to organise a 4WD and a good guide to find your way around Lafonia.

If the ferry that is planned to run between East and West Falkland ever gets commissioned it will probably run from New Haven, west of Goose Green and north of Kelp Harbour. The road to New Haven is under construction.

Islands off East Falkland

Although the two big islands – East Falkland and West Falkland – account for about 90% of the Falklands' land area a great deal of the interest for visitors is on the scatter of small islands roundabout. Some of these islands have managed to avoid the twin introduced scourges of sheep and rats. Sheep, particularly where they have not been confined and have been allowed to overgraze, have wiped out a great deal of native vegetation, including the tussock grass that once fringed so much of the Falklands' coastline. Tussock grass is the natural home of much birdlife, especially the small ground-dwelling birds, which have also fallen prey to rats. Islands where sheep are kept in their place and where rats have not got a foothold are far richer in birdlife.

The islands around East Falkland include Sea Lion Island, which is probably the most popular outer island in the Falklands because of its fine lodge and variety of wildlife. Today this is the only island in the Falklands where southern elephant seals continue to breed in any numbers, although they are seen on other islands. Nearby Bleaker Island has a spectacular stretch of coastline with large colonies of cormorants and rockhopper penguins only a few steps away from the comfortable cottage for guests. Lively Island is not on any regular itineraries, but it's interesting for being the largest rat-free island in the Falklands. Some cruise ships do call in on George and Barren Islands, both of which are rat-free, like nearby Speedwell Island. Although few people have ever landed on remote Beauchêne Island, this rock in the ocean has a stupendous black-browed albatross population. Finally, tiny Kidney Island (p88) is easily accessible from Stanley.

HIGHLIGHTS

- Walking the gently rolling terrain of **Sea Lion Island** (opposite), home to the Falklands' largest colony of elephant seals

- Checking out the 'gentoo highway' on **Bleaker Island** (p106)

- Visiting **Speedwell Island** (p108), site of a famous shipwreck and a classic castaway story

- Admiring the **Sheffield Monument** (p105) on Sea Lion Island, with a backdrop of thousands of rockhopper penguins

- Watching a black-browed albatross speeding down the wind off **Beauchêne Island** (p109), breeding site for 100,000 pairs

SEA LION ISLAND

The most southerly and isolated inhabited island in the Falklands is comparatively compact, but still has more wildlife in a smaller area than almost anywhere else in the islands. It's about 15km offshore from Bull Point or Porpoise Point at the southernmost extremity of East Falkland, and 117km from Stanley.

For most of its history, Sea Lion's isolation and difficult access contributed to the continuing abundance of wildlife. But much credit also goes to Terry and Doreen Clifton, who farmed the island from the mid-1970s before selling it in the 90s. The Cliftons developed the island with the idea that wildlife habitat and livestock were compatible uses. Through improved fencing and other conscientious management decisions, they made the island both a successful sheep station and a popular tourist site (the small number of sheep that still graze there are fenced off from the tussock zones). Originally it was popular for day trips from Stanley and the military base at Mt Pleasant, but today visitors come from all over the world.

The island's permanent population is only a half dozen people so, apart from the odd occasions when a cruise ship anchors offshore, it's pleasantly lonely.

AROUND THE ISLAND

Sea Lion is about 8km from one end to the other and only 2km across at its widest. Getting around on foot is made easy by the gently rolling terrain. One-fifth of the island is still covered by luxuriant growths of tussock grass and it's easy to envision what the rest of the Falklands must have looked like before sheep had such a devastating effect. At the eastern end a narrow peninsula runs to Northeast Point, while to the west it widens at the lodge and airstrip to low hills that fall more steeply into the sea along the south coast.

The island is dotted with small ponds and lakes, which are ideal for observing waterfowl although you may also find penguins and, even, elephant seals, rearing up from the still waters like antipodean hippos. Beaver Pond at the western end of the island is large enough for small seaplanes to land; it takes its name from the De Havilland Beaver floatplanes that used to operate from the pond from the 1950s until Falkland Islands Government Air Service (FIGAS) Islanders took over in the 1980s.

The grave near the vegetable gardens is of Susan Whitely, one of the three Falkland civilians killed during the 1982 war. She died in Stanley, only a few days before the Argentine surrender, when a British shell hit the house where she was staying.

WILDLIFE

Sea Lion Island is the most important breeding spot in the Falklands for southern elephant seals; every spring more than 500 females haul ashore to give birth. During the breeding (September–November) and moulting (December–April) seasons examples of their enormous bulk litter beaches and other suitable landing spots around the island. A long-term research project accounts for the cattle tags attached to the rear flippers of many of the island's elephant seals; some also have names sprayed with hair dye on their ample backs – Italian names, because it's an Italian-run project. The seal 'graffiti' is only visually intrusive, and makes it easier for researchers to identify specific animals without having to inspect the tags; the marks only last until the next moult. You can read more about the project and perhaps meet some of the researchers at the Sea Lion Lodge.

The sea lions that have given the island its name are far less numerous; even at peak times there are less than 100 of them. They can be seen along the south coast, particularly on the narrow gravel beaches below the cliffs at East Loafers, and lurking among the towering tussock grass.

Since Sea Lion Island is free of introduced killers like rats and cats, it has an unusually varied collection of birdlife. Among the highlights of the island are breeding colonies of three of the Falklands' five penguin species. Gentoo penguins are most common on the sandy isthmus east of the lodge; Magellanic penguin burrows are in the tussock grass to the south; and rockhoppers hop at Rockhopper Point, which also supports an enormous colony of king cormorants. Southern giant petrels nest along the headland; and the Falklands' three breeding geese species are all common on Sea Lion Island, so this is a good place to practise identifying them.

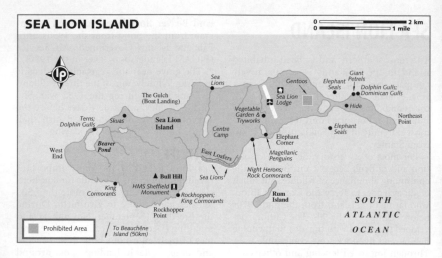

SEA LION ISLAND

0 _____ 2 km
0 _____ 1 mile

Sea Lions

Gentoos

Giant Petrels

Elephant Seals

Dolphin Gulls; Dominican Gulls

The Gulch (Boat Landing)

Sea Lion Lodge

Hide

Terns; Dolphin Gulls

Skuas

Sea Lion Island

Vegetable Garden & Tryworks

Northeast Point

West End

Beaver Pond

Centre Camp

Elephant Seals

East Loafers

Elephant Corner

Magellanic Penguins

▲ Bull Hill

Sea Lions

Night Herons; Rock Cormorants

King Cormorants

HMS Sheffield Monument

Rockhoppers; King Cormorants

Rum Island

SOUTH

Rockhopper Point

ATLANTIC

Prohibited Area

To Beauchêne Island (50km)

OCEAN

The skuas and sheathbills that hang around the penguin and cormorant colonies, or even march confidently right through them, are waiting for the same thing: the opportunity to grab something to eat. Skuas will even snatch a penguin egg from underneath a nesting bird and any disturbance that distracts a penguin or cormorant from its nest is a chance for one of these scavengers to do their dirty work. The gulls that hover overhead are there with similar intentions.

Johnny rook, the Falklands' noted bird of prey, and more correctly known as the striated caracara, is common on Sea Lion Island. They're cheeky and fearless, strolling confidently up to visitors and inspecting them quizzically, rotating their heads to take a better beady-eyed view. These handsome birds also pose proudly on fence posts, almost begging you to take a photograph. They have a well-earned reputation for making off with anything shiny and interesting. The much less attractive red-headed turkey vulture is also often seen on the island.

Small brown tussock birds hop right up to your feet, particularly on rocky stretches where they hope to make tasty discoveries under stones you dislodge. Other small birds include the pretty yellow-green black-throated finch, thrushes, snipe and fly-catching dark-faced ground tyrants.

Sea Lion Island is one of the best places in the Falklands to see killer whales (orcas), particularly when their favourite meal – seal

pups – are ready to leave their colonies. Killer whales also find arriving and departing gentoo penguins make a nice snack. They're often seen on approaches to the landing beach towards the eastern end of the island or you might glimpse them off the southern coast. Dolphins, particularly Peale's dolphin, are also regularly encountered around Sea Lion Island.

WALKS

Walkers should stay wide awake over much of the island's terrain: with so many birds nesting it's easy to stumble upon them almost anywhere. Some nest in the long grass, others burrow, and still others are at home on the beaches and sandy stretches. Stepping on a nest, putting a foot into a burrow or simply scaring a bird off its nest can all be dangerous, especially for the bird. For your own safety take care not to get between seals and the sea, and be especially wary when walking through tussock grass. Sudden encounters with a sleeping elephant seal or sea lion can be very frightening for both parties – particularly, when the seal awakes, for the walker. The official advice is to keep 5m away from seals or indeed any other wildlife. See p168 for more information on wildlife precautions.

East from the Lodge

Walking northeast takes you across grassland and past a pond where ruddy-necked and upland geese are often seen. Continuing on to

Stone runs (p37), Falkland Islands

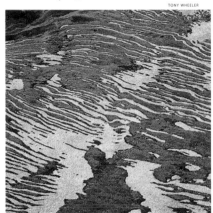

TONY WHEELER

TONY WHEELER

Cape Pembroke Lighthouse (p85),
near Stanley, East Falkland

The Neck (p127), Saunders Island, Falkland Islands

TONY WHEELER

Larsen Harbour (p160), South Georgia

The Tridents (p145), South Georgia

Drygalski Fjord (p160), South Georgia

Cumberland Bay (p158), South Georgia

the sandy isthmus the route goes past a large **gentoo penguin colony**. A handful of king penguins sometimes mix with the gentoos, looking slightly bewildered among their smaller cousins, like a gatecrasher at the wrong party. There's a prohibited area where visitors are asked not to disturb the colonies.

Continue past basking elephant seals to an **observation hide** at the start of tussock grass-covered Northeast Point, from where you can observe southern giant petrels nesting along the headland. Take care to approach the hide from the inland side in order not to disturb these nervous birds. Magellanic oystercatchers, with their long, bright orange-red bill and distinctive high-pitched call, are often seen along the beach.

Southwest from the Lodge

Heading southwest, walkers cross the airstrip towards the fenced-off vegetable garden. What looks like a crumbling stone barbecue just before the garden is actually the remains of an old tryworks (where penguins were rendered down to extract an oil used for lighting).

There are routes through the tussock grass past a small pond or along the edge of the tussock area towards the south coast. The pond is a favourite with Magellanic penguins and a variety of ducks, including Chiloé wigeon, and speckled and silver teal. It's still a wise idea to be alert for elephant seals, which can travel a surprisingly long distance from the shore.

As you re-enter the tussock grass along the coast a sign warns walkers to beware of 'lions'. It's the starting signal for the trail that runs along the clifftop looking across to Rum Island, which has its own dense tussock cloak. The tussock grass along this clifftop stretch is often more than head high. Here and at West End the cliffs sometimes rise as much as 25m above the sea. Take great care on the exposed clifftop in windy weather or when it's raining – the rocks can be slippery.

It is prohibited to climb down the cliffs in this area, but there are wonderful views down to the wave-swept rocky platforms where sea lions congregate during their December–February breeding season. From the clifftop you can see kelp geese foraging on the rocky coastal platforms, often accompanied by flocks of fluffy goslings in spring (November–December). Penguins can also be seen on the coastal platform and the kelp itself is spectacular.

The trail drops down to a beach at East Loafers then climbs back up through the tussock to open heathland running over the low-rise dome of 46m-high Bull Hill. Just above Rockhopper Point is the **Sheffield Monument**, honouring the 20 Royal Navy crew killed when the destroyer HMS *Sheffield* was hit by an Exocet missile 60km southeast of this point on 4 May 1982. The *Sheffield* sank nearly a week later while under tow towards South Georgia. The cliffs fall sheer into the sea at Rockhopper Point, where colonies of rockhopper penguins, and much more numerous king cormorants, are close and confused at the top. The sheer number of nesting birds attracts a wide variety of scavengers, including skuas, gulls, snowy sheathbills and striated caracaras. Tussock birds hop around your feet while you're watching the colonies. From the lodge it's a 4km to 5km walk to the point.

Skuas nest towards West End, past the old grass airstrip, and there's a variety of birdlife around Beaver Pond. Returning past the boat landing at the **Gulch** takes you past Magellanic penguin burrows and more elephant seals along the rocky, kelp-covered bay. At sunset penguins peer out from these holes.

SLEEPING

Sea Lion Lodge (☎ 32004, guests 25132; www.sealion island.com; full board per person low/high season f45/70-90; 💻) The lodge has been in operation since the mid-1980s. Managed by Jenny Luxton, it has six twin-bed rooms and one double, all with attached bathroom and telephones with international dialling. There are also two single rooms with a shared bathroom. There's central heating, hot water and 24-hour power, and the lodge has a lounge, dining room, bar, Internet access and even a small shop.

Visitors are given an introductory guided tour around the island in the lodge's Land-Rover so they know where the main wildlife sites are located. The 4WD can be hired for further tours although almost anyone can walk the length of the island in a few hours. To see the island in its entirety allow at least two full days, although guests sometimes stay for a week or more. The lodge is generally closed in June, July and August.

GETTING THERE & AWAY

A FIGAS Islander (£50 one way, 40 minutes) services Sea Lion Island from Stanley. During the summer high season there will be flights virtually every day. The clay-surfaced airstrip is just a couple of minutes' walk from the lodge. The old grass airstrip at the western end of the island is still used on rare occasions when the winds are totally wrong for the newer runway.

There is no harbour on the island; ship landings are usually made at the Gulch, on the north coast towards the western end of the island. The *Tamar* stops in at Sea Lion Island about every couple of months, but schedules are only decided a few weeks ahead of time.

Sea Lion island makes an excellent stop for expedition cruise ships and their Zodiacs can sometimes be seen pulled up on shore; landings on this windswept island's beaches can be exciting affairs.

BLEAKER ISLAND

It has been suggested that Bleaker Island should actually be named Breaker Island, on account of the waves breaking upon it, and once upon a time it was also appropriately known as Long Island. Visitors can enjoy a lot of wildlife in a very compact area and the wildlife sites of interest are all conveniently close to the settlement.

The island's self-catering Cobb's Cottage (p108) is named after Arthur F Cobb, who kept a diary of his life on the island between 1906 and 1923. It's more a collection of random observations of wildlife, island life and so on, but Cobb penned the memorable description of a rockhopper rookery sounding like 'thousands of wheelbarrows in need of greasing going at full speed'. His recollections include a fair amount about shooting things (like how to shoot a seal so it doesn't sink) and lots of egg collecting – or simply egg-breaking – to try to keep down the numbers of upland geese. Falklands farmers were concerned that the geese were getting to the grass ahead of the sheep. Until 1999 the island was owned by Falkland Landholdings Corporation, the company which had taken over the Falkland Islands Company's (FIC) holdings in Lafonia. The new owners intend to switch the emphasis from sheep to tourism.

AROUND THE ISLAND

Although Bleaker Island looks, at a glance, to be monotonously flat, in fact, it has some quite dramatic cliffs along its southwest coast. It is narrow and surprisingly long, and if you set out from Cassard Point to North Point you would probably cover 25km, although most visitors will spend their time in a much smaller area. From the airport and Sandy Bay Beach it's only about 3km south to the settlement area and Pebbly Bay. Some of the wildlife sites are so close to the settlement that it's quite easy to check if any sea lions have come ashore after dinner, or if all's well with the rockhoppers before breakfast.

The island's low silhouette and close proximity to the East Falkland mainland may be a reason for several of the shipwrecks on its shores. In 1906 the *Cassard*, a 1700 ton French steel barque, bound from Sydney to Cardiff with a cargo of wheat, went onto the point that bears its name at the southern end of the island.

WILDLIFE

Gentoo, Magellanic and rockhopper penguins all breed on Bleaker Island. Perched on the clifftop on the northeast coast, the rockhopper colonies are particularly photogenic. Rock cormorants perch on the southeast coast cliff faces, and king cormorants sit on the clifftops above them. Silvery and white-tufted grebes, speckled and silver teal and Chiloé wigeon are all regular visitors to Big Pond. Black-necked swans and even flying steamer ducks are less frequent sightings. The island's skuas are particularly numerous, but turkey vultures and sheathbills are also common.

Bleaker is not a breeding place for elephant seals or sea lions, but both species come ashore from time to time on Pebbly Bay.

WALKS

A round trip from the settlement can take most of the day and cover most of the island's wildlife possibilities. Start in the settlement itself at the **whale skeleton** behind the cow shed. The whale was brought here from where it beached itself. Just south of the settlement, **Pebbly Bay** is the place to look for elephant seals and sea lions. There's no telling when you might find these visitors on the beach: look first thing in the morning, at dusk or anytime you pass by.

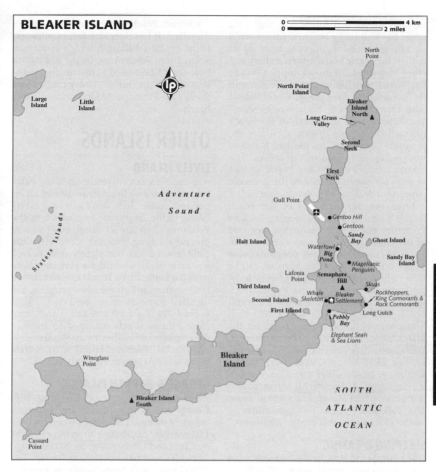

BLEAKER ISLAND

Large Island

Little Island

North Point

North Point Island

Bleaker Island North ▲

Long Grass Valley

Second Neck

First Neck

Adventure Sound

Gull Point

Gentoo Hill
Gentoos
Sandy Bay
Ghost Island

Halt Island

Waterfowl
Big Pond
Magellanic Penguins

Sandy Bay Island

Lafonia Point

Semaphore Hill ▲

Skuas

S i s t e r s   I s l a n d s

Third Island

Whale Skeleton
Second Island

Bleaker Settlement
Rockhoppers, King Cormorants & Rock Cormorants

First Island

Long Gulch

Pebbly Bay

Elephant Seals & Sea Lions

Wineglass Point

Bleaker Island

SOUTH

ATLANTIC

OCEAN

Bleaker Island South ▲

Cassard Point

ISLANDS OFF EAST FALKLAND

The most spectacular birdlife is found along the coastal stretch from the settlement, past Long Gulch and up the east coast to Sandy Bay. Although Bleaker Island may look very low lying, in fact it drops into the sea in spectacular cliffs along this coast; **Long Gulch** is only one of a number of dramatic inlets and clefts in the rock face. Much of this clifftop is fringed in tussock grass that is well fenced off from intruding sheep. Around 9000 pairs of king cormorants form the main seabird colonies along the clifftops, grouping together both inland from the tussock fringe and between the tussock and the cliff edge. The usual *eau de seabird* permeates the colonies and when the breeze is blowing towards the settlement that ineffable essence can also drift into your accommodation. Wet weather can make it particularly powerful. On the ocean side of the tussock the cormorants are joined by 500 or more pairs of rockhoppers.

The seabird colonies also feature the usual hangers-on, including dolphin gulls, snowy sheathbills and a large number of skuas. The skuas nest in the grass inland from the tussock fringe and just to the north of the tussock zone, towards Sandy Bay. The northern end of Sandy Bay also attracts these efficient predators.

Rock cormorants perch perilously on the rock faces of some inlets, often clinging to ridiculously tiny ledges. Further along the narrow, steep-sided inlets give way to a larger bay and rocky beaches, where you'll see kelp geese and flightless steamer ducks in their inevitable pairs, oystercatchers and other shorebirds. Tussock-topped Sandy Bay Island is offshore and, as you round the headland to Sandy Bay, Ghost Island (also tussock topped) lies closer to shore. You have to walk the length of the beach to reach the gentoo 'highway', where the penguins congregate on the beach before trudging uphill to their hilltop colony. The gentoo colonies on Bleaker Island do not seem to have been effected by the dramatic population declines of 2002–03 (see p47).

From the northern end of the beach there's a choice of routes looping back to the settlement. If you cross to the west side of the island, more gentoos come ashore along this coast. Magellanic penguins come ashore on both sides; their burrows can be seen right across the island. Alternatively, you can walk inland via Big Pond, which supports a wide variety of wildfowl. South of the pond, climb to the top of 27m-high Semaphore Hill, the highest point on the island, before descending to the settlement. With binoculars you can see the buildings on Sea Lion Island, 29km away to the southwest. In the other direction you can see clear across Lafonia to Mt Maria (658m) just outside Port Howard and 84km away. The Falklands' main TV transmitter is mounted on top of this central highpoint.

SLEEPING & EATING

Cobb's Cottage (☎ 21355; fax 21357; malvina@horizon .co.fk; self-catering/camping per person £20/10) There is room here for up to five people in two twin rooms and one single. The shiny new and modern cottage was built in 2000 and contrasts with some of the older facilities around the islands. The cottage has 24-hour power, a bathroom with shower and a living, dining and kitchen area with TV and stereo/radio. The kitchen is particularly well equipped. Overflow accommodation is available if the cottage is full.

The settlement **store** is well stocked; you can even get beer and very reasonably priced wine.

GETTING THERE & AWAY

FIGAS (£40 one way; 10–15 minutes) flights service Bleaker Island from Stanley.

Cassard Point, at the southwest end of the island, is less than 1km from Driftwood Point on East Falkland, which is in turn 32km from North Arm. In the old days a boat would be rowed across to the mainland to pick up visitors. Today cruise ships usually land their passengers on Sandy Bay beach.

OTHER ISLANDS

LIVELY ISLAND

Although it's not currently on many Falklands itineraries – there are no tourist facilities and cruise ships don't call in – Lively Island is the largest rat-free island in the Falklands. Rats are so dangerous to small ground-dwelling birds that the pretty little Cobb's wren has completely disappeared from any island where these predators have gained a foothold. Falklands Conservation's (FC) current rat elimination program has focussed some attention on Lively Island because there are rat-infested islands very close by and if rats managed to transfer the results could be disastrous. Remarkably, rat-infested Northeast Island at its nearest point is only 150m from Lively Island.

GEORGE & BARREN ISLANDS

At the southern end of East Falkland, George and Barren Islands are both now privately owned. They were owned for over 150 years by FIC before they were bought by Chris and Lindsey May in 2001. George Island is about twice as large as Barren. The Mays live on the islands during the summer months and continue to run some sheep.

Here there are gentoo and Magellanic penguins, sea lions and elephant seals, breeding colonies of giant petrels and sooty shearwaters; and, because the islands are rat free, small birds including Cobb's wrens and tussock birds. Minute, tussock-covered Tiny and Emily Islands lie just offshore from Barren Island.

Cruise ships occasionally call at George and Barren Islands.

SPEEDWELL ISLAND

Originally known as Eagle Island, this large island lies just north of George and Barren Islands at the southern end of East Falkland. The wreck of the *Isabella* here in 1813 played a pivotal role in a classic castaway story (see the boxed text p138). After the *Isabella* was wrecked, six men under the command of Captain Brooks took one of the ship's 5m open longboats on an epic 31-day voyage to the River Plate in South America.

Speedwell Island was also the site for the wreck of the British barque *Perthshire*, which went down off Blind Island, a tiny island closer to the East Falkland mainland, on 28 April 1885. The wreck was known as the 'salmon ship' because it was carrying a cargo of tinned salmon. The *Perthshire* had sailed out of Portland, Oregon, with the *Yarra Yarra*, which just one day later went down with all hands at Beaver Island. Eagle Passage separates Speedwell Island from the Lafonia region of East Falkland where the *Belleville*, a French-built, three-masted iron schooner broke adrift in Flores Harbour in 1936. The prominent wreck was carrying coal for a Falklands sealing company.

Today Ron and Yvonne Larsen run the **Speedwell Island Farm** (☎ 32001; fax 32010) but they do not offer accommodation. The island is rat free so it has a large population of small birds.

There is a FIGAS (£55, 45 minutes) flight to Speedwell from Stanley.

BEAUCHÊNE ISLAND

Named by Jacques Gouin de Beauchêne on board the *Phelypeaux* in 1701, this tiny island 50km south of Sea Lion Island is the most remote outpost of the Falklands. Ships approaching Stanley from Ushuaia often turn past the island, which is home to enormous colonies of seabirds and large rockhopper penguin rookeries.

It's estimated that over 100,000 pairs of black-browed albatrosses, more than 20% of the world's breeding population, nest here and clouds of them can be seen around the island. Black-browed albatrosses seen riding the air currents off Sea Lion Island will also be from Beauchêne. The population of rockhopper penguins is scarcely less impressive, numbering perhaps 70,000 pairs. Beauchêne has exceptionally deep peat deposits, and investigators digging down through the layers have determined that fur seals were on the island for over 10,000 years until they were almost wiped out by sealers. The island is cloaked in tussock grass, which is virtually the only vegetation that grows here.

Landing on the island is very difficult, but it certainly has been done; the names of men who lived there during the 1800s are carved on flat rocks at the boat landing place on the east coast.

ISLANDS OFF EAST FALKLAND

West Falkland

West Falkland is about a third smaller than East Falkland. The islanders like to joke that West Falkland doesn't have the three Ps – policemen, postmen or priests – but it also doesn't have much of a fourth P – population. The island's scattering of settlements has been steadily losing numbers, particularly over the last 20 years, and today the population has fallen to less than 100 people. One of the few hopes for arresting this precipitate decline is increased tourism.

The first recorded landing on one of the main islands of the Falklands was made just north of Port Howard in 1690, and the first British settlement in the Falklands was made at Port Egmont on Saunders Island, off the north coast of West Falkland, in 1765. The main island was not settled until the late 1860s, when pioneer sheep farmer James Lovegrove Waldron founded Port Howard. In short order, British entrepreneurs established stations at Hill Cove, Fox Bay, Port Stephens, Roy Cove, Chartres and many offshore islands. One of the most interesting experiments was the founding of the Keppel Island mission for Indians from Tierra del Fuego.

West Falkland has outstanding wildlife sites and good trekking in its interior. There are four main ranges in West Falkland. East–west across the north of the island is the range extending all the way from Falkland Sound to Mt Adam (the highest peak at 700m) and then dropping down to Byron Heights at the extreme northwest corner of West Falkland. Starting from Mt Maria, just west of Port Howard, the Hornby Range runs northeast to southwest, paralleling Falkland Sound. There are other groups of mountains north of Fox Bay, including Mt Sullivan and Mt Philomel, and down in the south there are high points to the east of Port Stephens. The west coast is a maze of inlets and bays with cliffs often falling over 500m straight into the sea.

Only a few of the West Falkland sites have formal tourist infrastructure, but for independent travellers there's a great deal of interest on the island.

HIGHLIGHTS

- Standing at the first **landing site** (p114) on the Falklands near the pretty little settlement of Port Howard
- Testing your fly-fishing skills in the **Chartres** and **Warrah Rivers** (p117)
- Picnicking in the Falklands' only forest at **Hill Cove** (p118)
- Taking in the views from atop **Mt Maria** (p116)
- Spotting wildflowers on **Narrows Island** (p117)

WEST FALKLAND

GETTING AROUND

As on East Falkland the road system has improved dramatically in recent years. Of course there is no bitumen or paved road anywhere on the island, but a good quality gravel road now runs from Port Howard on the east coast all the way to the two Fox Bay settlements to the south – there are plans to extend this road to Port Stephens in the extreme southwest. Spurs turn off this road to the Chartres settlement and to Roy Cove and Hill Cove. Elsewhere a system of rough tracks, many of them discernible only to the local eye, can be used by 4WDs and motorcycles.

The Port Howard Lodge had a Land-Rover, which could be rented for £40 a day plus fuel, but it was written off by two tourists in early 2003 and it's an open question whether its replacement will also be available to outsiders. Land-Rover tours are run from the lodge – a day trip to the Fox Bay settlements, Hill Cove or the Gladstone gentoo colony on Port Purvis costs £25 per person with a minimum of two people. Shorter tours around the settlement can also be made.

PORT HOWARD

West Falkland's oldest farm is the largest sheep station to survive the major agrarian reform of the 1980s. For more than a century it belonged to JL Waldron Ltd, but in 1987 it was sold to local managers Robin and Rodney Lee, who kept the farm and settlement intact rather than subdividing it. Robin Lee was one of the classic Falklands characters, like Kay McCallum in Stanley or Rob McGill on Carcass Island, but sadly Robin died in 2000.

Until quite recently there were still 40 people living in Port Howard, running the 80,000-hectare station with over 40,000 sheep, 800 cattle and its own dairy, grocery, abattoir, social club and other amenities. Unusually for the Falklands, employees were given the opportunity to purchase their houses and the tidy little settlement with its uniform white-with-green-trim buildings still looks as neat and well kept as ever. Today the population is only about 15 and there are grave concerns for its long term survival. It's a pity because the settlement, nestled into a valley beside the deep inlet, looks idyllic. It's at its best in spring when the gorse, planted as hedges around fields, or sometimes as avenues, is in bloom. Port Howard has been designated as the West Falkland terminus of the projected ferry across Falkland Sound, but it's hard to justify a ferry service when the entire population of the West Falklands has dropped below 100.

Port Howard is a very scenic settlement at the foot of Mt Maria, at the north end of the Hornby Range. The summit, about 5km west of the settlement, makes a good morning or afternoon hike. Although there is wildlife, most of it is distant from the settlement, whose immediate surroundings offer opportunities for hiking, horseback riding and fishing. It is also possible to view summer shearing and other camp activities, and there is a small museum of artefacts from the 1982 war, when Argentine forces occupied the settlement.

From Port Howard it would be possible, in several days, to hike up the valley of the Warrah River, a good trout stream, and past the Turkey Rocks to the Blackburn River and Hill Cove settlement, another pioneer 19th-century farm. Where the track is unclear, look for the remains of the old telephone lines. Ask permission to cross property boundaries and remember to close gates. There are other, even longer, hikes south towards Chartres, Fox Bay and Port Stephens.

SIGHTS

A settlement tour takes visitors to the sights around the town and out to see the **Mirage** wreck from the Falklands War, 15km to the west. Port Howard is postcard pretty, with nearly every building in the settlement painted in the same colour scheme of white with green roof, doors and windows. Overlooking the settlement from the hillside to the west, the **single shepherds' quarters** is one of the few buildings surviving from the previous round of painting, which was white with red trim. In fact two of the buildings in Port Howard, the school and the first building as you enter town from the Purvis Airport, survive from the earlier settlement at nearby **Second Creek**; they were moved here when Second Creek was abandoned around the end of the 19th century. The other houses are mainly from the 1920s,

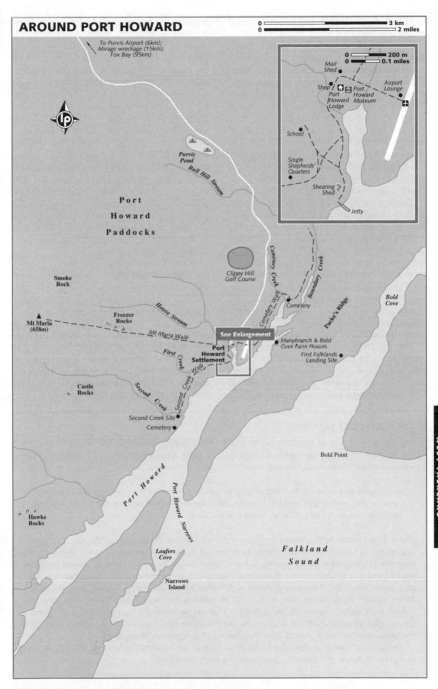

AROUND PORT HOWARD

0 ——————— 3 km
0 ——————— 2 miles

To Purvis Airport (6km);
Mirage wreckage (15km);
Fox Bay (95km)

Inset (enlargement):

0 ——— 200 m
0 ——— 0.1 miles

Mail Shed

Shop
Port Howard Lodge
Port Howard Museum

Airport Lounge

School

Single Shepherds Quarters

Shearing Shed

Jetty

Main map:

Purvis Pond

Bull Hill Stream

Port Howard Paddocks

Smoke Rock

Clippy Hill Golf Course

Cemetery Creek

Cemetery Walk

Boundary Creek

Cemetery

Bold Cove

Mt Maria (658m)

Freezer Rocks

House Stream

Mt Maria Walk

See Enlargement

Port Howard Settlement

Packe's Ridge

Manybranch & Bold Cove Farm Houses

First Falklands Landing Site

First Creek

Castle Rocks

Second Creek Walk

Second Creek

Second Creek Site

Cemetery

Bold Point

Port Howard

Port Howard Narrows

Hawke Rocks

Loafers Cove

Falkland Sound

Narrows Island

WEST FALKLAND

and are all of similar design with metal plates attached to a wood frame.

The Port Howard Lodge is very much the centre of the settlement and there's a small **war museum** next to it, open any time. A Mirage wing and a couple of guns stand outside; inside the collection is a small jumble, not all of it well labelled. Poke around and you'll find ejector seats from the Harrier and one of the Mirages which crashed nearby. There's an assortment of Argentine weapons, some examples of the mines they left behind, and a few bits and pieces of almost anything else an army might need, from uniforms to cooking equipment.

There were about 1000 Argentine troops in Port Howard during the Falklands War, but at ground level the conflict never really came to West Falkland – a number of aircraft were brought down on the island; there was the odd air raid and there were high-profile events like the SAS raid on Pebble Island, but otherwise the war bypassed West Falkland. Those 1000-odd troops were still in Port Howard when their surrender was finally negotiated, and they were running very low on supplies.

The road from the centre of the settlement down to the jetty passes a cut in the hill face where 350-million-year-old fossils were found in the shale and iron mudstone. Upstream a little you can see the building housing the settlement's hydro power plant. A pipeline brought water down from the slopes of Mt Maria to the plant, which was used until 1999. It's all still there and there are none of the popular wind power generators in the settlement itself, so it's a mystery why the plant isn't in use. The current diesel generator provides power mornings and evenings although the Port Howard Lodge has 24-hour power from a battery backup.

Just before the jetty, the spacious **shearing shed** is a hive of activity during the summer shearing season. The last shearing usually takes places in late January and the gun shearers have their names and daily tallies, typically over 400 sheep, marked on the rafters. Night herons are often seen around the jetty and Commerson's dolphins play in the harbour (particularly at high tide) during the summer months.

West of town towards the Purvis Airport, the **Clippy Hill Golf Course** has nine holes and, although some of the fairways might be classified as roughs in other parts of the world, there is a hazard that is probably unique – an adjacent minefield. Port Howard is particularly renowned for its fishing (see p117). Other possibilities include croquet on the Port Howard lawn (if you can find the equipment); and a couple of kayaks in the shed behind the lodge show there are certainly other things to be done.

THE BOLD COVE LANDING

Captain John Strong of the 270-ton, 40-gun, 90-crew *Welfare* made the first recorded landing on the main islands of the Falklands on 29 January 1690. A cairn and plaque to mark the event were unveiled 300 years, to the day, later:

> Wednesday this morning we weighed and stood unto an harbour on ye west side and there came to ane anchor and sent our boat on shoar for fresh water and we did kill abundance of geese and ducks but as far as wood there is none.

These days Captain Strong would have found plenty of wood; there may still be very little growing on the Falklands but there's plenty of driftwood washed up on almost every beach (along with the plastic and glass of modern flotsam). What might be much more surprising is all the sheep carcasses washed up on the beach: a small bay down at the east end of the beach is used as a local culling point for excess sheep, which after killing are simply heaved onto the beach to be washed away by the tide. Apart from his historic landing Captain Strong also gave the Falklands its name – indirectly. He called the channel between the two major islands Falkland Sound after Viscount Falkland who would later become First Lord of the Admiralty. Later the islands themselves were named after the channel that separates them.

The landing spot is on Bold Cove, the other side of the headland behind the Bold Cove and Manybranch farms. Ask there for permission to enter their land.

WALKS
The Cemetery & on to Purvis Pond

The cemetery walk makes an excellent short stroll or can be extended to a longer walk. From the Port Howard Lodge, walk down to the 'Port Howard Airport Terminal' and across the runway, checking there are no approaching aircraft. As you cross the runway note the building on your left, which houses a local farmer's aircraft. Surprisingly there are only a couple of private aircraft in the Falklands. Across the runway you enter an avenue, edged by gorse hedges, that leads you straight towards the coastline, looking across to two farms: Manybranch Farm where the white house has a red roof, and Bold Cove Farm where the white house has a green roof. The spinning wind-powered electricity generators have quickly become a familiar Falklands sight. Behind the farm buildings rises Packe's Ridge with its rocky spine.

Turn left through the gate and follow the coastline northeast for about a kilometre to the head of the bay, where you hop across the small Bull Stream and climb up to the white-fenced cemetery. The graves include a number of Lees, the local farm owners, including that of energetic local luminary Robin Lee, who was involved in many Port Howard projects. The Port Howard Lodge's excellent reputation was due to his wife Hattie Lee. In the northeast corner of the cemetery a tall wooden cross marks the grave of SAS Captain John Hamilton, who died in the Falklands War. There's also an unmarked grave of an Argentine soldier. In the southwest corner is the grave of Arthur (Togo) Hall, a shepherd who committed suicide and is said to haunt the house at White Rock where he used to live.

There are several alternatives from the cemetery. You can simply retrace your steps back to the settlement (the round trip will take about an hour, a total distance of about 4km). Or you can leave the cemetery towards the west, enter the field by the metal gate and continue across fields until you reach another pathway lined by gorse hedges back to the settlement. A slightly longer alternative would be to continue until you reach the main road and then cross to the Clippy Hill Golf Course.

For a longer walk continue north of the cemetery until you hit a track, follow it east until you reach Boundary Creek and then follow the creek upstream to Bull Hill. Continue along Bull Hill Stream past the road to the Purvis Airport road and Purvis Pond.

Second Creek Settlement

From the Port Howard Lodge, walk down towards the shearing sheds and the jetty, then take the road uphill to the single shepherds' quarters (an easy-to-identify building since it's the only red-and-white building among all the green-and-white ones). In fact all Port Howard's buildings used to be red and white; presumably someone picked up some bargain-priced batches of green and white paint but it wasn't quite enough to redecorate every building in the settlement. From this red-and-white standout, walk towards the coast – you'll quickly be stopped by the minefield warning signs. All you have to do now is keep the minefield fence on your left shoulder.

At First Creek the 4WD track cuts straight through the minefield to cross the creek, signs warn you not to leave your vehicle as you drive along this track, which is fenced in on both sides (but presumably since you're not in a vehicle this sign does not apply!). The track can be impassable at high tide. Beyond the creek you follow the signposted fence again until you leave the minefield zone to the safety of Second Creek. You may have to explore a little way upstream to find a narrow enough place to hop across the creek.

This was the site of the original settlement. It was shifted to Port Howard's current location around the end of the 19th century, along with three buildings; one of them has since disappeared but two still stand. As you walk down to the bay's edge at Second Creek a few scattered remains of the old leather tanning factory lie on the ground: bricks from Stourbridge in the English West Midlands and pieces of machinery from Leeds and London. There's a view from here out through the Narrows (the entrance to Port Howard's harbour) to Narrows Island. Walk along the coast a short distance to Second Creek's tiny cemetery with the graves of Eliza Fanny Shilling and Emily Jane Dixon, both of whom died in 1895, presumably before the settlement moved to its present location. The round-trip walk is five or six kilometres and takes a couple of hours.

WEST FALKLAND

Mt Maria

Rising due west of Port Howard, the walk to the top of 658m-high Mt Maria is very simple since you can see it so clearly. Leave the settlement by the social club, across the road from the Port Howard Lodge, crossing the stream by the footbridge next to the house behind the club. Follow the stream and the old hydro-power pipeline as it climbs gently uphill. The walk is soon interrupted by a minefield fence, which cuts across the stream; you have to diverge slightly towards the coast to get around it.

WARNING

Never enter a minefield. Apart from the obvious danger of blowing your leg off, you can be fined up to £1000 just for entering one.

Continue climbing to the picturesque outcrop known as Freezer Rocks, starting at around 200m altitude. There's a hole in the rocks that very neatly frames the entrance through the Narrows to Port Howard Bay, with Narrows Island appearing the other side of the entrance. From there it's gently on up to the summit, marked by a plethora of communications dishes and aerials. TV and radio broadcasts for almost all of the Falklands (apart from Stanley) comes from here, and if the weather is clear there's a superb view in all directions. To the north you can see all the way past the islands along the north coast of West Falkland. Mt Adam, the highest peak in West Falkland, rises due west and you can see to the sea to the west and south. In the other direction Falkland Sound, with its many islands, is directly below you. You can see clear across the flatlands of Lafonia to the east coast of East Falkland. Mt Maria is clearly visible from Bleaker Island, over 80km away. From town to Mt Maria is around 5–6km and takes roughly 1½ to two hours one way.

SLEEPING & EATING

Port Howard Lodge (☎ /fax 42187; www.port-howard .com; porthowardlodge@horizon.co.fk; full board including smoko, breakfast, lunch & dinner Dec-Mar £65, Apr-Nov £60; ☐) This lodge is a Falklands favourite. The former manager's house is a classic of its era with a beautiful conservatory that feels like the tropics when the sun comes out. There are nine rooms, all en suite and centrally heated – two doubles, four twins, two singles and one children's room with bunk beds – a dining room, lounge and bar. It's all beautifully kept and simply breathes an old Falklands flavour. The antique West Falkland telephone exchange equipment in the hallway with its list of names and numbers spells out the decline in the settlement's population. Guests can use the settlement's nine-hole golf course. There's a payphone (☎ 25125) for guests' use, faxes can be sent at £3 a page and the Internet can be accessed with the office computer.

For years the lodge has had a particularly high reputation for its food, a reputation which appears to have survived despite the departure of Hattie Lee, who was responsible for the kitchen's accolades. The range of breakfast cereals on offer is also fairly amazing. The lodge's bar operates on an honour system and there's a wine list with a selection of wines at £10 and £11.

There's camping on the other side of Port Howard Harbour at **Bold Cove Farm** (☎ 42178; fax 42177); some basic groceries are available but it's no distance in to Port Howard, which has a small shop. Campers can use the farmhouse bathroom.

GETTING THERE & AWAY

There is a Falkland Islands Government Air Service (FIGAS) flight from Stanley, which takes about 40 minutes and costs £50. Port Howard has two quite separate airports; which one is used depends upon the prevailing winds. Purvis Airport, used for east–west landings, is about 6km west of town, just past the golf course. In a place notable for its roller-coaster runways this is one of the flattest. The town airport is walking distance from Port Howard Lodge and is used for north–south landings – in contrast to the Purvis runway this is one of the hilliest in the Falklands.

The MV *Tamar* (for details see p177) also comes into Port Howard on its regular runs around the Falklands; and in 2002, for the first time, the expedition company Quark sent the *Professor Multanovskiy* around the Falklands. When its Russian captain threaded the vessel through the Narrows it clearly made a great impression on the Port Howard residents, who still talk about it.

AROUND WEST FALKLAND

FISHING

Fishing is a major activity at Port Howard Lodge and many of its guests will be there on fishing trips. The Warrah and Chartres Rivers both offer excellent sea trout fishing, with fish over 5kg regularly being reeled in. Fishing in the Warrah River or in Many-branch Creek is free to lodge guests; there's a daily fee of £15 to fish in the Chartres River. The lodge charges £20 per person for return transport to the Warrah River, and £25 to the Chartres or Manybranch Rivers. A ghillie (fishing guide) costs £55 per day per group.

There's a fishing record book in the lounge of the Port Howard Lodge where visitors can record where they fished, how many fish they caught, the total weight caught, the largest fish and even what flies they used. Looking back through the recent records the biggest sea trout in 2003–04 weighed in at over 6.5kg. Popular flies were Ally's Shrimp, Dunheld, Toby, Silver Spinner, Thunder Stroat, Blue Laser and the wonderfully named Woolly Bugger. Fishing for mullet is also popular right in Port Howard Harbour and in the tidal reaches of Manybranch Creek. See p163 for more information on fishing in the Falklands.

NARROWS ISLAND

South of Narrows Passage is Narrows Island. From Second Creek or Freezer Rocks it appears to be directly outside the passage, although in fact it's some distance to the south. The island is nearly 2km long, but just over 200m wide at its widest and for much of its length not much more 50m wide. It's one of only a few islands in Falkland Sound that has not been seriously overgrazed. The great diversity of habitat includes good stands of tussock grass at both ends, diddle-dee in a very small area and some huge balsam bogs in the middle section. The island is noted for its unusual variety of wildflowers and there are information sheets at Port Howard, which you can fill in to help extend research on the island. Sea lions beach on the island and may be encountered in the tussock grass (see p169). Various birds nest here (see p168).

Unfortunately getting out to Narrows Island is not straightforward. Robin Lee, whose boat is still moored near the jetty at Port Howard, used to run trips out to the island before his death, but there have been no trips for the past couple of years. If there's an opportunity to get there it would be worth taking. Commerson's dolphins often follow boats on the trip out to the island. Cruise ships may put passengers ashore by Zodiac.

GLADSTONE BAY

A day trip from Port Howard takes visitors to Gladstone Bay on Port Purvis, east of Shag Point on Purvis Bay. The route to the bay turns off the Fox Bay road soon after leaving Port Howard and runs across open country between Mt Caroline and Mt Jock to the bay. There's a large colony of gentoo penguins at Gladstone Bay, which doesn't seem to have been affected by the recent crash in gentoo numbers at other sites in the Falklands.

WARTIME WRECKAGE

Ten or 11 aircraft crashed on West Falkland during the war including a Harrier, which was hit by a ground launched missile as it flew low over Port Howard. The pilot, Jeff Glover, ejected, was rescued from Port Howard Creek by the Argentines with a rowboat, and became the only British prisoner of war during the conflict. He was flown back to Argentina and not released until nearly a month after the war ended. His aircraft slammed into the ground near the two farms across the creek, but there's little trace of it today.

The remains of the Argentine air force Mirage C403 is much more visible, starting with one of its wings on the right (north) side of the road about 15km west of Port Howard. Fragments, including most of the engine, are scattered for another couple of hundred metres to the west. Another Mirage C404 and a Skyhawk crashed in the same vicinity. It's hard to tell which of the Mirages the wing by Port Howard Lodge came from since the final number has been painted out. Port Howard also claimed a Dagger (the Israeli-built Mirage clone) C409 to the south of Mt Adam. Two Skyhawks C309 and C325 crashed between Mt Doyle and Mt Sullivan, near the River

Doyle and the west coast. Two Argentine Puma helicopters came down close to the east coast of West Falkland, north of Swan Island, and an Agusta helicopter just to their south.

WEST TO FOX BAY

The main road in West Falkland runs west from Port Howard almost to Chartres, a settlement on the west coast, before branching north to Hill Cove and south to Fox Bay. The road passes the golf course, Purvis Airport and, at 8km, the turn-off north to the Warrah River estuary. There are kilometre markers all along the road but they're haphazard: sometimes there will be a marker every kilometre, sometimes nothing for 5km or more. For much of the way west the road runs through a wide flat valley with parallel mountain ranges to the north and south. Turkey Rock is a prominent feature on the range north of the road.

The road enters Harp's Farm 20km from Port Howard. There's nobody there anymore and the buildings are used only at shearing time. Between the 27km and 28km point, an outside house evocatively known as Rat Castle lies a little north of the road. At 34km there's a borrow pit on the south side of the road – a quarry where material was dug out for the road construction. It turned out to be a treasure-trove of fossils and even today it's very easy to spend just a few minutes rummaging through the rock pile to turn up interesting looking fossils of sea creatures. Typically they'll be brachiopods from the Emsian age, the youngest period of the early Devonian, 385 to 390 million years ago.

The turn-off north to Hill Cove is at 45km and only 5km further along is the turn-off to Chartres. Just another kilometre beyond the turn the road runs beside a pretty little gorge, where a tributary runs its last stretch before joining the Chartres River. A modern and a much more picturesque old bridge crosses the tributary at this point. Nearly everybody from West Falkland came together here for a millennium party at the end of 1999.

The road continues past the Little Chartres settlement and you can cross the Chartres River either by bridge or ford. Take the bridge. Chartres River was named after Dr William Chartres, the surgeon on the survey vessel HMS *Philomel*, which visited the

Falklands between 1842 and 1845. In turn, the settlement was named after the river. Just past 60km there's a small stone cairn by the road marking the turn-off to the Hawk's Nest Ponds. Although the ponds are only a stone's throw away they're not visible from the road. Black-necked swans, night herons and yellow-billed teal are all birds you may see on these ponds. From there to Fox Bay the road runs through a landscape dotted with ponds but, surprisingly, there's not that much birdlife to be seen.

FOX BAY

John Byron, commander of HMS *Dolphin*, named Fox Bay after the *warrah* – the Falklands' only native land mammal until it was driven to extinction after the arrival of Europeans – when he stopped by on his round-the-world trip in 1765. The settlement is divided into two separate communities, Fox Bay (aka Fox Bay East) and Fox Bay West, on opposite sides of the bay and has a total population of 20–30 (making it larger than Port Howard). Until 2000 the Falkland Mill produced yarn for Falklands knitwear. Warrah Design, a knitwear company, still operates from the old farm manager's house. Fox Bay was noted for its large gentoo penguin colony, but this was particularly badly hit by the mystery ailment that affected so many Falklands penguins in 2002–03. Fox Bay East has a large stone corral built in 1942, many years after most of the other corrals around the Falklands. Close by is another corral dating from 1972, more than a century after some of the oldest examples, making it probably the last to be built in the islands.

The very well equipped **Gavin & Deirdre Marsh's Self Catering Cottage** (☎ 42079; fax 42063; gmarsh@horizon.co.fk; per person £10) can accommodate up to nine people and has central heating, a washing machine, gas cooker and TV with video and DVD.

The drive from Port Howard is about 95km. There's a FIGAS flight from Stanley to the airport at Fox Bay (£65).

HILL COVE

From the turn-off from the Fox Bay road, the route to Hill Cove curves around Mt Adam, and a spur turns off west to Roy Cove on King George Bay. This road was completed in 1998–99 and in Hill Cove there's a roadside memorial commemorating the completion of 80km of road construction in 1999. As you descend from the saddle between Mt Adam and Mt Fegan, the mountain slopes down to the sprawling settlement of Hill Cove and there are fine views north to Carcass, Saunders and Keppel Islands.

Hill Cove's principal claim to fame is the Falklands' only forest. Originally planted in 1898, there were additional plantings in the 1920s and today there are bigger trees and more of them than you'll see anywhere else on the islands. Unfortunately the spruce trees that form the core of the forest have been hit by the blight known as green spruce aphid. Many of the tightly packed large trees in the centre are looking brown and unhappy, although the trees around the periphery are still doing fine. The owners point out that the spruce trees were probably getting towards the end of their expected life span and they hope to replant them. The forest area is home to crowds of small birds, particularly black-chinned siskins and Falkland thrushes. Behind the forest is the Hill Cove cemetery with, as usual, many graves of those who died young but also the grave of Ann Rebecca Butler, who marched on to the age of 94 before dying in 1924.

Hill Cove Farm raises miniature horses, which will probably be on view in one of the paddocks. The farm covers 7000 hectares and includes another of the Falklands' surprising number of nine-hole golf courses. Fishing, birdwatching, walking and even lending a hand on the farm are all possibilities for guests who stay here. Right at the end of the headland is a military helicopter refuelling depot.

Instead of returning to Port Howard by the same route it's possible to loop back by a track running along River Harbour and then climbing over the range past Turkey Rocks to descend to the Port Howard–Fox Bay road. This cross-camp route definitely requires local knowledge to follow.

Run by Shelley and Peter Nightingale, **West Lagoon Farm** (☎ /fax 41194; www.westlagoons .com; pnightingale@horizon.co.fk; full board incl smoko per person £33; 🖳) has full board, central heating and sleeps up to five people. There are more rooms in a separate house in the settlement. Away from the settlement there's a cabin out on the farm where the cost is £17 per person on a self-catering basis.

You can drive the 80km from Port Howard or get a FIGAS flight from Stanley to the airport at Hill Cove (£65).

ROY COVE & CROOKED INLET

A new road turns off the Hill Cove road and runs west past the Crooked Inlet settlement to Roy Cove, which was originally settled in 1872. Crooked Inlet is a pretty little settlement with old houses among the gorse bushes.

The very comfortable self-catering cottage, **Crooked Inlet Farm** (☎ /fax 41102; per person £20), has two double and two twin rooms. It has recently been modernised and includes a large kitchen. The creekside cottage has great views of the picturesque settlement and across King George Bay to Rabbit, Hummock and Middle Islands. Vehicle hire is available at £30 per day. There's road access from here right across West Falkland.

PORT STEPHENS

Open to the blustery South Atlantic and battered by storms out of the Antarctic, Port Stephens' rugged headlands are unquestionably the most scenic part of the Falklands. Thousands upon thousands of rockhopper penguins, cormorants and other seabirds breed on the exposed coast, only a short distance from the settlement's sheltered harbour. Until recently this was the centre of one of the Falkland Island Company's (FIC) largest stations. Like many other settlements, Port Stephens has no formal tourist facilities, but is well worth a visit.

Less than an hour's walk from the settlement, Wood Cove and Stephens Peak are excellent places to see gentoo penguins, rockhopper penguins and other birds (see p168). Unfortunately, the mystery crash in penguin populations in 2002–03 also hit these colonies. The peak of Calm Head, about two hours' walk, has superb views of the jagged shoreline and the powerful South Atlantic.

Visitors interested in exploring Port Stephens and trekking in the vicinity should contact Peter or Anne at Port Stephens Farm (p120), or Leon and Pam Berntsen at **Albemarle Station** (☎ 42309).

Port Albemarle & the Arch Islands

One interesting longer trek goes from the settlement to the abandoned sealing station at Port Albemarle, and the huge gentoo penguin colonies near the Arch Islands. Hoste Inlet, where there is a habitable outside house, is about five hours' walk in good weather. The sealing station, another post-WWII Colonial Development Corporation blunder, is four hours further. Like the Ajax Bay freezer, the sealing station is a monument to bureaucratic ineptitude, but photographers and aficionados of industrial archaeology will find its derelict power station, boilers, rail track, water tanks, jetty and Nissen huts surrealistically intriguing. On the south shore of West Arm the sealing station was set up in 1950 with a licence to take 5000 male seal lions and bull elephant seals a year. However, by this time seals were already in short supply and when it consistently failed to reach that number it closed in 1953. In the 1920s the Falklands had a sea lion population approaching half a million. Today it's down to less than 5000. There is a habitable shanty with a functional Rayburn stove nearby, but the larger outside house on Mt Alice is not in good condition.

The massive penguin colonies are an hour's walk beyond the sealing station. The Arch Islands, inaccessible except by boat, take their name from the opening that the ocean has eroded in the largest of the group – and it is large enough to allow a good-sized vessel to pass through.

Port Stephens Farm (☎ 42307; fax 42304) Peter and Ann Robertson allow camping on their property. There is no charge but there are also no facilities, so campers must be completely self-sufficient.

Visitors to Port Stephen have to come by land or sea since there are restrictions on the use of the airstrip.

DUNNOSE HEAD & SPRING POINT

Spring Point is on the peninsula between Port Philomel and Queen Charlotte Bay. It's possible to camp at Ron and Fiona Rozee's **Spring Point Farm** (☎ 42001). Meat and vegetables can be bought from the farm and other supplies can be arranged if you give enough notice. The settlement even has a stone corral from the gaucho era. There's plenty of coastline with coves and white-sand beaches, and the birdlife includes striated caracaras and red-backed hawks. There's no road here; the only way to get to Spring Point is by sea. To find out what life is like at Dunnose Head check its website at www.falklandwool.com.

Islands off
West Falkland

CONTENTS

The scatter of islands around the two main islands – East Falkland and West Falkland – are prime sites for Falklands visitors, whether they're passengers on a cruise ship that stops at just one or two islands, or actually staying in the Falklands and visiting a number of islands. West Falkland has some of the most interesting of these outer islands, including some of the most popular and some of the most difficult to reach.

Carcass Island and Westpoint Island have proved particularly popular with cruise ships; both were pioneers as Falklands ports of call. Rob McGill on Carcass and Rodney Napier on Westpoint are attractions almost as important as their islands! Carcass Island is rat and cat free so it has a wide variety of small birdlife.

Saunders Island is larger and, although it does not have the small bird populations, there are huge breeding colonies of black-browed albatrosses as well as breeding groups of four types of penguin. A stay at the isolated Portakabin at The Neck is a Falklands highlight for many visitors. Saunders Island also has traces of the first British settlement in the Falklands at Port Egmont. Pebble Island is another of the larger islands, with interesting waterfowl as well as penguins and cormorants. The Special Air Service (SAS) raid on the island during the Falklands War was one of the most dramatic events during the conflict and the island has wreckage and memorials from the war. Sandwiched between Saunders and Pebble Islands is Keppel Island, which is uninhabited today but has a fascinating history because of its missionary establishment.

Off the southwest corner of West Falkland is Weddell Island, while to its west lie Staats and Beaver Islands, both with some interesting introduced animal species. Further northwest again is New Island, recently purchased by two private buyers and turned into two separate nature reserves. Finally, at the extreme northwest end of the Falklands are the remote and rugged Jasons, uninhabited islands with important – and spectacular – wildlife populations.

HIGHLIGHTS

- Staying in the Portakabin at The Neck on **Saunders Island** (p126) and visiting impressive albatross colonies

- Ignoring the name and enjoying the cheeky tussock birds and delinquent Johnny Rooks on **Carcass Island** (p129)

- Pondering the strange story of Captain Charles Barnard, the castaway of **New Island** (p136)

- Studying the penguin and albatross colonies on **Westpoint Island** (p133)

- Counting yourself lucky if you can make a landing on one of the remote and wild **Jason Islands** (p139)

PEBBLE ISLAND

Elongated Pebble, separated only by very narrow channels from the north coast of West Falkland, has varied topography, extensive wetlands and a good sampling of wildlife, including Magellanic, gentoo and rockhopper penguins. It was a frontline site in the Falklands War and there's still evidence of the conflict, including aircraft wreckage and a memorial for HMS *Coventry*, which sank 15km off Pebble Island in around 100m of water. After the war a team of divers spent six months on the wreck.

Pebble Island has 10,000 sheep – one of the highest stocking ratios in the Falklands since there's nearly a hectare for each sheep. At one time there were even more and the sheep population peaked at 13,000. The island also has cattle and pigs (Old English Saddleback and Gloucester Old Spot pigs): Pebble Island pork and ham finds a ready market in other parts of the Falklands. Less useful are the 150 feral goats, reminders of an ill-conceived 1992 plan to raise cashmere goats for their fine wool, when the price for sheep's wool was in steep decline. Raising the goats turned out to be tricky, expensive and extremely time consuming so the project came to nothing. The goats, on the other hand, found Pebble Island very much to their liking and have had a devastating impact on any tussock grass they can get their teeth into. Attempts are now being made to cull the goats down to 30, fence them in and have another go at cashmere wool production.

AROUND THE ISLAND

Elephant Bay cuts into the island, almost dividing it into two halves, each with a quite different character. The northwest half is marked by a chain of hills: from the settlement northwards there's First Mt (277m), Middle Peak (215m) and Marble Mt's twin peaks, Marble Mt North Peak and Marble Mt South Peak, which are both just under 238m.

The settlement is roughly in the middle of the island. Pebble Island is another Falklands settlement with a nine-hole golf course. Sand yachting on the Elephant Bay Beach has, in the past, been another Pebble Island activity.

THE PEBBLE ISLAND SAS RAID

Pebble Island was the site for one of the most dramatic events of the Falklands War. About 150 Argentine troops had been sent to the island to establish an air base, equipped with six of the feared Pucara ground attack aircraft and five other aircraft. On the night of 14 May 1982 a contingent of 45 British SAS troops were landed by helicopter, made their way to the airstrip, destroyed or damaged beyond easy repair all of the aircraft and escaped with only slight injuries to two of their number. As a result the 25 island residents spent the next 31 days locked up in the settlement's main house, let out only to keep the farm in shape each morning.

WILDLIFE

The island has three large colonies of gentoo penguins, colonies of Magellanics all along the north coast and rockhoppers at a number of places. The devastation that hit other penguin colonies (see p47) around the Falklands in 2002–03 did not seem to hit Pebble Island so hard.

The presence of rats on Pebble Island has considerably reduced the variety of small birds, although long-tailed meadowlarks and rufous-chested dotterels are often seen along the tracks.

Red-backed hawks are regularly seen perching on lookouts, but striated caracaras don't find Pebble to their liking: juvenile birds sometimes turn up for a spell but then move on when they are mature. Of course, upland geese can be seen everywhere.

The scattering of ponds across the eastern end of the island make this one of the most interesting islands for waterfowl. Black-necked swans are particularly prolific on Pebble Island and are found on many ponds – curiously, Swan Pond doesn't seem to attract many.

WALKS

Pebble Island is big and it is an island for driving rather than walking: it's 30km from one end to the other and a round-trip drive from the settlement to Shanty Point takes all day.

You will find that there are opportunities for walkers close to the settlement.

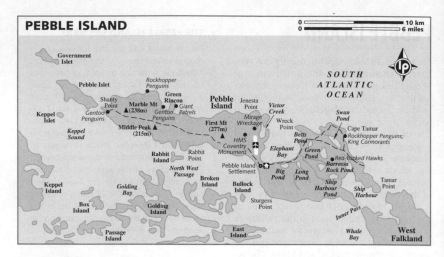

PEBBLE ISLAND

Northwest to Shanty Point

The northern circuit is a 50km round trip that takes all day, skirting the hills that form a spine to the island's northwestern half with various stops along the way.

Leaving the settlement, the route passes by the wreckage of the only **Argentine aircraft** remaining from the SAS raid (see the boxed text p123). Ironically, the aircraft, which was firmly bogged on the soft runway at the time of the attack, was a Short Skyvan, manufactured in Belfast, Northern Ireland.

Beyond the airstrip and scattered for several hundred metres towards the sea are fragments of an Argentine air force Mirage or Dagger. A second Mirage also slammed into the island, coming down just northwest of the first Mirage and scattering for a kilometre or more. Off to the northwest of the airstrip and settlement is a **memorial cross** to the sinking of HMS *Coventry*, with the names of the crew members who died inscribed on a plaque.

Depending on the season, all sorts of birds may be seen as you cross the rolling land towards the coast. There's a **gentoo penguin colony** to the south of Green Rincon headland. Gentoos regularly shift their colonies, sometimes moving 100m in one direction, sometimes 200m in another, but for the 2002–03 breeding season the colony moved 3km inland from the beach to the east of the headland. The change meant the tiny penguins' long walk at the beginning and end of each day could have been short-ened by a kilometre or so if they'd used the next beach to the west. Giant petrels along this stretch of coast have been nesting on their very exposed site for 20 years.

Quartz in rocks on Marble Mt are the reason for the glitter that has given the peak its name. A **memorial** on the northern slope of Marble Mt, not far from the sea, marks the crash site of an Argentine Learjet. The aircraft was on a reconnaissance mission over the Falklands just a week before the end of the war when it was shot down by a missile from HMS *Exeter*. Three bodies were retrieved from the remains soon after the war, but in 1995 two more were discovered in the wreckage. The remaining aircraft fragments were removed and the two bodies buried here; they are the only Argentine Falklands War casualties who are not at the Argentine cemetery at Darwin on East Falkland (p98).

The island's largest **rockhopper colony** is down at this end and these penguins are joined by an occasional pair of macaroni penguins. You may be lucky enough to come across some of the semi-translucent pebbles that have given the island its name. They're found mainly on north-facing beaches, but in recent years have become much more difficult to find. The hunting may be better on Pebble Islet, just off the northwest end of Pebble Island, but getting there would not be easy, you'd have to hitch a ride on a local boat going across. There's a bowl full of Pebble Island pebbles in the lodge. At the western end of the island there's another **gentoo penguin colony** near Shanty Point.

Southeast to Tamar Point

The route southeast takes you across flat land dotted with ponds and lakes. Almost immediately after leaving the settlement the route runs along the long beach of Elephant Bay (if the tide is out). These days elephant seals rarely show up on this beach, which is sometimes used as an alternative runway, but Commerson's dolphins may be seen inshore. Southern sea lions sometimes haul out on islands off the north coast and sometimes on the coast itself.

The route towards Tamar Point, which is separated by only a very narrow channel from the coast of West Falkland, passes close to **colonies** of Magellanic, rockhopper and gentoo penguins, with king cormorants adding to the activity. The usual threatening skuas loiter around the colonies. Royal albatrosses may be seen from Tamar Point in late summer or early autumn. On the way back to the settlement the route passes by Swan Pond, Green Pond, Betts Pond, Long Pond and Big Pond, all of which may have black-necked swans and a variety of other waterfowl. The closer ponds and Elephant Bay are walking distance from the settlement.

SLEEPING

Pebble Island Hotel (☎ 41093; pebblehotel@horizon .co.fk; full board per person high/low season £65/50; 💻) This building was originally the settlement manager's house; today it's right in the middle of the farm settlement. The six twin or double rooms are all en suite and have tea- and coffee-making facilities. There's a computer for Internet access.

At the west end of the island, **Marble Mountain Shanty** has accommodation in a single room with bunks for four and self-catering facilities. It's been closed for a couple of years because the spring that supplied the accommodation with water ran dry, but it may be reopened at some point.

GETTING THERE & AWAY

Falkland Islands Government Air Service (FIGAS; £55, about 40 minutes) flies from Stanley to Pebble Island.

The *Tamar* (p177) makes its usual circuit past Pebble Island. There's a pier close to the settlement.

Island trips can be arranged with one of the settlement's 4WDs; a day trip might cost £25 per person, minimum of two people.

KEPPEL ISLAND

This island was named after Viscount Keppel, who accompanied Anson around the world from 1740 to 1744 and went on to become Britain's first Lord of the Admiralty. In 1853, the South American Missionary Society established an outpost on Keppel Island to Christianise Yahgan Indians from Tierra del Fuego, and teach them to become potato farmers instead of hunter-gatherers. The mission was controversial because the government suspected that Indians had been brought against their will, but it lasted until 1898, despite the Indians' susceptibility to disease. Contrast the unmarked but discernible Yahgan graves with the marked ones of the mission personnel. One Falklands governor attributed numerous Yahgan deaths from tuberculosis to their:

> delicacy of constitution...developed owing to the warm clothing which they are for the sake of decency required to adopt after having been for 15 or 20 years roaming about in their canoes in a very cold climate without clothing of any kind.

It's likely that hard physical labour, change of diet, European contagion and harsh living conditions in their small, damp stone houses played a greater role in the Yahgans' demise than any inherent delicacy of constitution. The mission was undoubtedly prosperous – by 1877 it was bringing in an annual income of nearly £1000 from its herds of cattle, flocks of sheep and gardens. After the mission closed the island continued to operate as a farm until 1911.

In 1988 the island was bought by Englishman Lionel Fell. It has been uninhabited since 1992, so FIGAS can't fly there because there has to be someone present on the ground to man fire-fighting equipment when flights arrive or depart. The only way to get there would be by boat. The farm buildings remain in good shape and there are several interesting ruins. The former chapel became a wool shed, while the stone walls of

ISLANDS OFF WEST FALKLAND

the Yahgan dwellings remain in fairly good condition. The mission bailiff's house stands intact, though in poor repair. Keppel is also a good place to see penguins.

SAUNDERS ISLAND

Named after Admiral Sir Charles Saunders, this island boasts both history and wildlife. Saunders sailed with Lord Anson around the world in 1740, and it was after this voyage that Lord Anson recommended that Britain establish a settlement here. The suggestion was not followed up immediately but Port Egmont, on the eastern side of the island, did become the site of the first British settlement in the Falklands. The opportunity to stay in the isolated Portakabin at The Neck and observe four varieties of penguin, plus cormorants and albatrosses, is one of the island's attractions. The albatross colonies, which dot the north coast, also attract visitors.

In the 1980s Saunders Island passed by inheritance into the hands of Argentine descendants of Scottish pioneer sheep farmer John Hamilton, who also had extensive properties near Río Gallegos. For years, islanders agitated for the farm's expropriation, but the owners finally consented to sell the island to the Pole-Evans' in 1987. Although tourism is becoming increasingly important, sheep are still the core of the Saunders economy. There are 9500 sheep, plus a couple of pigs, some cattle and 30 or so cashmere goats. Cashmere wool fetches more than 10 times as much as sheep wool, but getting the wool is a pain: the goats need to be combed, shorn at just the right time and only have the best wool for a limited number of years.

At the moment, tourism still plays a secondary role to the island's farming activities but the emphasis could shift.

WILDLIFE

Saunders Island has rats but, fortunately, some small birds, in particular dark-faced ground tyrants and Falkland thrushes, manage to co-exist with them. Although penguins can be seen right along the north coast it's around The Neck where the largest numbers and greatest variety are present.

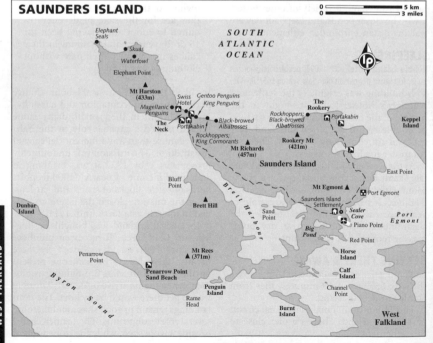

SAUNDERS ISLAND

Numerous colonies of black-browed albatrosses, numbering more than 10,000 breeding pairs, are major attractions. Other islands also have large numbers, but nowhere else are they so accessible. Adult black-browed albatrosses appear here from September to April and eggs are laid in October; the chicks hatch in December and by late February will have become balls of fluffy grey feathers perched awkwardly on nests that look far too small for them. The fledged chicks leave the nests in the second half of March or early April. In the early months of the year the colonies are a constant buzz of activity – adult birds come and go to feed their chicks or engage in the almost formal conduct which is part of albatross behaviour patterns. Just off the coast they wheel and dip in effortless flight, occasionally swooping low over their nests, dropping their legs and spreading out their feet to act as dive brakes.

Elephant seals are often seen at the appropriately named Elephant Point. Sea lions are less frequent visitors, swimming along the channel of clear water between the northern cliff edge and the kelp that grows just offshore. Peale's and Commerson's dolphins may also appear in this channel, while the spouts of southern right whales may be spotted further offshore.

WALKS

Visitors to Saunders Island tend to head off in two directions. Either they go northwest along the winding track to The Neck, from where they can walk to Elephant Point; or they travel north past the historic British settlement at Port Egmont and across the beach to the west of East Point to the Rookery with its albatross, cormorant and rockhopper penguin colonies.

The Neck

The Neck – the narrow, low-lying strip of sand that joins Elephant Point to the main part of Saunders Island – is one of the most spectacular wildlife-viewing places in the Falklands. Staying there in the Portakabin (p129) is a rare privilege, as the guest book entries make abundantly clear. You're 15km from the island settlement by Land-Rover (it takes about one hour, or four hours on foot), but you could just as easily be 100km or 1000km from the nearest concentration of humanity. What you are undoubtedly

close to is an awful lot of wildlife: there are thousands of penguins below the Portakabin on the beaches and lots more birdlife along the cliff faces to the east, not to mention plenty of sheep grazing among the nesting albatrosses.

The majority of the penguins on the beach at The Neck are gentoos. They congregate in several fairly distinct colonies and, like many other penguin colonies in the Falklands, their number took a dive in 2002–03. There are still many thousands, but not as many as before. On the south side of The Neck there's a rusting, cracked old cast iron **trypot** (a cauldron on three legs for rendering the blubber of penguins into oil). A single gentoo provided about half a litre. A fence warns you of the appropriate distance to keep back from a small colony of elegant king penguins on the east side of The Neck. Occasional macaroni and even the odd chinstrap penguin also turn up here.

Climbing up above the coastline as you move east there's a large mixed colony of rockhopper penguins and king cormorants. The rockhoppers have been hopping up this cliff face for so many years that they've scored deep grooves into the hard rock. A little further are colonies of black-browed albatrosses, again often mixed with other birds. These slopes, rising up to Mt Richards on the east side of The Neck, like the slopes of Mt Harston on the west side, are riddled with Magellanic penguin burrows.

Elephant Point

From The Neck it's 8km (as the upland goose flies) to the very end of Elephant Point and another 8km back. With some stops to view the wildlife and a pause for lunch it makes a good all-day walk. You can vary the walk by following the north coastline to the point and then climbing along the ridgeline for the views on the way back. Keep an eye out to sea as well because dolphins and whales are regularly spotted along this coast.

After you leave The Neck follow the sheep trails that contour along the side of Mt Harston. The prominent large rock labelled 'Swiss Hotel' is a popular camping spot (p129). The walk passes a couple of ponds where you may see a variety of waterfowl. As you approach Elephant Point, skuas nest close to the beach and will vigorously dive bomb walkers if they approach too close to eggs or chicks in their nests. A good high-speed swoop from a Falklands skua gets the heart beating faster (see p168). Watch for flightless steamer ducks and oystercatchers along this beach.

Elephant Point has a couple of sandy stretches along its north side where you may indeed encounter elephant seals, as well as the occasional sea lion. There are fine views west to Carcass Island (p129) and, further on, to the dramatic shapes of the Jasons (p139).

As you walk back to The Neck, climb to the ridgeline running to Mt Harston. As you ascend, the grass gives way to diddledee (small, evergreen shrub that produces bright red, edible berries) interspersed with vivid green patches of balsam bog. Off to the north, Wreck Island, visible as a line on the horizon as you walked closer to sea level, can now be clearly seen as a string of low-lying islands. Although you're further back from the coast it's much easier to spot whale spouts from up here. A 'standing man', the local name for a stone cairn, marks the summit of Mt Harston (433m). You actually have to continue a little beyond the high point before you can look down on The Neck and spot the Portakabin.

Port Egmont

Only a few kilometres west of Keppel Island, Port Egmont on the east coast of Saunders Island was the site of the first British garrison on the Falklands. Although built in 1765, it was not properly established until the arrival of Captain John McBride in early 1766. In 1770, three years after France had ceded its colony to Spain, Spanish forces dislodged the British from Saunders and nearly precipitated a war between the two countries. A year later a settlement was negotiated and the British returned, only to leave voluntarily in 1774. Following their second departure the Spaniards razed the settlement, including its impressive blockhouse, leaving the still remaining jetties, extensive foundations, and some of the buildings' walls, plus the garden terraces built by the British marines.

One British sailor left a memoir indicating how well developed the settlement was:

The glory of our colony was the gardens, which we cultivated with the greatest care, as being fully convinced how much the comforts of our situa-

tion depended on our being supplied with vegetables…We were plentifully supplied with potatoes, cabbages, broccoli, carrots, borecole, spinach, parsley, lettuce, English celery, mustard, cresses, and some few, but very fine cauliflowers.

Today the remains are less than half an hour's walk from the modern settlement. Apart from the foundations and fragments of wall from some of the buildings and some works in the inlet there's little trace of the settlement. A **plaque** outlines the history of this first British foothold, while a short distance inland there's a small, fenced-off **cemetery** with five British graves: three of seamen from HMS *Jason* in 1766 and 1769, and two from HMS *Favourite* in 1769 and 1770. Captain George Farmer of HMS *Favourite* was commanding the settlement when the Spanish commander Juan Madariaga turned up with five ships and 1500 men. Outnumbered, Farmer soon capitulated and surrendered the base to the Spanish. None of the graves result from this encounter in June 1770.

The Rookery

Another winding track across camp (anywhere in the Falklands outside Stanley) leads to the eastern slopes of Mt Egmont then descends to the coast, crossing a stream and running along the beach for a spell before climbing to The Rookery. Along this northeast coast below Rookery Mt (421m) for many kilometres back towards The Neck there is colony after colony of black-browed albatrosses.

Look out for whales and dolphins, which are clearly visible from these clifftop lookouts. Small corners of tussock grass survive on some of the steeper cliff edges or on small headlands inaccessible to sheep. Rockhopper penguins are also found along this coast; there's one spot where a stream tumbling down the hillside provides a convenient cold shower for rockhoppers keen on a clean up before they head back to sea.

Southwest Saunders

The southwest part of the island is comparatively infrequently visited. Dominated by Mt Rees (371m), it is separated from the rest of Saunders Island by Brett Harbour and joined to it by a very narrow isthmus.

Big Pond, just south of the settlement en route to this part of the island, is good place for viewing waterfowl.

SLEEPING & EATING

Saunders Island Self-Catering (☎ 41298; davidpe@ horizon.co.fk; self-catering/full board (by prior arrangement) per person £20/40) Run by David and Suzan Pole-Evans, these two cottages are the settlement (with other possibilities waiting on the sidelines). Both are traditional island houses, homely and sprawling affairs with a variety of bedrooms, bathroom, toilets, well-equipped kitchen, lounge and other facilities. The Old Military R&R Centre was used by the British forces after the Falklands War and sleeps up to eight in four rooms. They left the sign on the noticeboard announcing that it's the 'Saunders Island Hilton'. It may indeed be slightly more luxurious than Stone House Cottage, which dates from 1875, has three bedrooms and accommodates six.

Portakabin (first 1-2 persons/extra £80/40) For many visitors the opportunity to stay at The Neck is a highlight of a visit to the Falklands. As a result, the Portakabin can be booked out far ahead so inquire as early as possible. The faded lettering on what was once a shipping container indicates that the Portakabin was originally the Goose Green heliport. Initially there was just a kitchen-bedroom-living area with an outside chemical toilet; water had to be carried from a nearby spring. Subsequently a bunkroom was added, and then a bathroom with running water and flush toilet. The main living area now has two beds that double as couches in the daytime, chairs, a heater, stove, sink and a table with a couple of benches. The bunkroom accommodates up to four people, the main room another two. It's utilitarian living, but entries in the visitors' book indicate that it's less spartan than people had been led to expect. Of course it's self-catering.

The big attraction of a stay at The Neck, however, is that you can go out to watch the wildlife first thing in the morning, see the penguins come home in the evening or make a last check on the albatross chicks before you turn in. When night falls you can be comfortably warm inside and sense that you're a long way from anywhere. Your morning alarm might be striated caracaras clattering across the roof.

Swiss Hotel (camping per person £10) It's possible to camp here ate an overhang on the hillside, just beyond the isthmus at The Neck. It's big enough to shelter a tent. The sign comes courtesy of a group of visiting Swiss backpackers who made a long photographic visit to the island. Come prepared, as there are absolutely no facilities.

Portakabin (per person £20) Another Portakabin has recently been installed at The Rookery. Originally for the use of a visiting albatross researcher, it's very much like The Neck's Portakabin was in the early days, with just the one room and an outside chemical toilet.

Since Saunders is one of the few islands that encourages camping, there has been talk of setting up a bunkroom at the settlement as a further attraction for visiting backpackers.

The settlement's small **shop** has a surprisingly wide selection of tinned, dry and even frozen food and drinks, and fresh bread (sometimes), eggs, meat and milk can also be supplied.

GETTING THERE & AWAY

FIGAS (£65, under an hour) flies from Stanley to Saunders Island.

Saunders Island is popular with cruise ships, which land passengers at either the north or south beach of The Neck, depending on the prevailing conditions.

GETTING AROUND

Saunders Island is rather large to walk around easily, so the island's Land-Rovers (The Neck per person £20, one hour; The Rookery per person £15, 40 minutes) are the transport of choice.

CARCASS ISLAND

Despite its unappealing name, small but scenic Carcass is one of the most popular islands in the Falklands; book well ahead, since Stanleyites like to visit the island for weekends and holidays. The island's name comes from HMS *Carcass*, the sloop that arrived in 1766 with the frigate HMS *Jason* and the store ship HMS *Experiment* to establish the first British settlement at Port Egmont (opposite). In early 1767 HMS *Carcass* surveyed the waters around the island that now bears its name.

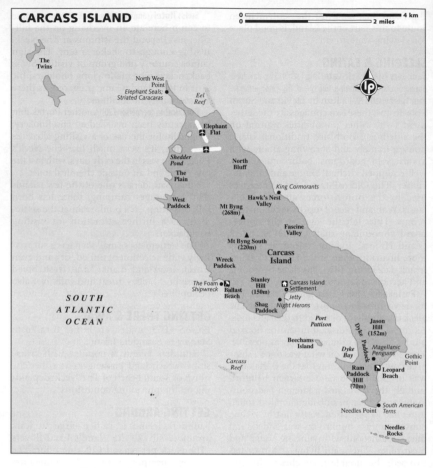

CARCASS ISLAND

0 ⸺ 4 km
0 ⸺ 2 miles

The Twins

North West Point
Elephant Seals;
Striated Caracaras

Eel Reef

Elephant Flat

Shedder Pond

North Bluff

The Plain

King Cormorants

West Paddock

Hawk's Nest Valley

Mt Byng (268m)

Fascine Valley

Mt Byng South (220m)

Carcass Island

Wreck Paddock

The Foam Shipwreck
Ballast Beach

Stanley Hill (150m)

Carcass Island Settlement

Jetty

Shag Paddock
Night Herons

SOUTH ATLANTIC OCEAN

Port Pattison

Jason Hill (152m)

Beechams Island

Dyke Bay

Magellanic Penguins

Gothic Point

Carcass Reef

Ram Paddock Hill (70m)

Leopard Beach

Needles Point

South American Terns

Needles Rocks

Carcass is off the northwest tip of West Falkland; beyond it are only the remote Jasons. The island is small, scenic and has always been free of rats and cats, and as a result has lots of small birdlife. The island has been owned by only three families, starting with Charles Hansen, a Danish seamen and sealer who took a lease on Carcass, the Jasons and some other nearby islands in 1872. The island remained with his descendants until Cecil and Kitty Bertrand followed from 1954 and the present owners Rob and Lorraine McGill took over in 1974. Lorraine runs Stanley House (the boarding house in Stanley for schoolchildren from camp) for much of the year, but Rob is a more than capable host and a key reason for the island's popularity.

Carcass still supports up to 1000 sheep and a handful of cows for island use only, but tourism is now the main money spinner.

Carcass Island had the historic shipwreck of the *Foam*, an 88-ton schooner built in Portsmouth in 1848 for Lord Dufferin and used for the explorations which led to his account *Letters from High Latitudes*. The ship came to the Falklands in 1863 and between then and 1882 did 59 round trips to Montevideo in Uruguay. Purchased by Carcass Island's first owner, Charles Hansen, he used it until 1890 when a gale blew the *Foam* ashore at Wreck Paddock not far west of the settlement. Only scattered wreckage remains at the site, but until recently the settlement's 1870s Valley Cottage, which burnt down in

2003, used the ship's steps as a steep stairway to the upstairs bedroom.

AROUND THE ISLAND

Carcass Island is about 8km long and 2km across at its widest point. A range of hills runs along the eastern side of the island, rising to its highest point at Mt Byng (268m), just north of Mt Byng South (220m). Jason Hill (152m) at the southern end of the eastern range is another prominent highpoint and Ram Paddock Hill (70m) is towards the southwest tip of the island.

Flecked with kelp, Port Pattison is the island's sheltered bay. The settlement with its small pier and ramp is at the north end of the bay. There's a beach at Dyke Bay at the southern end of Port Pattison and a longer sweep of sand at Leopard Beach. The only really flat areas on the island are Elephant Flat and the Plain at the northern end of the island where the airstrip is located.

The Carcass Island settlement is one of the most picturesque in the Falklands. The dense stand of trees around the settlement confirm that trees *can* grow on the Falklands. The Monterey cypress trees were planted in the 1930s, while more recent arrivals are cabbage palms and New Zealand flax, both introduced from New Zealand. The settlement garden is bordered at one end by a towering box hedge, an amazing sight since it has been clipped into a vertical surface a good 7m high.

WILDLIFE

Free of cats, rats and mice, Carcass supports a population of small birdlife, particularly around the settlement gardens. A walk along the island shoreline is accompanied by cheeky dark brown tussock birds that fly up to greet you or hop right up if you slow down. Stand still and they will jump on your shoes, just in case you've managed to kick up any tasty titbits. Tiny, light brown Cobb's wrens are another common shoreline sight. They will skitter along just in front of you, popping under stones or pieces of driftwood as you approach, but flitting out again as soon as you pass or if you pause for a few seconds. They're the certain sign that an island is rat free; no island with rats also has these tiny wrens. Black-chinned siskins, black-throated finches, Falklands thrushes and grass wrens are also seen.

Upland geese and smaller numbers of ruddy-headed geese are seen everywhere above the shoreline. Johnny rook, the striated caracara, can pop up almost anywhere, but particularly around the elephant seals at Northwest Point and around the settlement, where they can be heard sliding noisily down the metal roofs. Turkey vultures are also regular sights around the settlement. Night herons used to nest around the house until the Johnny Rooks worked out how to get at their nests and take eggs and chicks. Some can still be seen around the pier. Chickens have had an equally tough time of it with the Johnny Rooks; local character Rob McGill noted that they seem to prefer white chickens to other colours, 'probably because the white feathers flying everywhere look more spectacular'.

On the rocky beach in front of the settlement and elsewhere around the island, pairs of kelp geese and steamer ducks are regular visitors. Magellanic and black oystercatchers also appear on the shoreline, while shy South American terns nest right at the southern end of the island by Needles Point.

Carcass Island's penguin population took a dramatic dive in 2002–03 and the island's once dense population of gentoos virtually disappeared. While there are still plenty of Magellanic penguins, the numbers are actually far lower than in the past and the evening chorus of braying penguins no longer rings across the settlement at so high a volume.

Elephant seals regularly appear around Northwest Point and the occasional sea lion may be seen around Leopard Beach, although they do not breed there. Ship passengers coming ashore by Zodiac may see Commerson's and Peale's dolphins, which could also be spotted from the beach.

WALKS
North West Point

The walk to North West Point, 6km from the settlement, can make an interesting all-day excursion, or you can be dropped off at Shedder Pond, from where the walk to the point and back to the settlement will still take three or four hours with a few stops to view the wildlife.

From the settlement, the route up the island's central valley follows the variety of routes a Carcass Land-Rover would take to the airstrip. It's clear there's no single 'road' across the rolling paddocks! **Shedder Pond** will usually have a variety of waterfowl, while Magellanic penguins stand around, looking mildly bewildered as usual. From the pond you can walk along stretches of beach and hop across interludes of rock towards the northern tip of the island. You will probably have to divert into the tussock grass that cloaks the northern end of the island in order to skirt around groups of elephant seals monopolising the beach. Striated caracaras are also common, hanging around groups of elephant seals, clearly up to no good. The rocky coastline around the point is littered with all types of flotsam and jetsam, including large whalebones. Sitting on the rocks at the point you're clearly a long way from anywhere: there's just the background *harumph* of elephant seals, the wash of the sea and assorted squawks, chirps and quarks from a variety of birds.

From the point, which points decisively towards the Jasons, the walk back to the settlement starts out along the coast before climbing up onto the green hillsides that slope gently down before making their final rocky tumble into the kelp-strewn ocean. The grassy slopes are dotted with **Magellanic penguin burrows** and there are a couple of colonies of king cormorants. At Hawks Nest Valley, halfway back from the point and 3km from the settlement, turn inland and climb gently south to top the saddle before dropping down to the settlement. A diversion to climb Mt Byng gives fine views north to the Jasons on a clear day.

Leopard Beach

It's a 3km stroll to Dyke Bay or Leopard Beach at the southern end of the island. Many cruise ship passengers are dropped off here and walk to the settlement. Leopard Beach has a fine stretch of white sand running for a kilometre. Tussock grass fringes the coast at this end of the island and backs up the whole length of Dyke Bay.

There are many Magellanic penguins' burrows behind this beach and at a number of places along the walk, so walkers should take care not to disturb them or to step on their burrows (see p168). South American terns nest below Needles Point at the extreme southern tip of the island. These birds are extremely vulnerable to disturbance so visitors should take great care not to alarm them, particularly when they're incubating their eggs between October and January.

Although they do not breed on the island, the occasional southern sea lion can be seen basking on Leopard Beach or on the grassy slopes around Gothic Point.

Settlement Stroll

A short stroll from the settlement takes you down to the pier where you may see night herons. Beyond here there are dense stretches of tussock grass, a real contrast to many other islands where the tussock is seriously depleted. It's a popular home for Magellanic penguins and for small ground-dwelling birds. You can rock hop around the point and beyond the tussock climb up to the top of Stanley Hill at over 150m overlooking the settlement and topped by the telephone transmitter dish and a stone cairn.

SLEEPING

Carcass Island (☎ 41106; per person with meals £55) Rooms are available in the settlement house. Meals are taken with the family in the house, where there's a licensed bar for soft drinks, beer, wine and pre-dinner gin-and-tonics. Electric power from the diesel generator is backed up by a much quieter wind-powered generator, which provides up to 75% of the settlement's power requirements.

There used to be self-catering accommodation in the nearby Valley and Rose Cottages, but the former burnt down in 2003 and the latter is now used for staff accommodation.

GETTING THERE & AWAY

The 200km FIGAS (£75) flight from Stanley is one of the longest in the Falklands, and takes more than an hour direct, longer if there are stops at islands in-between. The grass airstrip is about 3km northwest of the settlement and one of the island's Land-Rovers meets incoming passengers.

There's a loading ramp for unloading provisions or loading wool bales, but visiting cruise ships normally drop their passengers by Zodiac at Dyke's Bay on Port Pattison or Leopard Beach at the southern end of the island, depending on the prevailing winds. From there it's a pleasant 3km stroll to the settlement where tea and cakes in the capacious kitchen is a Falkland Islands highlight for many visitors. This warm welcome, along with the island's prolific small birdlife, has made Carcass a particularly popular stop for visiting cruise ships.

WESTPOINT ISLAND

Off the northwest corner of West Falkland, Westpoint Island is 12km southwest of Carcass Island. It's about 5km from north to south and 3km across at the widest point. The island is a very popular stop for cruise ships, but although it has an airstrip it's not easy to visit from Stanley because the runway is very weather dependant.

Mt Ararat (242m) to the north, and Cliff Mountain (369m) and Mt Misery to the south tumble almost directly into the sea on the west coast, giving the island the highest cliffs in the Falklands. A valley crosses the island between these two highlands from the settlement on the east coast to the Devil's Nose, a spectacular promontory on the west coast. A fast channel only about 400m wide, known as the Woolly Gut, separates Woolly Gut Point on the island from Hope Point at the end of the West Falkland promontory.

Although the island has rats and mice (cats have recently been eliminated), the owners were conservation pioneers who replanted tussock grass at a time when it was seen as a pointless thing to do. The island was originally known as Albatross Island and in the late 18th and early 19th century was a pioneering centre for sealers in the Falklands. There was farming activity here as early as the 1860s, although the first independent sheep farming operation was

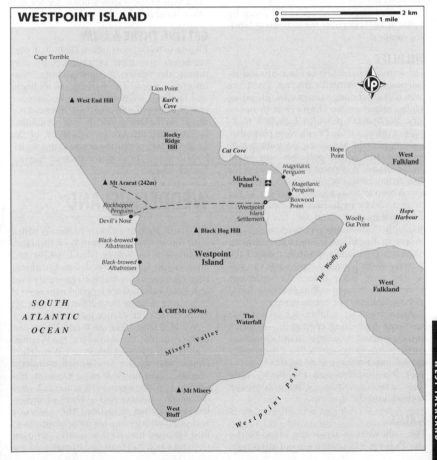

established by Arthur Felton in 1879. Felton used the remains of a stone hut from the sealing era as his first home and started to replant the tussock, which had been devastated by wild cattle released by the sealers.

Lily and Roddy Napier, the current owners, are direct descendants of Arthur Felton and have followed his early conservationist instincts, although the island continues to operate as a sheep farm. Their Falkland Islands tea and cakes in the farm house has become a major attraction for cruise ship visitors.

Lars-Eric Lindblad, who founded Lindblad Expeditions and was one of the pioneers of Antarctic and Falklands tourism, developed a special interest in the island and after his death in 1994 his ashes were scattered here.

The *Redwing*, tossed up on the beach by a gale in 1993, sits near the settlement landing ramp.

WILDLIFE

The island's population of black-browed albatrosses is of particular interest. There are over 10,000 breeding pairs in total, including a large colony on the Devil's Nose promontory. Westpoint's penguins include a rockhopper colony on the Devil's Nose plus other rockhopper and Magellanic penguin colonies. Kelp and upland geese are also found on the island. Westpoint Island is noted for its striated caracaras, but crested caracaras, which tend to be as reclusive and shy as the striated variety are fearless and forward, can also be seen. The island also has some remarkably fearless turkey vultures, which can be seen in the gardens around the settlement. Although the island's rats have reduced the number of small ground birds some can still be seen, particularly around the settlement where black-chinned siskins and long-tailed meadowlarks may be encountered.

Apart from its wildlife, the island also has some interesting vegetation – Felton's flower, named after the island's original farmer, club moss cudweed and the prickly coastal nassauvia are all endemic.

Peale's dolphins and the stocky little Commerson's dolphins often accompany Zodiacs into the shallows.

WALKS

The walk directly across the island to the Devil's Nose is the island's major attraction.

Over 2000 black-browed albatross breeding pairs nest here, along with 500 pairs of rockhopper penguins. It's just over 2km from one side of the island to the other, climbing past Black Bog Hill to an altitude of about 100m on the way, and passing a **bog** that at one time was heavily cut for peat to be used as fuel. Bird bones, many of them of striated caracaras, carbon dated to over 5000 years ago, have been collected from this peat bog in recent years.

Visitors can walk across the island in half an hour or ride over in just 10 minutes in the Napiers' Land-Rover. Once upon a time visitors to the island were conveyed in a decidedly out-of-place single-decker bus, an escapee from Wales. After visiting the wildlife a visit to the Napier's home for tea and cakes is another highlight of an island visit.

GETTING THERE & AWAY

Flights to Westpoint Island (£80, just over an hour) are often cancelled, especially during the winter, so most visitors come on cruise ships. The harbour is sheltered and landings from cruise ship Zodiacs are straightforward, either at the settlement jetties or on the landing ramp. The permanent landing facilities are an indication of the steady stream of visiting cruise ships, which have become the major source of income for the island.

WEDDELL ISLAND

Originally known as Swan Island, Weddell is off the southwest corner of West Falkland; further west is Beaver Island (p136) and New Island (p136). Weddell is the third-largest island in the archipelago – only East and West Falkland are larger – with several hills rising to more than 200m and one, Mt Weddell, to nearly twice that height.

Weddell Island, like the Weddell Sea (east of the Antarctic Peninsula) and the Weddell seal, are all named after James Weddell, a Royal Navy officer and British merchant marine, sealer and Antarctic explorer. His sealing trips between 1819 and 1822 were financially unsuccessful – years of merciless sealing had devastated the Antarctic seal population – but his futile attempts to find seals led him further south than even Captain Cook had managed to reach. Along

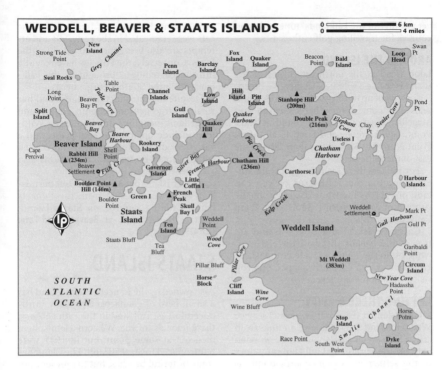

WEDDELL, BEAVER & STAATS ISLANDS

the way he took meticulous observations and his accounts of the Falklands are some of the earliest and most detailed. Coincidentally, he met up with Charles Barnard, the castaway of New Island (see the boxed text p138), and he may well have been the inspiration for Barnard to write the stirring account of his multiple mishaps.

Scottish pioneer John Hamilton, also a major landholder in Argentine Patagonia, acquired this western offshore island and others nearby to experiment on various agricultural improvement projects, including the replanting of tussock grass, forest plantations and the importation of Highland cattle and Shetland ponies; and the well-meaning but perhaps misguided introduction of exotic wildlife such as guanacos (still present on Staats Island (p136), Patagonian foxes (common on Weddell proper, and the cause of high lamb losses) and sea otters (apparently extinct). Despite the introductions, Weddell still hosts abundant local wildlife, including gentoo and Magellanic penguins, great skuas, night herons, giant petrels and striated caracaras.

During its sheep farming years the island was heavily overexploited: at one time there were over 20,000 sheep and Weddell's vegetation is still recovering from this serious overstocking. Hamilton, clearly a man intent on turning a quid in every way possible, introduced foxes in order to reduce the number of upland geese, which, it was theorised, were competing with sheep for grazing. In fact, the foxes preferred lambs to geese. He also had a go at rendering sea lions for their oil, which could then be used to produce paint! That idea was also a failure. Today the sheep population has been dramatically reduced and, like other islands in the Falklands, tourism is becoming increasingly important. The gorse hedges, used to demarcate the fields, have survived and make a fine flash of yellow when they're in flower in spring.

In the past the island has had accommodation in the farmhouse and in self-catering cottages, but they closed down in the 2003–04 season and stayed closed for the 2004–05 season. Camping on the island was also possible in the past. The island has yet another of the Falklands' nine-hole golf courses for travelling golf enthusiasts.

AROUND THE ISLAND

Loop Head at the northeast corner of the island is the best wildlife site: there's a breeding colony of up to 200 sea lions and elephant seals also come ashore here. Gentoo and Magellanic penguins can be found at Mark Point, Gull Harbour and Loop Head. Mark Point is an easy walk of less than 2km to the east of the settlement.

For walkers there's very rugged cliff scenery along the southeast coast or you can look out across the whole island from the summit of Mt Weddell (383m), 5km from the settlement.

Carthorse Island and Useless Island are two of the islands in Chatham Harbour, while off to the southwest side of the island Horse Block is a curiously shaped outcrop rising 67m above sea level.

GETTING THERE & AWAY

FIGAS Islander (£80, over one hour) service Weddell Island from Stanley. Landings from cruise ships are made either at the wooden jetty or on the shore at Gull Harbour, close to the settlement. Commerson's dolphins may be spotted as you come in to shore.

BEAVER ISLAND

A number of smaller islands are scattered between Weddell and New Islands. The largest of this group, Beaver Island, has a small settlement and is home to Antarctic sailing pioneers Jerome and Sally Poncet, who own both Beaver and Staats Islands (right). Their yacht *Golden Fleece* is available for charter in the Falkland Islands and further afield, and has been used for many film and other media projects in the region.

The island takes its name from the New England whaling ship *Beaver*, claimed to be one of the ships involved in the Boston Tea Party in 1773. Beaver Island claimed the British 1200-ton barque *Yarra Yarra* in 1885, which was en route from Portland, Oregon, to England in company with the *Perthshire*; the *Perthshire* also sank – just one day earlier on Blind Island. During the sheep farming era the island was overrun with feral cats as well as Patagonian foxes,

to the great detriment of the birdlife. The cats were eradicated in the early '90s and attempts are also being made to get rid of the foxes. Conversely, the Poncets have recently introduced reindeer, brought to the Falklands from the South Georgia herds.

Despite the introductions, the island has a fairly large gentoo penguin colony and Magellanic penguins are also seen. Wildfowl include upland and kelp geese, and a variety of ducks. Both striated and crested caracaras can be found and sea lions also visit Beaver Island.

Beaver Island has an airstrip, but permission must be obtained from the Poncets before landing here or on Staats Island; contact the Poncets at **Beaver Island Farm** (☎ 42315).

STAATS ISLAND

Also owned by the Poncets, Staats Island has a small herd of guanacos. Originally introduced to East Falkland in the 19th century, these 'camels' of the Western Hemisphere died out at some point, but in 1937 were reintroduced to Staats Island. The island has some beautiful beaches, but the presence of Patagonian foxes, combined with the lack of trees, ensures that few smaller birds can thrive. Adjacent to Staats Island is Tea Island, which has now had 30 years to recover from sheep grazing. The rare endemic Felton's flower is found on Tea Island. See above for details of access to Staats Island.

NEW ISLAND

At the southwestern corner of the Falklands, remote New Island is divided into two nature reserves: New Island North Nature Reserve is run by Tony and Kim Chater; Tony is the author of the photographic book *The Falklands*. New Island South Wildlife Reserve is run by Ian and Maria Strange; Ian is the author of the field guide *Wildlife of the Falkland Islands*. New Island is the most westerly inhabited island of the Falklands, but since there is no regular accommodation most visitors are from expedition cruise ships. The spectacular scenery, wide variety of breeding birds, dolphin sightings offshore, penguins, sea

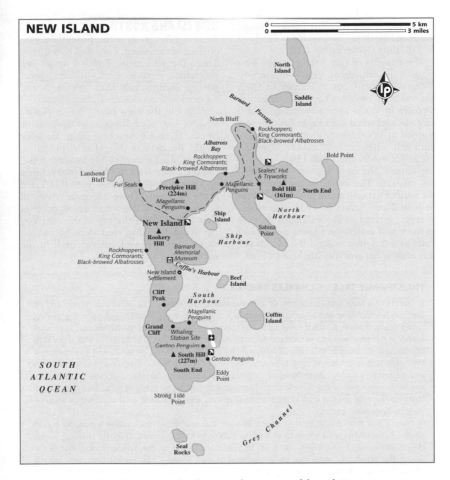

NEW ISLAND

0 _____ 5 km
0 _____ 3 miles

North Island

Saddle Island

Barnard Passage

North Bluff

Rockhoppers; King Cormorants; Black-browed Albatrosses

Albatross Bay

Rockhoppers; King Cormorants; Black-browed Albatrosses

Bold Point

Landsend Bluff

Fur Seals

Sealers' Hut & Tryworks

Precipice Hill (224m)

Magellanic Penguins

Bold Hill (161m)

North End

Magellanic Penguins

North Harbour

New Island

Ship Island

Rookery Hill

Sabina Point

Barnard Memorial Museum

Ship Harbour

Rockhoppers; King Cormorants; Black-browed Albatrosses

Coffin's Harbour

New Island Settlement

Beef Island

Cliff Peak

South Harbour

Magellanic Penguins

Coffin Island

Grand Cliff

Whaling Station Site

Gentoo Penguins

South Hill (227m)

Gentoo Penguins

South End

Eddy Point

SOUTH ATLANTIC OCEAN

Strong Tide Point

Seal Rocks

Grey Channel

lions and fur seals all help to make this a popular stop.

The island tilts dramatically, sloping up from sheltered bays and a natural harbour on the east side to wind-swept cliffs falling 170m to the sea on the west side. Climatically, New Island is one of the driest places in the Falklands, with annual rainfall much lower than the average.

Sealers and whalers were early visitors, and several operations slaughtered and rendered penguins for their oil. The stone corrals near the penguin rookeries are where the unfortunate birds were rounded up before being killed and processed. Rabbits and pigs had been released as early as the 1820s to provide fresh food for visiting ships. In

the 1850s and '60s there were attempts to exploit the island's guano deposits, and from the 1860s sheep were run on the island. From 1908 to 1916 a permanent shore-based whaling operation was established on New Island, but once that closed down sheep were once again the main activity until, in the late 1970s, the island was precisely divided into two equal-sized properties, which are both now operated as nature reserves. In 1987 all the sheep were removed from the island – except for a small flock kept in a controlled area – and the tussock grass has rapidly regenerated since then. The only settlement on the island is beside Coffin's Harbour, although a research field station operates on the south part of the island.

Coffin Island and six other islands around the main islands are reserves owned and run by Falklands Conservation (FC).

The remains of two wrecks can be seen close to the settlement. The 1800 ton iron *Glengowan* burnt out at Stanley in 1895. She was on her maiden voyage, sailing from Swansea in Wales to San Francisco with a cargo of coal when she caught fire. She was scuttled at Whalebone Cove and lay there until 1910 when her hulk was towed to New Island for use by the South Harbour whaling station. She now lies semi-submerged just offshore. The *Protector* lies beached at the head of the settlement harbour. She was built in Nova Scotia in 1943 as a minesweeper, arrived in the Falklands in 1949 to work as a sealer, then spent a couple of years as a freighter around the islands before ending her working life here in 1969.

NEW ISLAND NORTH

Although their reserve comprises the northern half of the island, Tony and Kim Chater live in the settlement. Both are artists and naturalists, and their work – which includes postage stamps, calendars, postcards and art work – is on sale from their house.

Walks in the New Island North Nature Reserve can start from Ship Harbour or North Harbour beaches. Ship Harbour South Beach has Magellanic penguins, steamer ducks and ruddy-headed geese, and the 2.5km walk to a **fur seal colony** climbs up a gentle slope past numerous thin-billed prion burrows. There are good views of Landsend Bluff, the westernmost point of New Island, from the top of the rise. You can avoid retracing your steps by turning south from the seal colony; back to the settlement is about 3km.

THE STRANGE TALE OF CHARLES BARNARD

In late 1812 a New England sealer, Charles Barnard, and a crew of 12 arrived at New Island on the brig *Nanina* to spend a summer season hunting seals. In April 1813, sailing in the sealing cutter *Young Nanina*, Barnard came upon the survivors of the wreck of the *Isabella* on Speedwell Island, at the southern end of Falkland Sound. Returning from Sydney in Australia with a drunken captain and passengers that ranged from military men to pardoned criminals and ex-prostitutes, their ship had struck a reef on 8 February, nine weeks earlier. Barnard agreed to carry the crew and passengers to the South American mainland, in exchange for the wreckage of their ship, and with a handful of the *Isabella*'s complement returned to New Island to collect the *Nanina*. Then, so the tale goes, a spell of bad weather ensued and they were unable to return immediately to Speedwell Island.

During this brief pause at New Island Barnard and four other men made a hunting trip to nearby Beaver Island and returned to find the *Nanina* had disappeared. Over the ensuing winter they made unsuccessful attempts to sail to Speedwell Island on the *Young Nanina*, but in the spring the other four men abandoned Barnard as well, leaving him completely alone on the island. Two months later the *Young Nanina* and its four crew turned up back on New Island, clearly with some difficult explanations to make.

They had sailed to Speedwell Island, expecting to find the *Nanina* at the site of the *Isabella*'s shipwreck, but there was no trace of her or the *Isabella*'s survivors. In fact, before Barnard originally discovered the wreck, many months earlier, seven of the *Isabella*'s castaways, led by a naval officer who earlier in the journey from Australia had proved a better seamen than the ship's captain, had sailed all the way to Buenos Aires in a longboat. A Royal Navy rescue party then set off back to the Falklands, arriving on 17 May, not long after Barnard originally sailed back to New Island to collect the *Nanina*. A month later, when the *Nanina*, without its captain aboard, turned up at Speedwell Island it was promptly seized as a war prize by the British and sailed off to England. A visit to New Island by the Royal Navy failed to find Barnard and the other four men, three of them crew from the *Isabella*.

In November 1814, after 18 months as castaways, the five men, now clad in seal skins, were rescued by the English whaling ship *Indispensable*. It was two years later before the penniless Barnard arrived back in the USA, after further adventures off the coast of Peru and Chile including a visit to Robinson Crusoe Island, the Chilean island where a shipwrecked English seamen provided the inspiration for that most famous of all castaway stories.

From Ship Harbour North Beach or from North Harbour Beach you can walk to colonies of black-browed albatrosses, king cormorants and rockhopper, Magellanic, gentoo and king penguins. The walk passes flocks of upland and ruddy-headed geese and goes via North Bluff. There are usually only a handful of king penguins, but the gentoo site numbers 6000 pairs and one of the black-browed albatross sites has 5000 nesting pairs. There are also innumerable prion burrows and a healthy population of skuas that prey on them. Striated caracaras are also common on the island's North End. Close to North Harbour Beach is the remains of a **sealers' hut** and the **tryworks** where penguins were boiled down for their oil. A loop walk from Ship Harbour North Beach to North Harbour Beach, or vice versa, would be about 5km. An all-day walk could start from North Harbour Beach and go via North Bluff, the two Ship Harbour Beaches and the fur seal colony all the way back to the settlement on New Island South, a total distance of about 10km.

NEW ISLAND SOUTH

The **Geoffrey C Hughes Field Station** in the settlement explains about the trust that operates the New Island South Wildlife Reserve. The **Barnard Memorial Museum** above the beach is built on the remains of the stone shelter Captain Charles Barnard of the sealer *Nanina* built when he and his four companions were marooned here from mid-1813 until late 1814 (see the boxed text opposite).

A short walk takes you straight across the island, rising from sea level at the beach to the top of the 170m cliffs on the west side. Black-browed albatrosses and king cormorants nest on these sheer and wind-swept cliffs, which are also home to a large colony of rockhopper penguins.

WILDLIFE

Of the Falklands' 61 breeding bird species, 41 are found on New Island. On the precipitous western coast there are large colonies of rockhopper, gentoo and Magellanic penguins. The rockhopper and gentoo populations were badly hit by the 2002–03 downturn in penguin numbers. A few king penguins live in the North Nature Reserve, where there are also black-browed albatrosses and striated caracaras, plus a substantial rookery of southern fur seals.

Visitors should take care when walking in areas where prions breed as their fragile burrows are easily collapsed by a careless foot (see p168). Movements around any wildlife should be smooth, slow and considered, but fur seal colonies should be approached particularly quietly and slowly while also keeping as low as possible (see p169).

SLEEPING

Facilities are few and access is difficult, but potential visitors should contact **Tony** or **Kim Chater** (☎ 21399), or **Ian** or **Maria Strange** (☎ 21185) in Stanley.

GETTING THERE & AWAY

New Island has an airstrip, but since there is no formal accommodation most visitors will be from expedition cruise ships. Ships normally anchor at Coffin's Harbour in front of the settlement.

JASON ISLANDS

Starting about 15km northwest of Carcass and Westpoint Islands, and stretching for 40km, Steeple Jason, Grand Jason and the scattering of other Jasons form the extreme northwest outliers of the Falklands. The two biggest islands in the group are Steeple Jason and Grand Jason, and spectacular topography, dense wildlife and difficult access make Steeple Jason a holy grail for Falklands' visitors.

Their remote location, swift tidal currents and a lack of both sheltered landing spots and fresh water, have ensured that the Jason Islands have never been inhabited, although sheep were grazed on the islands at one time.

The islands were discovered by the Dutch explorer Sebald de Weert on board the *Het Gheloove* in 1598, and named the Sebaldines after him. In 1766 they were renamed after HMS *Jason*. In 2002 Steeple Jason and Grand Jason were donated to the New York-based Wildlife Conservation Society by an American philanthropist and wildlife enthusiast. The other Jason islands are operated as reserves by the Falklands' government.

In his coffee table book *The Falklands*, Tony Chater relates interesting tales about the islands. In the early 1900s men would be

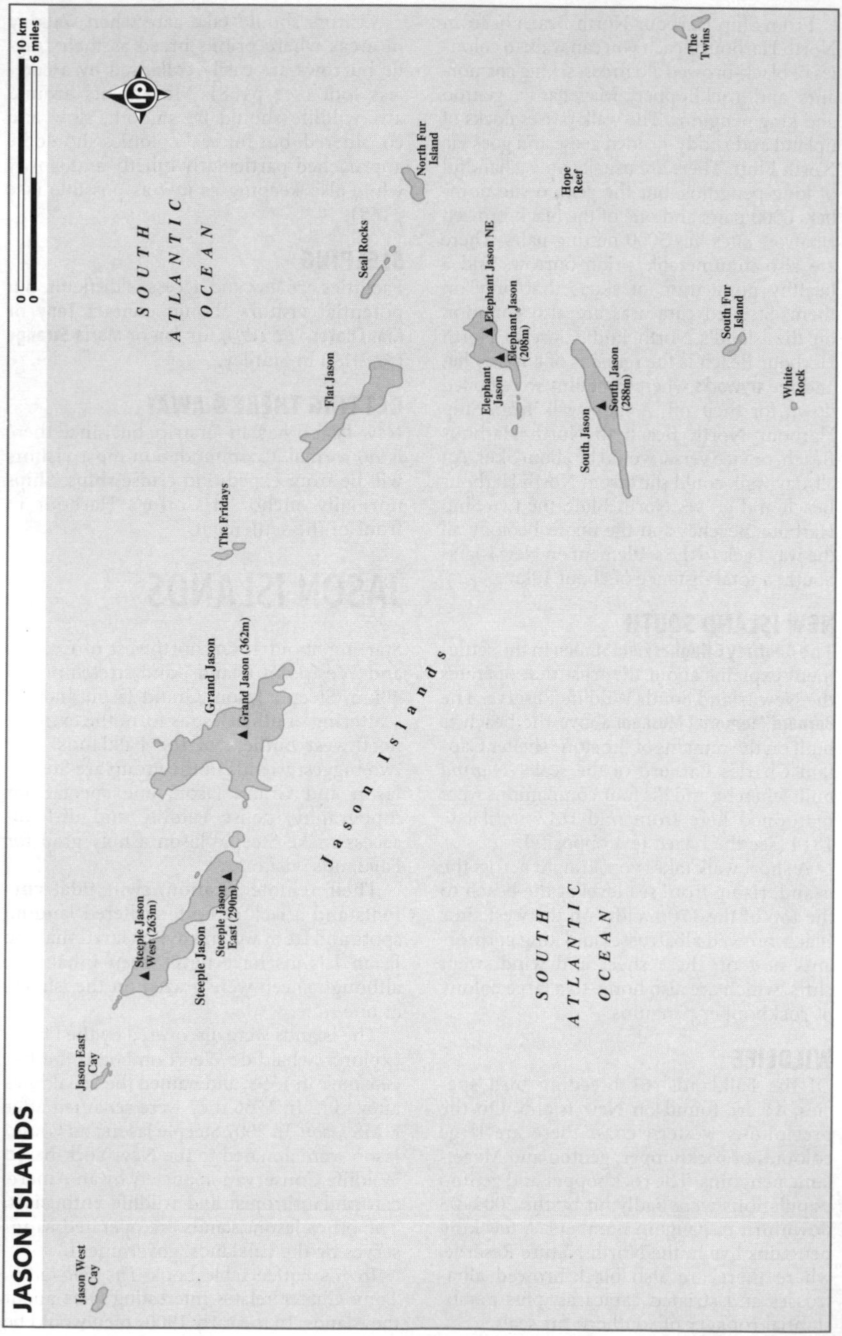

JASON ISLANDS

SOUTH ATLANTIC OCEAN

The Twins

North Fur Island

Hope Reef

Seal Rocks

Elephant Jason NE
Elephant Jason
Elephant Jason (208m)

South Fur Island

Flat Jason

White Rock

South Jason
South Jason (288m)

The Fridays

Grand Jason
Grand Jason (362m)

Jason Islands

Steeple Jason West (263m)
Steeple Jason
Steeple Jason East (290m)

SOUTH ATLANTIC OCEAN

Jason East Cay

Jason West Cay

0   10 km
0   6 miles

WHALING IN THE FALKLANDS

The first whaling ships touched on New Island in the 1770s and the island became a popular wintering point for whaling and sealing ships from North America. Coffin Island and Coffin's Harbour probably took their name from an American whaling captain; Coffin was a frequently encountered name among New England whaling captains. Barnard Passage is named after the sealing captain Charles Barnard, who made a lengthy unplanned stay on the island (see the boxed text p138).

There was a whaling operation out of New Island during the 1905–06 summer season; and from 1908 to 1916 the Falklands' only permanent whaling station was based here, as a direct result of the success of whaling on South Georgia. The immediate profitability of CA Larsen's whaling operations at Grytviken sparked a rush of applications for whaling licences, but when the British administrators decided that, initially at least, three stations were quite enough, the whaling company, Salvesens turned to the Falklands instead. The station and its equipment, dismantled and relocated from Iceland, was delivered to New Island on Christmas Eve 1908 and the first whale was killed less than a month later. In September 1909 Salvesens also opened a South Georgia whaling station at Leith, an operation which consistently proved far more profitable than their Falklands operation. In 1916 the New Island station was closed, some say because there were simply not enough whales, and some of the equipment was shifted to South Georgia. Some remains of the old station can still be seen at South Harbour.

---

dropped off on Steeple or Grand Jason Island to sheer sheep. Having worked through one flock they would then row across the dangerous channel to the other island, repeat their labours and then wait for a spell of good weather so they could be picked up. Chater also tells of the two main islands' purchase as a nature reserve for a total of £5500 in 1970. Its English owner, he records, intended to supply penguins from Steeple Jason to appear in the movie *Batman Returns*.

Steeple Jason also had a dramatic early shipwreck. The *Leopold* was a Belgian barque of 1200 tons with a crew of 20. Visibility was so poor when she ran ashore on the north coast of the island that a crewman was perched on the very end of the jib boom to keep watch for land. The first sign of it was when he was pitched ashore; he turned to see the ship slide back and sink almost immediately, carrying the rest of the crew down with it. The sole survivor was rescued 18 months later in, hardly surprisingly, less than excellent condition.

STEEPLE JASON

Regularly cited as the most breathtaking island in the Falklands, Steeple Jason has the world's largest population of black-browed albatrosses, and the penguin population includes colonies of rockhoppers that may be nearly as numerous. The island is shaped like an elongated figure eight, rising to the

rocky peaks of Steeple Jason West (263m) and Steeple Jason East (290m) at both ends, but narrowing and falling to a central isthmus that barely joins the two halves together. The island's area is 8 sq km and it stretches nearly 7km from end to end and is about 1.5km wide at the widest point.

Black-browed albatrosses number more than 150,000 breeding pairs, the main part of the **colony** stretching for 5km along the southwest coast. But that's only the starting point for the island's exceptional density of wildlife: in the early '90s a survey counted nearly 200,000 pairs of rockhoppers and more recent counts have still approached 100,000. There are smaller colonies of gentoo and Magellanic penguins, and the rare striated caracara is so numerous that visitors report being followed, hungrily, by up to 100 birds.

Southern giant petrels and king cormorants also breed on the island, and predators include Falklands skuas as well as the striated caracaras. The skuas and caracaras will aggressively defend their nesting areas, and if you are dive-bombed it's a sign that you are getting too close. However, giant petrels are notoriously nervous of intruders and will quickly abandon their nests, allowing predators like the skuas to take eggs or chicks (see p168).

Small numbers of fur seals also come to the island's beaches. The island's vegetation is still recovering from the sheep grazing days but the tussock grass is already well established. The last flocks of sheep were removed from Steeple Jason in 1968. Earlier visitors had herded together, clubbed and rendered their way through the island's penguin population, leaving trypots as reminders of their dirty work.

Most visitors to Steeple Jason come from visiting expedition cruise ships. Landings can be fraught affairs and are usually made on one side or other of the isthmus.

OTHER JASONS

Separated from Steeple Jason by a channel only 3km wide, Grand Jason is larger (14 sq km) and higher (362m) than its sister island. Like Steeple Jason, sheep were run on Grand Jason at one time and there was an even earlier population of goats.

Flat Jason, Elephant Jason and South Jason all lie between Grand Jason and West Falkland. Despite their small area, Elephant Jason towers 208m from the sea and South Jason an even more impressive at 288m. Tiny Jason East Cay and Jason West Cay lie beyond Steeple Jason to the northwest. There's a long-standing Falklands legend of the wreck of an Elizabethan-era ship on Jason West Cay; it's said to be one of Sir Francis Drake's party, which disappeared from his fleet around the Straits of Magellan in 1578.

South Georgia

CONTENTS

With snowcapped peaks and glaciers plunging towards the sea, South Georgia has been described as an alpine mountain range rising straight out of the ocean. But in the summer months there are swathes of green and it has one of the world's most extraordinary collections of wildlife. If you want to see king penguins or fur seals this is the place to come – there are fur seals by the million, while single colonies of king penguins can number in the tens of thousands. There are also substantial numbers of elephant seals as well as a variety of other penguin species. South Georgia and its outlying islands are also the home for a substantial proportion of the world's albatross population, including important colonies of the most extraordinary of these astonishing birds, the gigantic wandering albatross.

The dramatic increase in Antarctic tourism has focussed attention on the island, but scenery and wildlife are far from the only attractions. There's also a long and colourful history of whaling and a series of abandoned whaling stations along the north shore. Each of them is a snapshot of the whaling era, but Grytviken, the biggest and longest surviving station, also boasts a superb museum. Nearby is the British scientific base at King Edward Point.

Finally there's the Shackleton story and the extraordinary finale to the *Endurance* expedition. After his ship was crushed in the Antarctic pack ice, Ernest Shackleton made a dramatic journey by open boat to South Georgia and an equally dramatic walk across the uncharted island to the whaling station at Stromness. For fit and well-equipped adventurers the possibility of following this amazing trek has become one of the key Antarctic challenges. Years after his historic journey Sir Ernest suffered a heart attack and died at Grytviken; he's buried in the abandoned whaling station's cemetery.

HIGHLIGHTS

- Visiting the Shackleton grave and South Georgia Museum at **Grytviken** (p150)
- Pondering the 25,000 to 50,000 pairs of king penguins living in penguin paradise at **Salisbury Plain** (p156)
- Seeing the magnificent wandering albatross at aptly named **Albatross Islet** (p156)
- Following Shackleton's heroic **walk** (opposite) across the island – South Georgia's number one adventure
- Admiring the exceptional variety of wildlife and fabulous scenery at **Gold Harbour** (p159)

SIGHTS & ACTIVITIES
The Shackleton Walk

Shackleton's crossing of South Georgia was first repeated in 1964 by a British military group – they hauled sleds and hit terrible weather including a 36-hour blizzard. A ski planted in the snow outside their tents was snapped in two by the wind. In recent years the feat has been repeated by a number of private expeditions and by groups from expedition cruise ships. Usually the group will be dropped off at King Haakon Bay and the ship will continue round to the north coast, sometimes as part of a circumnavigation of the island, to pick the walkers up three or four days later. Typically the crossing involves two nights camping en route, although an extra night is always allowed for and if conditions are especially severe the crossing can take much longer. It's not unknown to be pinned down waiting out a blizzard.

As the crow flies – or perhaps some bird more appropriate to the Antarctic – it's only 35km from Peggotty Camp to Stromness whaling station, but the actual walking distance is about 50km. In good conditions it would not be a particularly difficult walk: the maximum altitude reached is about 650m and, apart from the sharp drop down from the Tridents, the ascents and descents are generally fairly gentle. Conditions on South Georgia are unlikely to be good. It's that simple fact that is the key to the walk; you might be lucky and make the crossing in 'good conditions', but it's far more likely that you will have bad weather, or even *very* bad weather to contend with. Shackleton's achievement in making this walk in 36 nonstop hours, with miserable equipment and while still exhausted after the long open-boat voyage to South Georgia, was an amazing feat – but he was also incredibly lucky to have good weather for the crossing. The couple of days during which the Shackleton party crossed was a narrow window with virtually the only good weather for months.

In addition, in many ways the conditions for the walk were better in 1916 than they are nearly a century later. Global warming and glacial retreats have made the terrain at some points along the walk much more difficult. In his account of following Shackleton's footsteps for the IMAX film about the *Endurance*, William Blake's comments

how mountaineers of the calibre of Conrad Anker and Reinhold Messner, with modern equipment and clothing, still took over 10 hours to cross the Crean Glacier, when Shackleton and his companions took only five. A smooth snowfield in Shackleton's era has become a heavily crevassed glacier, although conditions are probably not quite as bad as the IMAX film makes it look.

The walk today will vary with the time of year as well as weather conditions. In November or December, early in the season, walkers may have to face wilder weather, but better snow cover may make for easier walking. Later in the season reduced snow cover will lead to more crevasses to negotiate and may involve more floundering through deep and soft snow. However, some patches of snow may be gone completely and walking may be easier across bare ground.

Aurora Expeditions, the Australian adventure travel company that visits South Georgia with their Russian-crewed vessel *Polar Pioneer* gives this summary of requirements for joining a Shackleton walk:

- Experience in travelling roped-up in heavily crevassed alpine terrain
- At least one winter snow camping experience, including familiarity in carrying a heavy pack in snow
- Ability to carry a 15kg to 20kg pack for four days, for up to 10 hours a day
- Above average fitness
- Significant outdoor experience in extreme weather conditions such as high alpine, Himalayan or general mountain terrain
- Your own personal equipment such as rucksack, gaiters, crampons, ice axe, climbing harness and cross- country skis or snowshoes
- Above all, a good sense of humour and an understanding that there is a good chance that the crossing could be thwarted by weather

DAY ONE – PEGGOTTY CAMP TO THE TRIDENTS

From Peggotty Camp, where Shackleton and his two walking companions left the other three and set off on the walk, the route starts to climb immediately, following a stream at first. It takes about two hours to climb to the Shackleton Gap at about 400m. If snow conditions are good it may not be

SHACKLETON'S ENDURANCE EXPEDITION

After narrowly failing to reach the South Pole on the *Nimrod* expedition in early 1909 – but saving himself and his companions – Ernest Shackleton set his sights on an Antarctic crossing. The threat of a German expedition attempting the same journey helped Shackleton to raise funds, as nationalistic Britons sent in contributions to the 'first crossing of the last continent'. His plan was simple but ambitious: Shackleton would sail in *Endurance* to the Weddell Sea coast, establish a base, then trek across the continent via the South Pole. At the top of the Beardmore Glacier, the crossing party would be met by a group that had landed at Ross Island by *Aurora*, sailing from Hobart.

Even as *Endurance* prepared to sail, WWI was engulfing Europe. Britain declared war on Germany on 4 August 1914 and Shackleton immediately offered *Endurance* and her crew for service. Winston Churchill, then First Lord of the Admiralty, wired his thanks, but the expedition was told to proceed. *Endurance* sailed from Plymouth on 8 August 'to carry on our white warfare', as Shackleton put it. After calling at Madeira, Buenos Aires and South Georgia, the expedition pushed into the Weddell Sea pack and soon found itself squeezing through ever-narrower leads.

By 19 January 1915, *Endurance* was caught. The ship, inexorably crushed by the grinding ice floes, finally sank on 21 November. Shackleton and his men lived on the pack ice for five months before they sailed three small boats to uninhabited Elephant Island in the South Shetlands. Shackleton and five others then crossed 1300km of open sea in the 6m *James Caird* (which Henry McNeish, the ship's carpenter, had decked over with spare timbers) to seek help from the whalers at South Georgia. Departing on 24 April 1916 it took 16 exhausting days at sea, completing one of history's greatest feats of navigation.

---

necessary to rope up during this first part of the walk. From the top of the gap there are fine views back down over King Haakon Bay. From Shackleton Gap the route tracks over the featureless Murray Snowfields, climbing to around 500–550m to reach the first night's campsite before the Tridents.

DAY TWO – THE TRIDENTS TO FORTUNA GLACIER

The Tridents, a series of rocky peaks, marks the ridge between the Murray Snowfields and the Crean Glacier. It was here where the Shackleton party inspected the first two of the four saddles looking down onto the glacier before reluctantly opting for the fourth – they decided to simply slide down into the unknown. The smooth snowfield his party slid down is now more likely to be heavily crevassed so the quick 'human toboggan' ride down onto the glacier is no longer an option.

It's a long day's walk of 10 to 12 hours to climb up to the Tridents, descend onto the Crean Glacier and then climb up to the second night's campsite on the Fortuna Glacier. At the bottom of the descent from the Tridents the altitude is about 250m and from there the walk climbs back up to about 550m at the high point. The second night's camp can really be made anywhere across

the glacier; the further you get on the second day the less distance to be covered on the third. During the Falklands War two British Wessex helicopters crashed on the glacier; their remains may still be seen.

DAY THREE – FORTUNA GLACIER TO STROMNESS

From the second night's camp the walk continues across the Fortuna Glacier, which runs northeast towards the sea. A spur of the glacier turns off to the east and drops down to Fortuna Bay. It's a four- to five-hour descent from the campsite, across the glacier and then steadily down to sea level. At the start of the descent Shackleton thought they were on their way down to their goal, the station at Stromness. It was only when he remembered there was no glacier descending to Stromness Bay that he realised there was still one more bay to go. The glacier doesn't run all the way to the sea; even in November you leave the snow and start walking across bare ground before the coast. The walk edges around the bay, passing the large king penguin colony at the head of the bay and crossing the river running off the Konig Glacier. This will probably require taking shoes off and wading through icy water.

It takes about three hours to walk around the bay to the start of the walk up to the

Their landfall was at King Haakon Bay, on South Georgia's uninhabited southwest coast, and the whaling stations were on the island's northeast side. Although no-one had previously penetrated further than a kilometre or so from the coast, Shackleton decided to try to cross the island. With Tom Crean and Frank Worsley, he hiked for 36 straight hours across the mountains and crevassed glaciers to reach the whaling station at Stromness Harbour. As they neared the station, impassable ice cliffs forced them to lower themselves down an icy, 9m waterfall. Upon their arrival at the station, on 20 May 1916, their long beards, matted hair and ragged clothes caused the first people they met to flee in disgust.

At the home of the station manager, where they bathed and where they were fed and clothed, Shackleton asked, 'When was the war over?' 'The war is not over,' the manager answered. 'Millions are being killed. Europe is mad. The world is mad.'

That night a whaler was dispatched to pick up the three men left behind at King Haakon Bay. Over the next four months Shackleton led three failed rescue attempts to reach the 22 men still stranded on Elephant Island. He was finally able to pick them up with the help of the *Yelcho*, a steamer lent by the Chilean government, on 30 August 1916 – nearly two years after they initially departed from the UK. It was 10 January 1917 before Shackleton also retrieved the *Aurora* party via New Zealand. The war, meanwhile, raged on long enough for two of Shackleton's men to die in the fighting.

Shackleton himself lived to mount one final assault on the Antarctic, the ill-defined *Quest* expedition. Upon reaching South Georgia, he suffered a massive heart attack and died on 5 January 1922 aboard his ship, moored at Grytviken.

---

saddle between Fortuna Bay and Stromness Bay. It's a steady climb, first through tussock and then across bare ground (or patches of snowfield early in the season) to the top of the saddle at about 300m. A small tarn before the saddle may be covered with ice and snow early in the season. From this point the ruins of the Stromness whaling station will be clearly visible below, and early in the season the descent may start with a Shackleton-style 'bum slide' down a snowfield. It's wise to avoid the waterfall, which Shackleton's party climbed through on their descent, by sticking to the higher ground on the way down. The low ground can be soft and muddy, and at the end there is a small stream to cross.

The walk into the back of the whaling station passes the station cemetery. Early in the season be prepared for angry male fur seals attempting to block your path into the station and down to the beach (see p169). From Fortuna Bay, up and over the saddle and down to Stromness takes about two hours.

Wildlife Viewing

South Georgia's wildlife is amazingly varied and abundant (see p400) despite the incredible slaughter that took place just a century ago. Although fur seals have enjoyed a spectacular recovery whales are still

rare around South Georgia. It's estimated that South Georgia has a total population of more than 50 million birds. Two of the offshore islands – Annenkov Island and Bird Island – are designated as Sites of Special Scientific Interest (SSSI) where landings are not allowed without special permission. Cooper Island is even more restricted; it's a Specially Protected Area (SPA), where nobody is allowed to land – not even for scientific studies – in order to preserve the environment.

ALBATROSSES

South Georgia is estimated to have 100,000 pairs of black-browed albatrosses, 80,000 pairs of grey-headed albatrosses, 5000 to 7500 pairs of light-mantled sooty albatrosses and 4000 wandering albatrosses. It's the magnificent wanderers that for many visitors top the list. Watching wanderers soar in the stiff Antarctic winds or coming in to land on a remote island, looking like a fully laden, flaps-out 747, feeding their huge but downy chicks, or engaging in their exultant courtship displays, is an experience not to be missed. 'I now belong to a higher cult of human,' biologist Robert Cushman Murphy wrote in *Log Book for Grace: Whaling Brig Daisy 1912–13*, 'for I have seen the albatross.'

CONSERVATION GUIDELINES

The South Georgia government makes the following recommendations to visitors:

- Know your capabilities and also the dangers posed by South Georgia's environment, and act accordingly. Plan activities with safety in mind at all time.
- Take note of, and act on, the advice and instructions from your leaders. Do not stray from the group.
- Be prepared for severe and changeable weather. Ensure that your equipment and clothing are of sufficient strength and quality to withstand Antarctic conditions. Remember that South Georgia's weather is unpredictable, so when ashore be prepared for the worst, however pleasant it may seem when setting out.
- Be aware of the location of the designated SPA and SSSI. Entry into these areas is prohibited except by special permit.
- Do not walk on to glaciers or snowfields without proper equipment and experience: there is real danger of falling into hidden crevasses.
- Avoid walking on fragile vegetation. A footprint on a moss bank may remain there a long time; trampling of vegetation, especially in wet and peaty soils, can cause significant erosion over time. Moss beds and the margins of streams and lakes are particularly fragile.
- Do not collect native plants.
- Always give animals the right of way.

If permission is given for overnight stays ashore, then the following points should be observed:

- All shore parties must have immediate support from their expedition vessel: there are no search and rescue facilities in South Georgia.
- If you carry it in, you can carry it out. Return all rubbish to your vessel. This also applies to any camping, climbing and mountaineering equipment.
- Use portable stoves and ensure all fires are kept small and controlled so there is no danger of igniting the surrounding vegetation or peat.
- Take care to extinguish completely all cigarette butts and ash.
- Do not use soap or detergent in freshwater streams or ponds. Carry water to the campsite and drain it into absorbent soil.
- Dispose of toilet wastes either directly into the sea or by burying in a shallow hole well away from fresh water.

Unfortunately we may not continue to see albatrosses. Every year the albatross population falls by 1%. South Georgia has one-quarter of the world's wandering albatrosses and they're under as much stress here as anywhere else. Human visitors are certainly a danger and we need to take great care not to intrude on their nesting sites, but there are other great dangers: the exploding population of fur seals will inevitably put pressure on albatross habitat, but the biggest is longline fishing.

Longline fishing in Antarctic waters has increased rapidly in recent years and although the 'bycatch' of other aquatic species is far less than with trawling the bycatch of birds can be horrendous. As longline fishers bait the hooks and pay out their 100km-long fishing lines, following birds, albatrosses among them, swoop in to try and snatch the bait. Too often these magnificent birds will end up hooked, dragged underwater and drowned. One death leads to another because it takes full time work by two parents to feed one chick. An adult albatross drowned on a longline will inevitably lead to the death of its chick.

There are answers: streamers can be tied on to the longlines to scare birds off; sinkers can carry the baited lines quickly underwater and out of the birds' reach; new designs of deployment gear can ensure the hooked lines are carried underwater before they are released. Funding these changes and ensuring that longline fishing boats practice seabird-safe procedures is a challenging operation. One charity working to protect albatrosses is BirdLife's (www .birdlife.net) Save the Albatross Campaign, which is supported by a number of international bird protection organisations.

FUR SEALS
Apart from small populations, which managed to survive on Willis and Bird Islands, the sealers virtually wiped out South Georgia's fur seals. During the 1960s and '70s, the Antarctic fur seal population increased about 15% annually and is still increasing at 10% per annum. Today South Georgia probably has more than three million fur seals, more than 90% of the total world population. Found mainly on the northwest coast, the seals are so numerous that they present a hazard to Zodiacs trying to land during breeding season.

PENGUINS
More than 2.5 million breeding pairs of macaroni penguins nest on the island, congregating in huge colonies on steep slopes. There are large populations of king penguins at St Andrew's Bay and at Salisbury Plain in the Bay of Isles on the northwest coast. Over 100,000 pairs of gentoo penguins nest in small colonies on sheltered bays and fjords.

GETTING THERE & AWAY
Everyone who visits South Georgia, apart from a handful of people on yachts, will be on a cruise ship. For full information about ships and yachts, see the Transport chapter (p177).

ENTRY FEE

Visitors to South Georgia are charged a landing fee of £50 per person, and visits must be approved in advance. See p182 for more details. Every South Georgia visitor gets (in return for their entry fee) an information package, which includes *South Georgia* by Robert Burton (1997) – a handy little 32-page colour illustrated booklet.

GRYTVIKEN WHALING STATION

Grytviken means 'Pot Cove' and is named for the sealers' trypots that were discovered there. It is the best harbour in South Georgia and was chosen by the Norwegian Captain Carl Anton Larsen as the site of the first whaling station. The site was a good choice: it is on a bay within a bay, and so is very sheltered; there was sufficient flat land to build on (there's even the remains of a football pitch!); there was plenty of fresh water and the climate is probably the most benign on the island.

On 16 November 1904 Larsen arrived with a small fleet of ships and whaling started five weeks later. Huge profits were made but by the 1960s whales had become so rare that the station was no longer economically feasible. After the 1961–62 season it was subleased to a Japanese whaling company, which on 4 December 1964 also decided South Georgian whaling was finished. A caretaker remained at Grytviken until early 1971.

During Grytviken's first years only the blubber from the whale was utilised. Later, meat, bones and viscera were cooked to extract the oil, leaving bone- and meat-meal as important by-products. Elephant seal oil, an important contribution to the station economy, was also produced from bull elephant seals, which were shot and flensed on the beaches around South Georgia.

Life for the station workers was arduous. The 'season' ran from October to March, when the workers put in 12-hour days. As many as 300 worked here during the heyday of the industry. A few stayed over winter to maintain the boats and factory. Transport ships brought down coal, fuel oil, stores and food for the workers and took away the oil and other products. Attitudes towards whaling were very different a generation ago and whaling was a highly respectable profession among Norwegians.

Grytviken has been named as an ASTI (Area of Special Tourist Interest) along with the area between Cumberland East Bay and Cumberland West Bay, bounded by Moraine Fjord, Hamberg Glacier, Mt Sugartop and the Lyell Glacier.

INFORMATION

There is a post office at King Edward Point with a very English-looking mailbox. Postcards and stamps can also be bought at the museum and there is a post box there. The museum shop has T-shirts, sweatshirts, patches, woolly hats, souvenirs, postcards, slide sets and a surprisingly good selection of books and maps. US dollars, pounds sterling, Visa and MasterCard are accepted. Proceeds from sales assist further improvements to the museum.

SIGHTS

South Georgia Museum

The superb museum is housed in the former manager's villa. It was opened in 1992 and is supported by the South Georgia government. Material has been collected from Grytviken and other South Georgia whaling stations; exhibits illustrate the lives of the whalers, and the history of the island and its wildlife. There's even the projector and the old signboard from the station's cinema, which opened in 1930 and was finally flattened by a hurricane in 1994.

Whalers' Church

The typical Norwegian church is the only building at Grytviken that retains its original function. It was consecrated on Christmas Day 1913. Inside are memorials to Carl Anton Larsen and to Ernest Shackleton, whose funeral was held here. There are also two bells, which visitors are invited to ring. The church's wooden structure deteriorated over the years, and storm damage to the roof in 1994 prompted a major restoration. Note the remains of the ski jump on the hill behind the church and the football pitch on the left.

The first pastor, Kristen Löken, had to admit that 'religious life among the whal-

ers left much to be desired'. The church has been used for a few baptisms and marriages. The first baptism was on Christmas Day 1913, and 13 births have been registered on South Georgia. There have also been four marriages – the most recent in 1999 – but the church has been used more often for funerals.

The Old Station

The large open space between the two main jetties was the flensing plan. Whale carcasses were brought to the iron-plated whale slip at the base of the plan and hauled onto the plan by the whale winch. The 40-ton electric winch has been removed. The blubber was slit by flensers armed with hockey-stick-shaped flensing knives. Strips of blubber were ripped off the carcass, like the skin from a banana, by cables attached to steam winches, which you can still see.

The blubber went to the blubber cookery, the large building on the right of the plan, where it was minced and fed into huge pressure cookers. Each cooker held about 24 tons of blubber, which was cooked for approximately five hours to drive out the oil. The oil was piped to the separator house for purification by centrifuging. The separator house, and the generator house behind it, have been destroyed by fire but you can still see the separators in the ruins. Finally, the oil was pumped into tanks behind the station. If there was a good supply of whales, about 25 fin whales, each 18m long, could be processed in 24 hours. They would yield 1000 barrels (160 tons) of oil.

When the whale had been flensed, the meat, tongue and guts were cut off by the lemmers (the men who cut up the whales), drawn up the steep ramp on the left of the plan to the meat cookery and dropped into rotating cookers. The head and backbone were dragged up another ramp at the back of the plan to the bone cookery, where they were cut up with large steam saws and also cooked. After oil extraction, the remains of the meat and bone were dried and turned into guano for animal feed and fertilizer. In later years, meat extract was made by treatment with sulphuric acid in a plant next to the blubber cookery. Meat extract was used in dried soups and other prepared foods.

WARNING

Many parts of Grytviken are unsafe. In 2002–03 most of the station was marked off-limits and visitors could only walk around the outer periphery. Even if more of the station is open, do not enter buildings that are boarded up and marked as off-limits. Fire is a serious hazard – so smoking is forbidden.

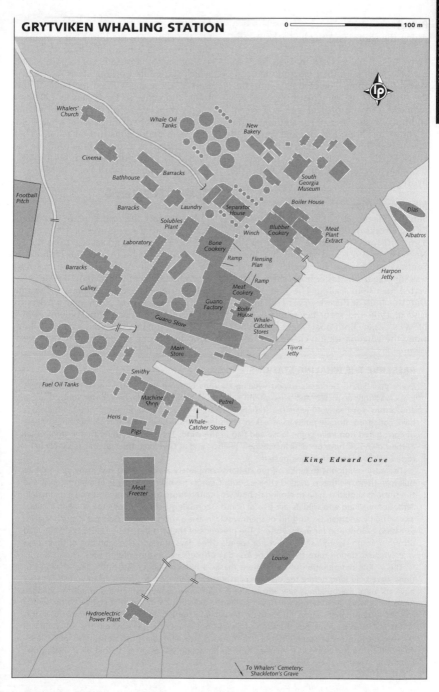

GRYTVIKEN WHALING STATION

0 [========] 100 m

Whalers' Church

Whale Oil Tanks

New Bakery

Cinema

Barracks

Bathhouse

South Georgia Museum

Football Pitch

Barracks

Laundry

Separator House

Boiler House

Solubles Plant

Blubber Cookery

Meat Plant Extract

Dias

Albatros

Laboratory

Bone Cookery

Winch

Barracks

Ramp

Flensing Plan

Harpon Jetty

Galley

Meat Cookery

Ramp

Guano Factory

Boiler House

Whale-Catcher Stores

Guano Store

Tijuca Jetty

Main Store

Smithy

Fuel Oil Tanks

Machine Shop

Petrel

Hens

Pigs

Whale-Catcher Stores

King Edward Cove

Meat Freezer

Louise

Hydroelectric Power Plant

To Whalers' Cemetery; Shackleton's Grave

Petrel

Along the shore, past the boiler house and guano store, is where the 35m, 245-ton *Petrel* lies. Built in Oslo in 1928, she was used for whaling until 1956 and then converted for sealing. The catwalk connecting the bridge to the gun platform has been removed and the present gun is a recent addition. In this area of the station are the engineering shops, foundry and smithy, all of which enabled the whalers to repair their boats. Further along the trail is the piggery, the meat freezer and, on the hillside, the hydroelectric power plant.

Albatros & Dias

Sunk beside the jetty in front of the museum lie the wrecks of the *Albatros* and *Dias*. The 33m, 210-ton *Albatros* was built at Sevlik, Norway, in 1921 and started her life at South Georgia as a whale catcher. When she was superseded by faster boats she was converted for use in sealing. The 33m, 167-ton *Dias* was built at Beverley near Hull in England in 1906 and spent her whole working life as a sealer. Both boats were abandoned when the whaling station closed.

Louise

On the shore are the burnt-out remains of the 53m, 1065-ton, wooden barque *Louise*, a sailing ship built in 1869 at Freeport, Maine, which started its working life as the *Jennie S Barker*. Later she worked the Baltic timber trade and came to Grytviken in 1904 as a supply ship. For a spell she provided accommodation at the whaling station while buildings were under construction ashore. Then she remained as a coaling hulk until she was burned as a training exercise by the UK's garrison at King Edward Point in 1987.

Whalers' Cemetery & Shackleton's Grave

This is mainly the resting place of whalers, but there are a few graves of 19th-century sealers. The oldest graves are from the *Esther*, which was hit by a typhus outbreak in 1846. A couple of those 1846 graves have reproductions of their memorial plates – the faded originals are on display in the museum. Nine graves of Norwegian whalers are the result of another typhus epidemic, which hit the station in 1912. The cemetery's abundant dandelions probably come from seeds

---

PRESERVE THE WHALING STATIONS

Every year South Georgia's ruined whaling stations become just a little more ruined. Access is increasingly restricted and a long-term solution is a major headache for the South Georgia authorities. For nearly 40 years the stations have been steadily deteriorating; wooden buildings have collapsed, storage tanks have leaked, abandoned ships have sunk at their moorings, sheets of corrugated iron have come loose and flap in the wind. The signs warning that visitors 'enter at their own risk' have become increasingly realistic and at Grytviken the station has simply been roped off and 'no entry' signs posted.

The easy solution is to fence off the stations completely and let them rust away or simply to bulldoze them. Neither is a good choice. South Georgia's whaling history is of great interest and the stations should remain to remind us how we hunted those great mammals to near extinction. Although walking and wildlife are two of South Georgia's great attractions the whaling stations are certainly another. Getting rid of them would make a trip to South Georgia a much less interesting proposition for many visitors. The presence of the whaling stations also takes the load off other South Georgia sites. If a visitor spends three days at island sites and one of those days is at whaling station ruins then it's one less day of pressure on the wildlife sites.

The visible deterioration of the stations masks a hidden danger: asbestos. The whaling stations were built long before the dangers of asbestos became known and a clean up will not only have to make the buildings safe and secure it will involve doing something about this danger. Reportedly work at Grytviken will have tackled the asbestos danger at that station by the end of the 2004–05 summer season. Cleaning up the whaling stations and making them safe for visitors is not going to be easy, but the stations should not simply be demolished. The SGSSI (British Dependent Territory of South Georgia & the South Sandwich Islands) administration gets £50 for every visitor to the island. If they want to keep attracting visitors they should be investing that money in a realistic long-term solution.

in the soil, some of which was imported from Norway to allow the dead whalers to be buried in a bit of home.

An impressive monument to one side of the little cemetery commemorates William Barlas, who had been deputy magistrate and then magistrate on the island for 21 years until 2 September 1941 when, his gravestone records, he was 'killed by an avalanche in the course of his duty'. The avalanche swept him off the path between Grytviken and King Edward Point and into the sea. The most recent grave is of the unfortunate Argentine Felix Artuso who was killed in a misunderstanding after the close of hostilities in 1982. His guards shot him when they thought he was making some sudden move to sabotage the submarine *Santa Fe;* he wasn't.

There are 65 graves in total, but it's that of Ernest Shackleton, at the back of the cemetery, which gets the most attention. He died on 5 January 1922 aboard his ship *Quest* moored in King Edward Cove. His granite stone bears the nine-pointed star that he used as a personal symbol. On the reverse of the stone is one of Shackleton's favourite quotations, from the poet Robert Browning: 'I hold that a man should strive to the uttermost for his life's set prize'.

The cross on the hillside above commemorates Walter Slossarczyk of the *Deutschland* expedition. He went missing from a rowboat in Cumberland Bay in 1911. A path leads to the cross, a good location for taking photographs of Grytviken. Finally, even higher up the hill, directly behind the cemetery, is a cross for the 17 men from a crew of 38 who died when the South African fishing vessel *Sudur Havid* sank off South Georgia during a storm on 6 June 1998. Most of the deaths were from exposure.

King Edward Point

Around the bay from the museum is the settlement at King Edward Point. The settlement was originally established in 1912 as a civil administration headquarters for the island while the Falkland Islands Dependencies Survey established a new base at King Edward Point in 1949–50. After the 1982 Falklands War the British military forces were based here, but in 2001 the last military personnel departed and the British Antarctic Survey (BAS), based on Bird Island since

1982, moved back to King Edward Point in a new building. Some of the older buildings were demolished at that time although the settlement's historic jail is still standing.

NORTH COAST & OFFSHORE ISLANDS

All the whaling stations are on the north coast of South Georgia – there are more sheltered bays, fjords and harbours along this coast and the weather is more benign. The less protected south coast is subject to icy blasts direct from the Antarctic continent, while the north coast is protected from these onslaughts by the central mountains.

SHAG ROCKS

These dramatically pointed rocks rise from the ocean 250km northwest of the main island in two distinct groups, each of three rocks. The highest point reaches 71m above sea level. The rocks take their name from the resident population of blue-eyed shags (cormorants). The Spanish vessel *Aurora* probably discovered the rocks in 1762, 'probably' because they didn't chart them very accurately. Although whalers and sealers knew of them and took precautions to avoid them, it was not until 1920 that they were charted with accuracy and not until 1956 was the first landing made (by an Argentine helicopter from the *Bahía Aguirre*).

About 18km east of Shag Rocks is Black Rock, which protrudes only 3m above the surface. In early 2003 A43B, a huge tabular iceberg measuring 74km by 24km grounded on the continental shelf between Shag and Black Rocks and the main island. Icebergs this big can take years to break up or melt down. In *The Island of South Georgia* Robert Headland tells of the 65km by 38km iceberg, which passed through this area in 1978, having been 'tracked by satellite for 15 years in the Weddell Sea'!

WILLIS ISLANDS

Shag Rocks are really an isolated outlier from South Georgia and the first real offshore islands to the west are the Willis Islands, named after Cook's midshipman Thomas Willis. It was Willis, described as a 'wild and drinking midshipman', who made the first sighting on 14 January 1775. Rising out of the sea to an altitude of 551m, the highest point on Main Island would certainly be hard to miss. Also in the group are Trinity Island, Verdant Island and several smaller islands, all separated from Bird Island by the Stewart Strait. Remarkably these islands have no permanent snow or ice.

The Willis Islands were some of the limited number of offshore islands where remnants of South Georgia's once flourishing fur seal population survived after the savage blitz by the late 18th- and early 19th-century sealers. In recent years fur seals have recolonised the main island with dramatic success although, perhaps surprisingly, there are not great numbers of them here. Like other offshore islands the group is free of rats and as a result is home to burrowing and ground-nesting birds, such as small petrels and prions; and South Georgia's unique pipit, which has been devastated on the main island by this accidentally introduced predator.

Albatrosses also nest on the Willis Islands, including 34,000 pairs of black-browed albatrosses, a third of South Georgia's total population. About 25,000 pairs of South Georgia's 80,000 grey-headed albatross are also found on these islands. The Willis Islands are also home to perhaps half of South Georgia's 2.5 million pairs of macaroni penguins.

BIRD ISLAND

From Willis Island Captain Cook continued past Bird Island, which he named 'on account of the vast numbers that were upon it.' His description still holds true: this is one of South Georgia's most important bird breeding sites, with 27 of South Georgia's 31 breeding species found here. In particular, Bird Island is home to more than 1000 pairs of wandering albatrosses, which breed here each year. Since it takes the gigantic wandering albatross more than a year to raise a chick, they breed (at the most) only every two years; this means that even greater numbers of this most impressive bird call Bird Island home.

In addition there are larger numbers of the smaller, but still impressively large, black-browed albatross (15,000 pairs) and grey-headed albatross (12,000 pairs). Bird Island has about 500 pairs of southern giant

petrels, 10% of South Georgia's total. There are about 50,000 macaroni penguins and the island is also home to gentoo penguins, although their population has been decreasing in recent years. Rats are not present on Bird Island and this has protected the smaller species, including the South Georgia pipit, but increasing numbers of fur seals and the damage they do to tussock has reduced the habitat available to blue petrels.

The density of birdlife, the number of wandering albatrosses and the fur seal population have inspired a great deal of scientific research on Bird Island, starting with US funded projects in the late 1950s. A scientific station was established on the island in 1962 and there have been projects running here almost every year since. Between 1959 and 1962 a great number of Bird Island's wandering albatrosses were ringed, a project that proved what an extraordinary range they wandered over.

One peripatetic bird was ringed on Bird Island during the 1958–59 summer season and then seemed to bounce back and forth between South Georgia and Australia – a round trip of over 20,000 km – annually for the next four years. In 1961 75 wandering albatrosses were dyed pink, prompting a great deal of head scratching by birdwatchers far from South Georgia.

Bird Island is categorised as an SSSI and as a result landings are not permitted without special permission. The island rises to a high point of 365m and is separated from the main island by Bird Sound; its north coast is mainly cliffs falling straight into the sea but there are beaches along the south coast.

ELSEHUL

Elsehul is separated from Undine Harbour on the south coast by a narrow isthmus; like Undine Harbour, Elsehul is one of South Georgia's main breeding grounds for fur seals. During the November to March breeding season the beach will be so crowded with aggressive male seals that landings are, to say the least, inadvisable (see p169). Of course there are great views from offshore and cruising past to observe the hectic activity on the beach and rocks is a favourite Zodiac pastime.

Macaroni penguins congregate on the slopes above the beach while petrels and smaller albatrosses also nest here.

RIGHT WHALE BAY

The fur seal 'problem' is also clearly evident at the height of the breeding season at Right Whale Bay, but the beach is long enough and the real estate behind the beach extensive enough that a landing should be possible. There often seems to be the odd blonde fur seal standing out from the masses at this typically jam-packed fur seal beach. A large king penguin colony extends back from the beach at the eastern end of the bay and there are smaller groups of king penguins and small groups of gentoos dotted around the bay; all of them often look perplexed about threading a way through the fur seal blockade.

Once you've found your own way through the seals' line of defence (see p169) a wide moraine outflow leads back up towards the snowfield leading to the Ernesto Pass. It makes a pleasant walk up from the busy beach.

WELCOME ISLETS

From Right Whale Bay or from ships approaching from the Bay of Isles the hole in the rock – described on marine charts as a 'natural arch' – is an easy identifier for this cluster of rocks rising from the ocean. The highest point in the cluster is 88m but except in ideal conditions it's hard to land here. From Zodiacs it's possible to spot macaroni penguins, blue-eyed cormorants and, inevitably, fur seals.

BAY OF ISLES

The area between Cape Buller and Cape Wilson, and inland to the height of the land, along with all the islands and rocks in the

---

CULL FUR SEALS?

Captain Cook can take some of the blame for the decline of the fur seal. His casual mention in the log of his 1775 visit to the island that there were plenty of fur seals around South Georgia inspired the sealing onslaught that followed. Fur seal skins found a ready market and by 1820 sealers had virtually wiped them out. Benjamin Morrell, writing of a visit in 1822, claimed that he had circled the entire island without finding a single seal.

In fact, remnant populations survived at isolated Willis and Bird Islands to the west and Cooper Island to the east. Well over a century passed and fur seal numbers had still not recovered from those late 18th- and early 19th-century depredations until suddenly, in the 1960s, the population began to explode. Every year the fur seal population of South Georgia – which is more or less the fur seal population of the world, more than 90% of them are found right here   grew by 10%. It's still growing at that rate and fur seal colonies are spreading from the two ends of the island towards the centre. Given that so many beaches are crowded with fur seals standing flipper to flipper it's remarkable that until 1977 a log was kept at King Edward Point for fur seal sightings. In *Antarctic Housewife* Nan Brown records how seeing a fur seal in the mid-50s was an event.

So what's the problem? Mankind nearly wiped them out, now they're back to being three million strong and growing rapidly; nothing wrong with that? Well, from the South Georgia visitor's point of view fur seals are an incredible annoyance. At many beaches during the breeding season getting ashore means running a gauntlet of foul-breathed, barking, threatening, stroppy fur seals. Male ('bull') fur seals that is, all convinced that these Zodiac-transported arrivals are intent on stealing the female ('cow') fur seals they've been so zealously protecting – that is to say, herding together for future mating purposes.

So big deal, surely tourists can live with difficult beach access? In fact, the fur seal population explosion affects more than just tourists. Seal hordes are flattening countless acres of fragile vegetation, hampering penguins getting to and from their colonies and, on Albatross Island, potentially threatening a really endangered species. While fur seal populations are zooming up by 10% a year the wandering albatross is declining by 1%, much of the decline pegged to birds entangled by longline fishing boats. Albatross Island has an overcrowded fur seal population and as the struggle for a few square metres of territory becomes more intense the breeding seals are pushing further and further back from the water's edge. Already you can encounter seals more than 100m above sea level on the 279m-high island. Pretty soon they may be encroaching on the nesting grounds of those very threatened wandering albatrosses.

Anyone for a fur seal cull?

bay, has been designated as the Bay of Isles ASTI. One of the most popular regions of South Georgia, the wide bay has a number of interesting landing sites including Albatross and Prion Islets, two important bird breeding grounds since they are rat free. Both of them have nesting sites for wandering albatrosses and giant petrels. There are also large populations of pipits on both islands.

Permits are required for landing on these two islets and must be applied for at least 60 days ahead. There are only four designated landing areas on Albatross Islet and just one on Prion; no more than one ship is allowed to land per day; visitors cannot number more than 65, must not stay more than four hours and must visit in groups of no more than 12, each led by a group leader. Visitors must not approach closer than 10m to an albatross or closer than 25m when albatrosses are going through their courtship rituals and displays. In fact, if you sit very quietly and still it's quite possible an albatross may come over to inspect you, and perhaps gently prod you with its huge bill.

In all there are about a dozen islands, islets and stacks in the bay. Of South Georgia's 31 breeding bird species, 17 are found here.

Salisbury Plain

Behind the landing beach stretches Salisbury Plain, a huge, flat expanse of green spreading out in front of the Grace Glacier. On the east side of the plain a hill rises above a massive colony of king penguins – it's been estimated at anything from 25,000 to 50,000 pairs and seems to have been growing in recent years. You can wander into the edges of the colony or climb the tussock-covered hillside to enjoy wonderful views. From a distance the huge mass of penguins makes patterns, the grey, black and white of the adults swirled through by the brown of their chicks. Sometimes the chicks' crèches are simply wavy swirls, other times they gather in circles. From the hillside don't only look down on the penguin colony: the views back towards the mountains or north to Albatross and Prion Islets and the numerous other islands that have given the bay its name, are also spectacular.

Fur seals also stake out their territories along the beach in increasingly large numbers and, as usual, they can make landing and walking back from the beach a challenging affair during the breeding season (see p169).

There are also smaller numbers of elephant seals. Surf and high winds can sometimes make landings difficult at Salisbury Plain.

Rosita Harbour

Although a licence for a whaling station at Rosita Harbour was held from 1909 to 1923 no station was ever built; the two whale catchers permitted by the lease were operated out of Leith Harbour. Rosita Harbour was known at first as Allardyce Harbour.

Albatross & Prion Islets

So long as fur seals don't make it impossible to land these islands are good places to see wandering albatrosses and their nests. Both islands are rat free so they are among the few places in South Georgia where pipits and burrowing seabirds can survive. Visitors are required to take great care not to introduce rats, although it's highly unlikely a modern cruise ship would have rats aboard and you would certainly notice any rats in your Zodiac! Visitors must also take care not to walk over seabird burrows and risk collapsing the tunnels, and there are very specific requirements for watching the albatrosses (see p168).

On Albatross Islet about 150 albatross pairs nest at the top of the island while on Prion Islet there are about 50 pairs. Their nests are interspersed with giant petrel nests, birds that in their own right look very large but are dwarfed by their neighbours. With a wingspan of up to 3.5m a wandering albatross makes anything else that flies look small. You may see albatrosses sitting on their eggs, sitting expectantly on a nest waiting for a mate, or a chick waiting for a returning parent to feed it. Both parents may be away for eight to 10 days at a time, leaving the chick to fend for itself. Ungainly chicks stand in the wind, practising their wing- flapping for that first big take-off and the departure for an initial flight that can last for years. Watching the dignified and intricate courting and display rituals between pairs of wandering albatrosses is another feature that makes a visit to these islands a very special occasion.

Albatross Island's big problem is fur seals. They've taken over the sandy isthmus where expedition ship Zodiacs try to land and, during the mating season, growl and roar at every intruder (see p169). As their population increases they are also moving further and further inland and up, potentially threatening the albatrosses' nesting sites. In November, when the pregnant fur seal cows have returned and given birth, the scene on the beach is completely chaotic. The angry bulls threaten each other just as fiercely as visiting humans, their harem of cows gathering round them in a tight circle with the pretty little black pups spilling over them. A newborn seal pup emerges into this world of noise and confusion, probably with a waiting skua trying to carry off the afterbirth. It's hardly surprising they're soon growling threateningly, just like the adults.

PRINCE OLAV HARBOUR

Just outside the mouth of Possession Bay a factory whaling station was in operation from 1911 to 1916. It became a shore station for the 1917–18 season, continuing that way until 1931. Although the South Georgia Company took up the expired lease in 1936 it was only in order to salvage equipment from the site. Interestingly this could have been the target for Shackleton's 1916 trek across South Georgia, rather than the much longer walk he did to the Stromness station. Shackleton thought the station would have closed down for the winter when he set out on his epic walk.

The *Brutus* was deliberately beached at Prince Olav Harbour to serve as a coaling hulk. Built in Glasgow in 1883 the 76m-long, 1700-ton, iron-hulled, three-masted sailing vessel started life as the *Sierra Pedrosa* and was towed here from Cape Town. After the station was abandoned in 1931 the ship was blown ashore in a storm. Brutus Island, just offshore in the harbour, is named after her.

Prince Olav Harbour's fur seals have a reputation for being particularly bad tempered, making Zodiac landings very interesting (see p169).

POSSESSION BAY

It was here that Captain Cook landed on 17 January 1775 and took possession of the island. He described his majesty's newest possession in less than glowing terms in the log book from his second voyage (1772–75):

The head of the Bay…was terminated by a huge Mass of Snow and ice of vast extent, it shewed a perpendicular clift of considerable height, just like

the side or face of an ice isle; pieces were continually breaking from them and floating out to sea. A great fall happened while we were in the Bay; it made a noise like Cannon. The inner parts of the Country was not less savage and horrible…the wild rocks raised their lofty summits until they were lost in the clouds, and the valleys lay buried in everlasting snow. Not a tree was to be seen nor a shrub even big enough to make a tooth-pick.

Possession Bay is not very well charted so visiting ships treat it with some trepidation. A fine glacier tumbles into the bay on the southeast corner, occasionally calving icebergs into the bay's waters.

FORTUNA BAY

Shackleton's party descended from the Fortuna Glacier on to the west side of the bay, followed the edge of the bay round to the east side and then climbed up over the saddle to drop down to the Stromness whaling station on Stromness Bay. There's a large king penguin colony at the head of the bay, backed up by the usual collection of elephant seals and fur seals.

STROMNESS BAY

Three whaling stations – Leith Harbour, Stromness and Husvik – were established in Stromness Bay and a rough track along the beach connected the three stations. During the whaling era the Leith Harbour station had a cinema and whalers would follow the track round from Stromness to catch an evening movie.

Hercules Bay

There is a large and very easily accessed macaroni penguin colony at this smaller bay at the entrance to Stromness Bay.

Leith Harbour

The whaling station at Leith Harbour opened in 1909 and from 1912 to 1918 also operated floating factories. There were no operations in the 1932–33 and 1940–41 seasons and from 1943 to 1945, before the station closed completely after the 1960–61 season. For the 1963–64 season it was subleased to a Japanese whaling company for four seasons but on 15 December 1965 it too admitted defeat; operation was no long economically feasible and South Georgia's whaling history came to a close. A caretaker stayed on for just one more month before the station was completely abandoned.

The Leith site, tightly squeezed up against a cliff face, presented some problems during its operating life. In 1911 an avalanche wrecked a couple of buildings, sweeping several of them into the sea. A repeat performance in 1929 killed the station's blacksmith and his two assistants.

Stromness

The abandoned whaling station at Stromness is a surreal site, like a ghost town taken over by seals. A great many aggressive fur seals and rather less touchy elephant seals have staked out the beach and taken up positions all around the town, even moving inside some of the buildings and occupying the cemetery. As a result Stromness can be something of an obstacle course (see p169).

Stromness was originally intended to be a floating factory site in 1906–07 but the opening was delayed when the mother ship was wrecked. Eventually a shore station commenced operation in 1913, but in 1931 the station was converted to a ship repair yard and for the rest of its life was an adjunct to the other South Georgia stations. There's a collection of propellers just south of the 'no entry' sign. With the winding down of whaling at the beginning of the 1960s it closed for good after the 1960–61 whaling season.

The station is best known for Shackleton's famous arrival at the manager's villa. The boarded up house is at the south end of the settlement and beside the front door, which faces away from the sea, a plaque briefly recounts the dramatic events. The old house is still in fairly good condition, including the bath tub in which Shackleton and his companions took their first bath in many months. Funds are being raised to eventually restore the historic building.

Grass Island

Not far offshore in Stromness Bay is Grass Island, a site of particular interest because brown rats were successfully exterminated here (with New Zealand expertise) in late 2000. Of course, there is always the danger that they could cross back if ice extends from the main island during winter, but the

successful elimination of rats, even on one small island, is cause for celebration.

Husvik

The whaling station at Husvik started as a floating factory site in 1907 and continued to operate in that fashion until 1913, although it also commenced as a shore operation in 1910. There were several interruptions over the years, including a complete shutdown after the 1930–31 season, until it reopened after WWII for the 1945–46 season. The station finally closed in 1960 and much of the equipment was dismantled and moved to Grytviken.

The station buildings are now very dilapidated although the BAS sometimes uses the old manager's villa as a field station during the summer months. Elephant seal, king penguin, insect and vegetation research is carried out here on the area from Fortuna Bay to Cumberland West Bay.

Husvik has a 'shipwreck' sitting securely on the slipway. The 32m, 179-ton *Karrakatta* was built in 1912 in Oslo. She was hauled out of the water for her coal-fired boiler to provide steam to power an adjacent engineering workshop. The boiler wasn't even removed from the boat; a hole was simply cut in her side and a steam pipe connected to the workshop.

Dammed by the Neumayer Glacier, the Gulbrandsen Lake near Husvik is one of the largest and most spectacular lakes on the island. Icebergs sometimes float across its surface and 12 terraces around the lake mark earlier water levels.

CUMBERLAND BAY

Cumberland Bay subdivides into Cumberland Bay West and Cumberland Bay East. Grytviken and the adjacent scientific and administration centre at King Edward Point lie on King Edward Cove, which leads off Cumberland Bay East.

Thatcher Peninsula

Many people might prefer to call it something else, but officially the spit of land separating the two Cumberland Bays is now named after the ex-British prime minister. Grytviken and King Edward Point are both on the peninsula along with the Hamberg Lakes and numerous streams and tarns. The Hamberg and Lyell Glaciers, dropping from the 2323m Mt Sugartop, mark the southern boundary of the 10km long peninsula. There are a surprisingly small number of fur seals on the peninsula and no reindeer, but plenty of rats. Despite the presence of that most harmful introduced species, and the fact that this is the part of South Georgia with the most intrusive human presence, there is still a great deal of wildlife and the peninsula's system of streams and lakes ensures that this is the best freshwater habitat on the island.

Hestesletten

Just south of King Edward Cove this is the only rival to Salisbury Plain as a flat area. The name translates as Horse Plain, named after the horses that were released here by the South Georgia Exploration Company in 1905. Some Manchurian ponies were also left here by an expedition in 1912 but neither group survived. The plain is backed by the Hamberg Lakes.

On 25 April 1982 British Royal Marines landed here to advance upon the Argentine forces at King Edward Point. The Argentines surrendered later that day.

GODTHUL

This whaling station had only a small land base to support a floating factory site. It operated from 1908 to 1929 with a four year interruption from the end of the 1916–17 season to the beginning of the 1922–23 season. Godthul lies between Cumberland East Bay and Ocean Harbour.

OCEAN HARBOUR

Known until 1955 as New Fortune Bay, the station commenced in 1909 but in 1920 the leaseholder amalgamated with Sandefjords Hvalfangerselskab and almost everything at the site was taken to that operator's station at Stromness. Old sealing trypots can still be seen at the site along with the toppled narrow gauge locomotive used in the whaling station. Ocean Harbour's other notable relic of the sealing and whaling era is the wreck of the *Bayard*, a 67m-long, 1300-ton, iron-hulled, three-masted sailing vessel built in 1864. The *Bayard* was moored at the station's coaling pier in 1911 when high winds tore her loose and swept her across the harbour, where she grounded.

The station's cemetery has the grave of Frank Cabrail, the steward of the sealer *Fran-*

cis Allen, who died on 14 October 1820. It's the oldest recorded grave on South Georgia, but the marker has gone and it is no longer known which of the eight graves it is.

ST ANDREW'S BAY

South Georgia's largest king penguin colony is here with more than 100,000 birds congregated on the gravel beach at the foot of the retreating Ross Glacier. In October and November breeding elephant seals can restrict access to the beach (see p169), so landing at the river edges may be easier. In any case, high surf can make landings difficult. The 481m peak of Mt Skittle overlooks the 3km-long beach from the north; the Hearney and Cook Glaciers tumble down to the bay.

ROYAL BAY

During the International Polar Year programme of 1882–83 a German expedition spent over a year here carrying out research projects. The group came on the *Moltke*, the first powered vessel to reach South Georgia. Moltke Harbour on Royal Bay is named after the ship. The foundations of the eight buildings at their site can still be traced. King and gentoo penguins and blue-eyed cormorants all breed at Royal Bay.

GOLD HARBOUR

Blending an exceptional variety of wildlife with some really fabulous scenery, Gold Harbour has huge numbers of king penguins along the beach, interspersed with smaller numbers of gentoos. The large numbers of elephant seals includes, at the end of the breeding season, a pup kindergarten at the western end of the beach where a glacial stream runs down into the sea. Fortunately fur seals are not present in such large numbers as at many other South Georgia beaches. The bay is overhung by the huge hanging Bertrab Glacier, while the headland overlooking the beach from the western end is a good place to look for nesting light-mantled sooty albatrosses.

COOPER BAY

Towards the southeast end of the island this bay has separate colonies of chinstrap and macaroni penguins. However, swells can make landings problematic on the beach at the chinstrap colony. Fur seals, elephant seals and giant petrels also breed here; the fur seals may make visits difficult (see p169).

COOPER ISLAND

Named after James Pallisser Cooper, Captain Cook's first lieutenant on his 1775 visit on the *Resolution*, Cooper Island is South Georgia's only SPA. The exceptional variety of breeding birds on this rat-free and tussock-covered island includes snow petrels, Antarctic prions and white-chinned petrels. There are also 12,000 pairs of black-browed albatrosses and 20,000 pairs of macaroni penguins; and the inevitable fur seal colony. This was one of the few places where fur seals survived the destruction of the sealing era. This is one of South Georgia's limited sites for chinstrap penguins.

The island rises to 416m at its highest point and there is permanent snow or ice on the high points.

DRYGALSKI FJORD & LARSEN HARBOUR

At the extreme southeast end of the island the wildlife includes a small Weddell seal colony in Larsen Harbour. This area is rat free and as a result birds like the South Georgia pipit and smaller burrowing petrels and prions, which are usually threatened by rats, may be seen. The mountain peaks tumble sheer into the bay and the glaciers calve icebergs into the bay's waters. It's a scene very reminiscent of the Antarctic Peninsula.

The southwest tip of the island was named Cape Disappointment by Captain Cook – his hope that he might have touched upon the southern continent turned to disappointment when he rounded this cape and decided it was just another island.

SOUTH COAST & OFFSHORE ISLANDS

UNDINE HARBOUR

Close to the western end of South Georgia and separated from Elsehul on the north coast by a narrow isthmus, Undine Harbour is another main breeding ground for fur seals. Landings are inadvisable during the November to March breeding season, but there are great views of the activity from offshore.

KING HAAKON BAY

This bay on the south side of the island's northwest corner is famous as the starting point for Shackleton's epic walk; the waters are poorly charted and boats entering the bay must take great care.

Cave Cove

Just inside the entrance to the bay, on its south side near Cape Rosa, is the tiny cove where Shackleton's party landed the *James Caird* at the end of their epic voyage from Elephant Island. Today fur seals are likely to put up some opposition to your landing, while elephant seals gaze on nonchalantly. Above the small niche in the rock face, where the men sheltered, a plaque recounts the historic arrival. It's possible to climb up the hillside to a fine view down on the cove and, in the opposite direction, out to sea. Giant petrels nest along the top, skuas skulk around while ducks float on the small tarn visible from the top.

After their landing on 10 May 1916 Shackleton and his men rested for five days, feasting on albatross. 'We have not been as comfortable for the last five weeks,' wrote Henry McNeish, the carpenter. 'We had 3 young & 1 old albatross for lunch with 1 pint of gravy which beets all the chicken soup I ever tasted.' When they arrived in the cove they had run out of drinking water and their first action was to throw themselves face first into the stream, which still trickles into the sea. On that first night in the cove, when they were still too weak to manhandle their boat ashore, swells tore off the rudder. Days later they were about to jury rig a rudder when, to their amazement, the original rudder floated through the narrow entrance to the cove.

Peggotty Camp

From Cave Cove the Shackleton party sailed up King Haakon Bay and made camp at the top of the bay. Here they stayed for another four days, waiting impatiently for good weather before Shackleton, Worsley and Crean set off on their epic voyage. Sheltering under the overturned *James Caird* they named the site Peggotty Camp after the poor but honest family in Charles Dickens' *David Copperfield* (who also sheltered in a home fashioned out of a beached boat). While waiting, McNeish extracted screws from the boat and set them in the walkers' shoes to help them cross the icy glaciers.

King penguins, fur seals and elephant seals inhabit the beach at Peggotty Camp. Peggotty Bluff is the dark bluff at the end of the beach, beyond the snout of the glacier.

UNDINE SOUTH HARBOUR

The Brogger Glacier tumbles down to the sea at the wide expanse of Undine South Harbour.

Ducloz Head

Between 1951 and 1957 Duncan Carse led four surveying expeditions into the inland areas and much of today's mapping is still based on his pioneering work. Despite those earlier visits his most extraordinary stay was in 1961. Carse wanted to experiment with living alone and in complete isolation, and became an Antarctic Robinson Crusoe when he was dropped off at Ducloz Head near Undine South Harbour. He had been given a lease on 4 hectares of land at a token rent of one shilling a year. Clearly sensing a bargain he paid the rent in advance for 10 years. On 23 February HMS *Owen* dropped him off, along with 12 tons of supplies, including a prefabricated hut which was assembled well back in the tussock in a sheltered cove.

HMS *Owen* dropped by again in early April to check on his wellbeing, but on 20 May a freak surge wave washed most of his supplies and the hut (along with Carse, fast asleep inside) into the sea. Remarkably he escaped and salvaged enough of his equipment to survive through the winter until he was rescued by a sealing ship, 116 days later.

Carse, clearly a man of many talents, was the voice of Dick Barton, special agent, from 1949 to 1951. This BBC radio serial ran for 711 episodes and in those pre-TV days just after the war it was enormously popular. At its peak it's estimated that it had an audience of 15 million, virtually every third person in the UK! Later he was the front man for the TV series *Travellers in Time*. Mt Carse, at 2331m the third highest point on the island, is named after him.

Mt Paget

South Georgia's highest mountain, 2934m Mt Paget, stands directly south of Grytviken,

but it's much closer to Undine South Harbour on the south coast. It's clearly visible from Grytviken and King Edward Point. A Combined Services Expedition from the British military made the first successful ascent on 30 December 1964.

ANNENKOV ISLAND

One of the sadly limited number of rat-free islands around South Georgia, Annenkov was originally named Pickersgill by Captain Cook on his 1775 visit to the island. It was renamed by the Russian explorer Thaddeus Bellingshausen after his 1819 visit on board the *Vostok* as part of his epic Antarctic explorations. He was no more impressed than Cook, commenting that there was, 'not a single shrub nor any vegetation'. Although he did not realise it, Bellingshausen was probably the first explorer to actually sight the Antarctic continent. The name Pickersgill was transferred to a group of smaller islands slightly to the east of Annenkov.

The island has 17,500 pairs of black-browed albatrosses and is one of South Georgia's three main wandering albatross breeding sites, with about 500 pairs. There are about 10,000 macaroni penguin pairs along with southern giant petrels and a variety of smaller petrels, fairy prions and the South Georgia pipit and pintail. Elephant seals are found on the island's beaches.

Annenkov lies 15km south of the main island and rises to Olstad Peak (650m) at its highest point. It's one of the few places in South Georgia with fossils and, like Bird Island, is an SSSI where landings are not permitted without special permission.

CLERKE ROCKS

Some 70km southeast of the main island, Clerke Rocks, like Shag Rocks, consists of two distinct groups. Also like Shag Rocks it is shags (cormorants) that are the principal residents. The rocks stretch over 11km with a highest point 244m above sea level. The rocks were named after Lieutenant Charles Clerke on board Captain Cook's ship *Resolution* when it passed by in 1775. The first landing was from the ship RRS *Shackleton* in 1961.

Directory

CONTENTS

ACCOMMODATION

Accommodation in the Falklands is limited and at times can be hard to find. It's wise to book ahead, particularly on the outer islands. Stanley is the only place with a real choice, ranging from B&Bs and guesthouses to two hotels. Despite all the housing construction, the Falklands suffer from a chronic housing shortage and rental housing is difficult to find.

Away from Stanley, the Port Howard Lodge in West Falkland and the Pebble Island Hotel function much like small hotels; in other settlements the possibilities range from rooms in the main farm building to specialised island resorts, such as that found on Sea Lion Island. Self-catering cottages are popular, and include traditional old farm cottages (Saunders Island or Carcass Island), attractively modernised old cottages (Darwin) or even brand new units (Bleaker Island). 'Self-catering' means that you cook for yourself – a particularly popular option

PRACTICALITIES

- Electricity: 220/240 volts, 50 cycles; plugs are identical to those in the UK
- Newspapers & Magazines: The weekly *Penguin News* is an intriguing insight into local events and concerns; the annual *Falkland Islands Journal* collects an interesting variety of articles, reports and reviews about the islands.
- Weights & Measures: Metric system

with Stanley residents when taking a break in camp. Self-catering doesn't necessarily mean you have to zip around the Stanley supermarkets before you head out to the airport: for an extra charge you can often take your meals in the main house. Alternatively, you can arrange with Stanley travel agents to have supplies sent along or you can buy supplies from small settlement shops.

More spartan accommodation is available at some locations, including 'Portakabins' – shipping containers fitted with doors and windows and once used by the military as temporary accommodation. The Portakabin at The Neck on Saunders Island gives wildlife enthusiasts the opportunity to stay right beside large penguin colonies.

In areas not frequented by tourists, islanders often welcome house guests. Many farms have 'outside houses', formerly used by shepherds working away from the main settlement, where visitors may stay with permission. Some are very comfortable, if a bit old; others are very run-down.

Camping in the Falklands is only possible with permission from the landowner. There are no organised camping sites and, even where camping is allowed, you often need to be completely self-sufficient. In Stanley it's possible to camp in the garden at Kay's B&B or at Scotia House, while elsewhere on East Falkland you can camp at Estancia, Fitzroy, Goose Green, North Arm, Port Sussex, Rincon Grande and Walker Creek. On West Falkland you can camp at Bold Cove, Port Stephens, Spring Point and West Lagoon. You can also camp on Saunders Island.

ACTIVITIES
Fishing

Fly-fishing is very popular and many visitors come specifically to fish the Falkland rivers. Sea trout are the Falklands fish of choice although mullet, a good eating fish, are also pursued. So what are sea trout? Brown trout that go to sea is the simple answer; if they stick to life in freshwater rivers they're brown trout, if they venture out into saltwater they're sea trout.

Brown or sea, the first *Salmo trutta* didn't arrive in the Falklands until 1940. When Charles Darwin visited the Falklands in 1833 and 1834 he noted two local freshwater fish: *Aplochiton zebra*, known locally as zebra trout, and *Galaxius maculatus*, a minnow. At that time the zebra trout was widespread, not only in Falklands rivers but also in some of the islands' many freshwater lakes and ponds. In 1939, just before the outbreak of WWII, rainbow trout, brown trout and American brook trout had all been introduced to rivers in Tierra del Fuego in South America, a move which inspired thoughts of similar introductions to the Falklands. In 1940 small numbers of all three trout types were brought over from Chile and released in the Falklands. The records of what was released where were subsequently lost, although it appears only the brown trout did well.

After WWII more introductions were made from Chile and from Britain, although again the records were remarkably imprecise. Nevertheless, by the early 1950s Falkland anglers began to find brown trout, rather than the smaller zebra trout, on their hooks. As the years passed, the fish began to get so large that it was clear they were leaving their river homes for the richer nourishment to be found at sea: the brown trout had become sea trout.

Today the size of the sea trout (although the really big ones, weighing more than 4kg, are relatively rare), their fighting qualities and their 'lack of shyness' (ie they're not very cautious about getting caught) are all attractions for visiting fishing enthusiasts. The one loser has been the local zebra trout, which is now only found in some of the most remote corners of West Falkland or in the bleak flatlands of Lafonia. Zebra trout are completely protected, but most sea trout fishing is also on the 'catch and release' principle.

Although sea trout are the main quarry, the sea fish known locally as mullet is also a worthy catch. In fact, *Eleginops maclovinus*, a member of the Antarctic rock cod group, is often caught in the shallow waters of estuaries and creeks. They can be caught with fly-fishing tackle and they're popular with anglers because they put up a fight. They would feature even more frequently on Falklands menus except for the fact that the islanders are simply not very partial to seafood of any type.

THE BEST & WORST

Best

- Colourful Stanley with its wriggly tin architecture and vivid paintwork
- Flights with the Falkland Islands Government Air Service (FIGAS) – great views and everyone gets a window seat
- The complete fearlessness of so much of the wildlife
- Icebergs looking like modern cut glass artwork when they litter the sea around South Georgia
- The multitude of penguins, including the regal kings, at Volunteer Beach

Worst

- Those damned sheep, shitting everywhere, eating everything and all too rarely fenced off
- Eau de Seabird – the ineffable pong of thousands of tightly packed penguins or cormorants
- Windy days, or any days when the weather's bad in the Falklands
- Getting bogged in 'soft camp', the marshy, muddy peat bogs of the Falklands
- The damage rats and cats have done to small birdlife

As with any outdoor activity in the Falklands, anglers should be prepared for the often rapidly changing weather and come equipped with suitable clothing to counter the chilling winds.

Fishing for Falklands Sea Trout by Peter Lapsley (2000) tells you everything you need to know about fly-fishing in the Falklands, including where to fish, how to fish and the best fly-fishing tackle.

FISHING PERMITS

The old system of obtaining a fishing licence from the post office has been superseded by daily permits, typically costing about £10. They are issued by the controller of fishing rights on each stretch of river. The controller of fishing rights is likely to be either whoever you're staying with or somebody next door.

WHEN TO FISH

The fishing season is from 1 September to 30 April, but December and January are not good months on the rivers (although fish can still be caught in the estuaries). From September to November, fish running the rivers tend to be smaller than those caught in February to April, and the more rainfall the better the trout. After periods of low rainfall there may be more fish in the estuaries, although seals have also learnt to exploit these opportunities. The Falklands' rivers have been compared to those of Scotland and north and west England; their levels vary with rain and the water sometimes has a brownish tinge from the peat.

WHERE TO FISH

Many visiting anglers start their fishing forays straight from Stanley where there are a number of good fishing guides, including Neil Rowlands of Hebe Tours. The Murrell, Malo and San Carlos rivers are the main rivers for sea trout in East Falkland. The Murrell is relatively short but conveniently close to Stanley. Fishing on the Malo is controlled by the Malo Angling Club, so you need to know somebody there to fish this river. The Malo has its source in the middle of East Falkland, very close to the source of the San Carlos, but flows off in the opposite direction (running east to reach the southern end of Port Salvador). The San Carlos River runs north and west to eventually reach Falk-

land Sound by Port San Carlos. It was in the San Carlos in late March 1992 that Alison Faulkner hauled in the record Falklands sea trout, a monster tipping the scales at over 10kg. Other prime fishing spots in East Falkland include the huge expanse of Port Salvador and, near Mt Pleasant, the Fitzroy River, Fitzroy Creek and Swan Inlet.

The Warrah River in West Falkland is only about 30km long, but can be surprisingly wide. It runs northeast to enter the sea on the north coast. The popular Chartres River is also short, running for just 15km to 25km before reaching the sea at Christmas Harbour, near the Chartres settlement on the west coast. Both these rivers are normally reached from Port Howard, which also offers interesting fishing in tidal waters very close to the settlement. There are also good fishing possibilities around Fox Bay and in other small streams. In West Falkland, the Port Howard Lodge is the main centre for fishing activity.

Golf

A current Falklands fad is golf, with 9-hole courses in Stanley and several camp settlements hosting popular tournaments. No-one will mistake Stanley Golf Course (or any of the others) for St Andrews, but gales and rolling terrain make for a challenging experience. There are certainly some unique hazards – such as hitting your ball into a minefield at Port Howard's Clippy Hill course.

Scuba Diving

The Falklands have good scuba-diving opportunities but this is cold-water diving; temperatures only rise to 14°C in summer and drop to as low as 4°C in winter. In summer the water temperature drops another 1.5°C at 20m depth, but in winter it stays pretty much the same. In these temperatures a drysuit is really a necessity; local divers say you can manage with a wetsuit in the summer, but only for about half an hour.

The Falklands' numerous shipwrecks are a prime attraction. There are over 200 recorded wrecks, some of which are protected or restricted sites that require a government-issued licence before you can dive them. Due to high winds and algal blooms, visibility is not always high during the summer months – dropping to just a few metres in shallow areas. The winds can also make diving difficult. In winter, the visibility is usually much better, sometimes reaching 20m.

For information about the numerous ship wrecks contact Dave Eynon's **South Atlantic Marine Services** (Map pp70-1; ☎ 21145; fax 22674; sams@horizon.co.fk; PO Box 140, Stanley) or visit in person at the boathouse on Ross Rd. Some equipment is available, but you will need to provide your own wetsuit or drysuit.

Walking & Camping

The possibilities for trekking and camping in the Falklands remain remarkably untapped for a variety of reasons. One is the severe lack of public land in the islands – apart from odd corners and offshore islands the Falklands are practically devoid of public parks and reserves. Land is almost all privately owned and permission must be sought before you can enter or cross it. There are none of the hard-won public rights of way found in Britain, or the public access to coastal areas, which is the norm in so many other parts of the world.

There is no denying that there are some landowners who just simply do not like outsiders encroaching on their land and, in some cases, there are good reasons for this dislike. Landowners regularly raise the dangers of fire and it's true that dry summer conditions and wind can make the Falklands into a tinderbox; peat fires have been known to smoulder for years.

However, there are places in the world that regularly face even more severe fire dangers – Australia, for example – and still manage to allow walking and camping. The danger that walkers might put themselves in – and the expense of rescuing foolish visitors – is cited as another reason for banning walkers. The Falklands' weather can be severe and sunny summer days can quickly give way to rain, cruel winds and very restricted visibility. Clothing and equipment suitable for Europe can prove seriously inadequate for Falklands conditions, and during the hard-working summer season landowners certainly do not want to be distracted by having to rescue unprepared outsiders.

Finally, it's also been suggested that the islanders' love affair with the Land-Rover is a reason for their disdain for unmechanised transport.

Nevertheless, the Falklands do offer great trekking and camping possibilities and it's a shame they aren't more open for visitors. One proposal that might satisfy concerned landowners is for strictly organised and guided walking trips, although the high costs involved would seriously discourage the young people most likely to be interested in exploring on foot. More encouraging, from the point of view of potential walkers, is the growing concern about the rapid decline in camp populations. The total population of West Falkland is now less than 100 people: settlements that once had 30 or 40 people often have only five or 10, and many smaller settlements have shut down completely. The 'outside houses' used by shepherds tending remote flocks have fallen out of use as motorcycles have proliferated. Using outside houses, in the same way as unstaffed backcountry huts are used along New Zealand walking trails, would be an excellent way for walkers to explore the Falklands.

Walks & Climbs in the Falkland Islands by Julian Fisher (1991) is a fairly basic introduction to walks around Stanley, together with short notes on rock climbs around the islands.

Wildlife Viewing

Wildlife is the major attraction for most visitors to the Falklands or South Georgia. Penguins, other shorebirds and marine mammals are easily approached, even at developed Falklands tourist sites such as Sea Lion Island and Volunteer Beach. However, there are other equally interesting, undeveloped sites on islands off East and West

---

SOUTH GEORGIA ACTIVITIES

It's quite possible that trekking, mountain climbing, scuba diving and kayaking opportunities will develop in years to come on South Georgia. There have already been kayaking trips to South Georgia – in 2004, **Expedition Kayak** (www.expeditionkayak.com) in the UK undertook a kayak circumnavigation of the island. Meanwhile, the main adventure activity on South Georgia is the walk following Shackleton's famous route. Of course, for most visitors to South Georgia, wildlife and the abandoned whaling stations are the major attractions.

Falkland. Keep a respectful distance from all wildlife. There are no wildlife developments on South Georgia.

Windsurfing

Windsurfing is possible in sheltered Falklands waters such as Stanley Harbour, but probably only the truly adept can avoid sailing to South Africa on the prevailing winds.

BUSINESS HOURS

Falkland Islands government offices are open weekdays from 8am to noon and 1.15pm to 4.30pm. Most large businesses in Stanley, such as the Falkland Island Company's (FIC) West Store (a supermarket with some general interest items), stay open until 7pm or 8pm, but smaller shops are often open only a few hours a day. On weekends, business hours are much reduced. All this changes when there's a cruise ship in port; shops are always open when there's a ship around. The few stores in camp, such as those at Fox Bay East and Port Howard, have a very limited regular schedule, but will often open on request.

CLIMATE
The Falklands

Despite a reputation for dismal weather, the islands' climate is temperate, although there are frequent high winds. In fact, it's rarely not windy and the wind-chill factor can

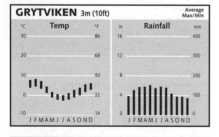

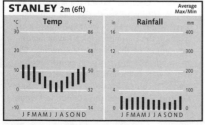

make the Falklands seem much colder than they really are. Cold weather often extends far beyond the actual June to September winter months. See also p9.

Maximum temperatures rarely reach 24°C, even in the summer months of December to February. Even on the coldest winter days the temperature usually rises above freezing at some time and rarely drops below –5°C. The mean annual temperature is about 6°C. Summer weather can be quite sunny; proximity to that famous ozone hole means that sunglasses and sun protection are a wise precaution.

The average annual rainfall at Stanley, one of the islands' most humid areas, is only about 610mm. The rainfall is fairly evenly distributed throughout the year; there are no noticeably rainy months. Snow is not uncommon, sometimes even falling in summer, but it rarely lies around for long.

Don't pack your swimsuit unless you plan to use the Stanley swimming pool. The waters around the Falklands are cold both summer (9° to 11°C) and winter (3° to 6°C). For scuba divers this is definitely drysuit territory. Antarctic icebergs drift north of the Falklands and the extreme limit of pack ice is only 300km to the south. Very large icebergs sometimes strand about 150km south on the Birdwood Bank and can actually cause temporary climatic changes.

For a current weather report from Mt Pleasant International Airport in the Falklands check the **Weather Underground** (☎ 32500; www.wunderground.com/global/stations/88889).

South Georgia

The Antarctic Convergence makes all the difference: South Georgia is not much further south than the Falklands and Grytviken is actually north of Ushuaia in Argentina, but south of the Convergence the weather is cold, cloudy and windy. There is little variation between summer and winter. In the northern hemisphere Manchester and Newcastle in England are at similar latitudes, but you'd have to get about 20 degrees closer to the pole to find similarly severe weather. The King Edward Point weather station, which kept records from 1905 to 1982, has recorded temperatures varying from –19°C to 24°C but the annual range of mean monthly temperatures is only about 7°C.

Over one metre of snow accumulates in the winter, but heavy rainfall (sometimes up to 100mm in a day) is more likely. The sea sometimes freezes in sheltered bays in winter and in some years the Antarctic pack ice extends all the way to South Georgia. In 1980 pack ice reached 200km beyond South Georgia and the island was effectively ice-bound. In 1978 a tabular iceberg measuring 65km by 35km, about half the area of the island, passed by South Georgia. Another large tabular berg was grounded on the continental shelf west of the island in 2002–03.

The northeast coast, sheltered by the central mountains, gets clearer and calmer weather than the southwest coast, which bears the full brunt of Antarctic weather. Sudden winds can blow up and can be a serious danger for small craft. These winds can be katabatic (when cold air funnels down valleys) or fohn (when air loses its water vapour and warms up as it crosses the mountains, leading to dramatic temperature increases). See also p9.

CUSTOMS

There are few customs regulations; limits and heavy taxes are imposed on importation of alcohol and tobacco, but both are readily available locally.

DANGERS & ANNOYANCES
Driving

Despite the signs at the outskirts of Stanley warning you to put your seat belts on as you leave town and take them off when you enter, it's wise to wear them all the time. Accidents do happen on Falklands roads; running off the road into the scenery is not a good idea, and in camp it can be a long time before help comes along.

Minefields

Near Stanley and in a few camp locations on both East and West Falkland, plastic land mines remain. Minefields are clearly marked and no civilian has been injured since the Falklands War. *Never* even consider entering one of these fields – the mines will bear the weight of a penguin or even a sheep, but not a human. A cow or two has had an unpleasant mine experience. Apart from the danger of blowing your leg off, you can be fined up to £1000 for entering a minefield.

Report any suspicious object to the **Explosive Ordnance Disposal** (Map pp70-1; EOD; ☎ 22229), opposite the Stanley police station, which distributes free minefield maps (handy for walks in the Stanley area). You can also acquire a free 'Danger Mines' warning sign, although a donation is appreciated. They have examples of the nine different types of mine that litter the Falklands: two each from Spanish, Italian, Israeli and Argentine mine manufacturers, and one from the USA. In all, 25,000 to 30,000 mines were left. They lie in 135 fenced-off areas totalling about 20 sq km. Since the end of the hostilities about 6000 mines have been cleared; to get rid of the lot would cost an estimated £50 million.

Walking

Trekking in camp is safe for anyone with confidence in his or her abilities, but it's better not to trek alone. Camp is so thinly populated that the consequences of an accident, however unlikely, could be very serious. Walkers in camp should be aware that so-called 'soft camp', covered by white grass, is boggy despite its firm appearance. This is not quicksand, but step carefully. In summer the grass can get very dry and when combined with the high winds there's a serious fire danger. Almost all of the Falklands is private property and permission must be obtained before venturing onto private land. Some farmers are very unenthusiastic about walkers crossing their land (see p165 for more information).

Weather

In general the weather in the Falklands is not terribly severe – it never gets extremely cold and it certainly never gets more than mildly warm (see opposite). But it does get very windy and the weather changes with remarkable speed; many walkers have set out on a mild day only to find the temperature drops, rain comes down and the wind picks up. In the Falklands the wind-chill factor can be horrendous and getting caught outside without adequate clothing (this is Gore-Tex country) can be a recipe for hypothermia. Add a Falklands mist to the often confusing uniformity of the countryside and you have a recipe for disaster. Never underestimate the weather and always come prepared for the worst.

For most visitors to South Georgia weather conditions are unlikely to be a problem in the relatively short time spent ashore. If you're feeling uncomfortably chilly it's easy to simply go back aboard the ship. If you are planning to spend longer ashore, on a walking trip for example, then you must be very carefully prepared and clothed (see p9).

Wild weather can be a problem on board ship and the old advice to always keep 'one hand for the ship' is a good one (see the boxed text on p178).

Wildlife

Wildlife generally doesn't present real dangers – there are no grizzly bears, crocodiles or poisonous snakes in the Falklands or South Georgia.

The biggest wildlife hazard is not to you, but to the wildlife (see p40). Walking carelessly through areas with ground-nesting birds can easily result in stepping on a nest or crushing the home of a burrowing bird. Many birds are easily scared off their nests, and any egg or chick left unattended – even for just a few seconds – will end up as a meal for one of the Falklands' endlessly vigilant predators. Any penguin colony will have skuas patrolling it, waiting for a moment's inattention.

BIRD PRECAUTIONS

Many of the birds in the Falklands and South Georgia are remarkably unafraid of humans, but care should be taken not to disturb them, particularly during the breeding season.

■ Always move carefully and slowly, and keep low when approaching colonies – and be prepared to retreat at the first sign of discomfort or alarm. The general rule is not to approach closer than 5m to any wildlife, but additional care must be taken with some species, such as albatrosses and giant petrels.

■ Take special care when birds are on their eggs or looking after chicks. If a bird is frightened off its nest the eggs or chicks can be taken with remarkable speed by predators, which are waiting for exactly this opportunity. Exposure to the weather can also be harmful for eggs or chicks that are left even for short periods of time. Some species are easily disturbed by intruders and will abandon their nest

and eggs if you approach too close. Giant petrels are particularly uneasy about disturbances while Dominican gulls (kelp gulls) and Antarctic terns only need to see a human to desert their nests.

■ If you're being dive-bombed by a skua you're too close – back off. Watch for any sign of behaviour indicating that a bird is alarmed. Although the danger is probably only to your nerves, skuas are undoubtedly the Falklands' scariest wildlife. Stalking around a penguin colony or swishing dangerously in to land among a group of cormorants they look like big, powerful birds. Skuas don't like people getting close to their nests when they've got chicks or eggs, and they'll show their displeasure by performing a live action replay of Hitchcock's *The Birds*. A large, brown, angry bird swooping at your head at 100km/h definitely raises the pulse. OK, they're going to miss you by a few centimetres, but how do you know that? And don't duck! Next time they'll fly in from behind and, expecting you to duck, will come in a little lower…

■ The other scary Falklands bird is the famed Johnny Rook, the striated caracara. These days this eagle-like predator is found only in the more remote locations on the Falklands. They're wonderful to watch: fearless, cruel and endlessly curious, always ready to investigate anything new. There are countless tales of Johnny Rooks picking up cameras or binoculars and carrying them off, usually followed with 'and dropping them 200m off the coast'. Falklands farmers all have tales of Johnny Rooks attacking lambs or troubled sheep. Walking on some remote island it's not unusual to find a Johnny Rook casually hopping behind you, probably with a thought balloon floating above its head saying, 'now if he just trips over that rock and breaks an ankle…'

■ Penguins might be cute, but they're not completely harmless: those beaks are powerful and sharp. In the Falklands never put a hand down a Magellanic penguin's burrow if you want to get it back in the same condition. Magellanics also have nasty fleas that are only too happy to transfer from penguin feathers to human ankles, if you spend too much time around their burrows.

- A number of petrel species and prions nest in burrows and the tussock areas on rat-free islands or bare soil areas above the tussock margin on coastal areas can be riddled with tunnels which collapse easily under heavy feet. Avoid areas where burrowing birds are found or, if you find yourself in such an area, escape by walking on the tussock tops.

RAT PRECAUTIONS

Rats now exist along most of the coast of the main island of South Georgia and have been disastrous for smaller birds. On the Falklands smaller birds only survive on the offshore islands, and rats have wiped them out on East and West Falkland.

There is great concern that rats may be carried to smaller islands off South Georgia, which are currently rat free. Larsen Harbour at the southeast end of the island, Cape Rosa at the entrance to King Haakon Bay, and the islands in the Bay of Isles are rat-free environments. These are regularly visited areas where great care should be taken that no rat has hitched a ride. Rats can easily enter open containers or boxes or even be inadvertently packed into one.

SEAL PRECAUTIONS

In South Georgia, fur seal numbers have been increasing rapidly in recent years and during the breeding season there are many beaches where it is not possible to land. Male fur seals can be very aggressive, can move extremely fast and bites are very likely to become infected even if they are not otherwise injurious. During the November to March breeding season the bulls fiercely defend their breeding territories against any intruders, while the cows are equally protective of their pups.

Fur seal breeding beaches are mainly at the two ends of the island. At the northwest end they extend from Schlieper Bay to Right Whale Bay, particularly at Elsehul and Undine Harbour. At the southeast end, Cooper Bay is the main fur seal breeding location. Observing the seals from Zodiacs offshore at these overcrowded beaches is not a problem, but no attempt should be made to land among them.

From February to April a large part of the fur seal population moves back from the beaches into the tussock grass. At this time most of the seals will move away if you give them warning of your approach. Curious young seals may actually come towards you, but it is a good idea to carry a stout stick or Zodiac paddle to gently ward off approaches. Tapping a seal under the chin will generally warn them off. Despite all the snarling confrontations, fur seals would rather not attack; the problem is that some beaches can be so crowded it's simply impossible to plot a path between one angry seal's territory and another's. Never get between any seal and its path to the sea.

Elephant seals breed from late September to early November and should also be treated with respect. Despite their bulk they can move very quickly and cows are extremely protective of their pups and the bulls can be very dangerous and unpredictable.

Seals have sharp teeth and, particularly during mating season, a nasty disposition. Seals aren't going to chase you down unless you get threateningly close or if you come between them and the sea. Give a seal an escape route and there's no problem. Nasty seal surprises happen when you meet them unexpectedly in high tussock grass; if you're blocking the only exit route, and that's a corridor no wider than your hips, the result may be unpleasant. If there are seals around always enter tussock with caution. See also p42.

FOOD & DRINK

Wool has long been the staple of the Falklands economy and mutton the staple of the diet. The old joke that the islanders eat '365' – mutton every day of the year – has the follow up that it should really be called '364', since on Christmas Day they substitute lamb. In fact, there are cows and pigs on some farms, and goats have also made an appearance – although Jamaican goat curry does not, yet, appear on Falklands menus.

At least meat is cheap and many islanders have their own kitchen gardens (although vegetarians may have a hard time of it). Greenhouses are becoming increasingly common and Stanley has a hydroponics market, which turns out vegetables including tomatoes and lettuces throughout the year.

Stanley snack bars offer fast food, such as fish and chips, hamburgers made with beef or mutton (better than it sounds), sausage rolls

---

FALKLANDS FOOD

The following is a select list of some of the items you may find on a Falklands menu.

Calamari With all that squid being caught around the islands by European and East Asian fishing boats it's hardly surprising that a little of it manages to find its way onto Falklands menus.

Chacarero A traditional Chilean sandwich with grilled steak and topped with cheese, tomatoes, steamed green beans and a hot sauce.

Diddle-dee Berries This heathlike shrub produces bright red berries in late February/early March. They're edible, if slightly bitter, and are used to make preserves.

Empanadas Those tasty turnovers, one of the most popular Chilean or Argentine snacks, are equally at home in the Falklands. Empanadas can be filled with vegetables, cheese, egg or a variety of meats, and can be baked or cooked.

Lamb or mutton Dubbing it '365' is unfair, but in various forms sheep does find its way onto the Falklands plate with great regularity. Falklands pay-packets used to include regular supplies of meat.

Mullet Correctly a type of Antarctic rock cod, the Falklands mullet is popular with anglers and is good to eat.

Teaberry Whalers and sealers used the leaves as a substitute for tea, but the pink coloured berries (picked in autumn) are delicious fresh or can be used to make teaberry cake or pie.

Trout The favourite quarry of Falklands anglers, the sea trout appears all too rarely on island menus.

Upland Goose This very common Falklands bird occasionally makes it to the menu as goose pâté.

---

and pasties. There are a handful of surprisingly good restaurants and Falklands home cooking can be excellent. On the other hand, a couple of weeks in the Falklands can be a reminder that the old British habit of cooking vegetables until they're limp still prevails in odd corners of the empire. Disappointingly, despite the trout-stocked rivers and endless coastline, the islanders are not very keen on seafood and, when it does appear on Stanley menus, it's likely to be frozen and imported. On the other hand, you may encounter the odd menu item indicating that the Falklands really are very close to South America.

Stanley has several well-patronised pubs where beer and hard liquor (whisky and rum) are the favourites, though wine has gained popularity in recent years. Gato Negro (black cat) is the Chilean house wine of choice, although you'll also find European, Australian, New Zealand and South African wine on sale as well as the excellent Chilean varieties. All drinks are imported.

HEALTH
The Falklands

No special health precautions need be taken when visiting the Falklands, but carry adequate insurance. There are excellent medical and dental facilities at the King Edward VII Memorial Hospital, a joint civilian–military facility in Stanley.

Despite relatively cool temperatures, unsuspecting visitors may suffer severe sunburn after experiencing the deceptive combination of the wind and the sun. In the event of inclement weather, the wind can contribute to hypothermia.

Because RAF flights from Brize Norton to Mt Pleasant may be diverted to West Africa or Brazil due to bad weather, the British Ministry of Defence (MOD) recommends that passengers on its flights make sure their yellow fever vaccinations are up to date.

South Georgia

Most cruise ships will have a doctor or someone with medical expertise on board. There are no medical facilities on South Georgia and no form of medical evacuation. The high intensity of sunlight means visitors should take precautions, although there usually won't be much skin showing to get sunburnt. The extremely dry air can lead to dehydration so remember to drink plenty of liquids.

The chief health problem is liable to be seasickness. The waters around South Georgia can be stormy so if you're prone to motion sickness the trip may be uncomfortable. Some voyagers find that one or other of the commercial motion sickness remedies does the trick and there will usually be a choice available on board (just in case you haven't brought your own). Fresh air, eating sparingly and a lower deck cabin (less rock and roll) can all help. You may be lucky and enjoy a calm voyage.

HOLIDAYS & EVENTS

On both East and West Falkland, the annual sports meetings have been a tradition since the 19th-century advent of sheep farming. With most people living a very isolated existence, these events provide a regular opportunity to get together and share news, meet new people and participate in competitions, such as horse racing and sheep-dog trials.

The rotating camp sports meeting on West Falkland at the end of the shearing season, usually in late February, carries on this tradition best, hosting 'two-nighters' during which islanders party till they drop, go to sleep for a few hours, get up and start all over again. Independent visitors should not feel shy about showing up, but it is best to arrange accommodation in advance. This will usually mean floor space for your sleeping bag. In Stanley there are sporting events between Christmas and New Year.

National holidays include a holiday unique to the Falklands: Margaret Thatcher Day – although the official government website notes that this is 'not a public or government holiday'. Falklands Day is also not a public or government holiday. If you are in the islands late February or early March, Camp Sports is a great opportunity to see sheep-shearing contests.

New Year's Day 1 January
Margaret Thatcher Day 10 January
Camp Sports Late February or early March
Good Friday March/April
Queen's Birthday 21 April
Liberation Day 14 June (or first Monday after if the 14th is a Saturday or Sunday)
Falklands Day 14 August
Spring Holiday First Monday in October
Battle of the Falklands (1914) 8 December (or first Monday after if the 8th is a Saturday or Sunday)
Christmas Day 25 December (also a holiday on the Monday if Christmas falls on a Saturday)
Boxing Day 26 December
Stanley Sports 26-27 December

INTERNET ACCESS

There are no Internet cafés in Stanley but there are a number of locations with computers set up for Internet access. **Cable & Wireless PLC** (Map pp70-1; ☎ 20804; Ross Rd; ☽ 8am-12 noon & 1.15-4.30pm Mon-Thu, 8am-12 noon & 1.15pm-4.15pm Fri) sells prepaid cards that give you 20 minutes' access for £3. It's not cheap and often not very fast. There are several machines in a room adjacent to the Jetty Centre Tourist Office that are open the same hours as the tourist office. The Dolphin Guest House, Waterfront Guest House and Malvina House Hotel (see pp79–80) all offer Internet access. In camp, the Pebble Island Hotel (p125) and the Port Howard Lodge (p116) both offer Internet access.

LANGUAGE

The Falkland Islanders speak English, perhaps with a trace of southern latitudes such as you will hear in the accent of Australians or New Zealanders. There is also some borrowed Spanish, particularly in geographical terms, place names and, a hangover from the gaucho days, in names for horse gear.

MAPS

Topographic maps of the Falkland Islands, prepared by the Directorate of Overseas Surveys, are available from the **Secretariat** (Map pp70-1; ☎ 27141; Thatcher Dr, Stanley). They can also be purchased at map outlets like Stanfords in London. There is a two-sheet, 1:250,000 map of the entire islands that is suitable for most purposes, but for more detail the islands are also covered in 29 1:50,000 sheets. They're interesting, but out of date: many sheets date from before the Falklands War and have none of the recently constructed roads or airstrips. They're also severely lacking in older man-made features, such as shipwrecks or the old corrals from the gaucho era. Even the original British settlement at Port Egmont on Saunders Island fails to appear. These large-scale maps are much cheaper in Stanley than in the UK; you can purchase the whole 29-sheet set for a bargain £25.

The Ordnance Survey's 1:643,000 map of the Falkland Islands is not very detailed but it was published in 1998 and is more up to date on road construction. For maritime charts, contact the **Customs & Immigration Department** (Map pp70-1; ☎ 27340; fax 27342; customs.fig@horizon .co .fk; ground fl, Byron House, 3H Jones Rd, Stanley) on the east side of town. Commercial maps of the Falklands include:

Falkland Islands Explorer (Ocean Explorer Maps, 1:365,000) Available in the Falklands and overseas, this extremely clear map shows the main centres of interest along with a great deal of wildlife and historic information; there's also a town plan of Stanley on the reverse. It's not completely up to date with recent road building and it's not very detailed.

Falkland Islands/Islas Malvinas (ITMB Publishing, 1:300,000) This map is widely available outside the Falklands and includes fairly detailed information on wildlife sites, although it's also somewhat out of date and doesn't show recent road building.

Islas Malvinas (Auto Mapa 1:500,000) Spreading this map out before a Falkland Islander and asking which way it is from Puerto Argentino to other settlements on the Isla Soledad might not go down too well, but if you're in Ushuaia it might be interesting to check the Falklands from the Argentine perspective. It's very out of date.

For South Georgia, Admiralty Chart 3597 covers the island at a scale of 1:250,000. Charts 3585, 3587, 3592 deal with the various bays and harbours around the island.

3585 Undine Harbour, Elsehul, Fortuna Bay, Larsen Harbour, Gold Harbour, Moltke Harbour, Right Whale Bay, Blue Whale Harbour, Cape Buller to Cape Constance, Rosita Harbour, Prince Olav Harbour

3587 Leith Harbour, Stromness and Husvik in Stromness Bay, Jason Harbour, Maiviken, King Edward Cove, Grytviken, Cobbler's Cove, Godthul

3592 Approaches to Stewart Island, Stewart Strait and Willis Island, Bird Sound, Bird Island and mainland South Georgia

South Georgia (MicroMap) is a handy small map that comes in the South Georgia visitor's information package. *South Georgia Explorer* (Ocean Explorer Maps, 2002) is at 1:250,000 scale and has a great deal of information on sites of interest, South Georgia personalities, history, wildlife and a timeline. It's available in Stanley in the Falklands. *South Georgia DOS 610* (Directorate of Overseas Surveys, 1958) is at 1:200,000 scale and is the definitive map of the island; much of the work on this map being based on Duncan Carse's 1950s explorations and surveys.

MONEY

The legal currency is the Falkland Islands pound (£), on a par with sterling. There are bank notes for £5, £10, £20 and £50, and coins for 1p, 2p, 5p, 10p, 20p, 50p and £1.

UK sterling notes and coins circulate alongside the local currency, but Falklands currency is not legal tender in the UK, nor on Ascension Island, where flights to and from the UK make a brief refuelling stop. Ascension/St Helena bank notes and coins are not legal tender in either the Falklands or the UK. Get rid of Falklands currency before you depart the islands, unless you want to keep it as a souvenir.

There is only one place visitors can spend money on South Georgia – at the museum shop in Grytviken, where they take UK pounds sterling or US dollars in cash.

The **Standard Chartered Bank** (Map pp70-1; ☎ 21352; fax 22219) is the only banking operation. Visitors intending a longer stay may want to transfer funds to this bank.

Cash

Euros and US, Canadian, Australian and New Zealand dollars can be changed at the bank; forget about trying to change any South American currency.

Credit Cards

Visa and MasterCard are increasingly widely used in the Falklands, but American Express, Eurocard and Diners Club cards are only accepted at a few outlets. There are no ATMs in the Falklands, but you can get a cash advance at the Standard Chartered Bank on a Visa or MasterCard for a 3% fee (minimum £2) plus a communication charge (usually £1.50).

In South Georgia the Grytviken museum shop accepts Visa and MasterCard credit cards.

Personal Cheques

Cheques from British banks can be cashed with difficulty, and from other countries with extreme difficulty.

Travellers Cheques

Travellers cheques are accepted with a minimum of bureaucracy.

PHOTOGRAPHY & VIDEO

Colour and B&W print film are readily available at fairly reasonable prices. Colour slide film is hard to find: bring all you need. Colour print processing is available in Stanley.

The Falklands are extremely photogenic and the clear air, the light and the often remarkably fearless mammal and birdlife flatter photographic skills. Apart from the possibility of using far more film than expected, visitors should take some precautions. If you're on a ship and making Zodiac landings protect your camera from salt spray and beware of errant waves. Remember that weather conditions can change rapidly and without warning. On the Falklands or South Georgia winds can also cause problems:

beware of sand blasting along windswept beaches – and trying to avoid camera shake when it's difficult even to stand up can be a challenge. The intense light can make a polarising filter useful.

POST

Postal services to and from the Falklands are reliable. There are airmail services once or twice weekly to and from the UK, but parcels larger than about 0.45kg arrive or depart by sea four to five times yearly. If you're expecting mail in the islands, instruct correspondents to address their letters to: 'Post Office, Stanley, Falkland Islands, via London, England'.

In South Georgia stamps can be purchased and mail posted in the very English-looking mailbox at the King Edward Point Post Office. Delivery is via the Falkland Islands and it can be two months or more before a ship collects the mail. The museum also handles mail.

RADIO & TV

Radio is the most important communications medium on the Falklands. The Falkland Islands Broadcasting Station (FIBS) produces local programming and also carries news from the BBC. It broadcasts on 530 kHz on the AM/MW band island-wide, at 88.3 MHz on the FM band in the Stanley area and 102 MHz from Mt Maria on West Falkland. Do not miss the nightly public announcements to which locals listen religiously – particularly the next day's Falkland Islands Government Air Service (FIGAS) airline schedule, which actually broadcasts the names of all passengers for each flight.

There are also programmes from the British Forces Broadcasting Service (BFBS), which broadcasts at 550 kHz on the AM/MW band, at 96.5 MHz on the FM band island-wide and 98.5 from the Mt Pleasant Airport (MPA).

TV is available through BFBS, which broadcasts same-day programmes from the UK, and there is also a limited range of cable TV in the principal Stanley hotels.

SHOPPING

With all those sheep it's hardly surprising that knitted woollen sweaters are one of the Falklands' prime souvenirs. See p82 for shopping possibilities.

TELEPHONE

The Falklands' international country code is ☎ 500, which is valid for numbers in Stanley and in camp. Cable & Wireless PLC operates both local and long-distance telephone services; all local numbers have five digits.

Calls made on a phonecard cost 6p per minute in the Falklands, £1 per minute to the UK and £1.10 per minute elsewhere. Phonecards are on sale from Cable & Wireless PLC (see p69) and other outlets in Stanley for £5, 10, 15 or 20.

Scratch off the strip on the back, which reveals a number, then dial 141 from any phone and follow the instructions. Once you've connected you can make calls to Falklands numbers or to anywhere overseas up to the remaining value on the card. These cards are convenient because they work from public or private phones.

In camp many people communicate on the ham radio 2-metre calling channel VHF 145.500.

TIME

The Falklands are four hours behind Greenwich Mean Time (GMT, also known as UTC). From September to April, Stanley goes on daylight-saving time so it's only three hours behind, but camp remains on standard time. The difference between 'Stanley time' and 'camp time' can often lead to confusion. In summer when it's 12 noon in Stanley, it's the same time in Santiago or Punta Arenas, 8am in San Francisco, 1pm in New York, 3pm in London and 2am the next morning in Sydney.

South Georgia should be two hours ahead of Argentina, but in fact the official South Georgia time is only one hour ahead (three hours behind GMT/UTC). So when it's 12 noon in South Georgia it is 3pm in London. In fact many ships visiting South Georgia out of Ushuaia simply keep their clocks on Argentine time. During the summer visiting season there are plenty of daylight hours so the time is really irrelevant.

TOURIST INFORMATION

The local Falklands tourist office is the **Falklands Islands Tourist Board** (☎ 22215; fax 22619; www.tourism.org.fk; Shackleton House, Stanley); the islands also have representation in the UK (see p174).

Visitors to South Georgia pay, in their cruise cost, a £50 entry fee to the island. In return they get a tourist pack that includes a useful and colourful South Georgia information booklet, a map of the island, a certificate that they've been there and various other information sheets.

VISAS & DOCUMENTS

All nationalities, including British citizens, must carry valid passports to visit the Falklands. For non-Britons, visa requirements are generally the same as those for visiting the UK, although Argentines must obtain a visa in advance. For details, consult **Falkland Islands Government Office** (☎ 020-7222 2542; fax 7222 2375; rep@figo.u-net.com; Falkland House, 14 Broadway, Westminster, London SW1H 0BH) or the Falkland Islands Tourist Board (see p173). In Punta Arenas, Chile, contact **LanChile** (☎ 61-241 232, 241 100; Lautaro Navarro 999) or the **British Consulate** (☎ 61-211 535; Cataratas del Niágara 01325).

Visitors normally get a one-month visitor's permit on arrival. Officially, visitors must have an onward or return ticket and sufficient funds or credit cards to finance their stay; they must also have at least their initial night's accommodation booked. In practice, arrivals who don't have pre-booked accommodation are held in the arrivals area while rooms are found. As Stanley can be completely booked out, it's a good idea to book ahead for your first night. International Tours & Travel and Stanley Services are two Stanley travel agents who can book accommodation, tours and flights throughout the Falklands (see p185 for contact details). Alternatively, you can contact most places in the Falklands by email.

There are no particular entry requirements to South Georgia, but you can get your passport stamped at the King Edward Point British Antarctic Survey (BAS) station.

WORK

Stanley's labour shortage has eased over the last few years and work is more difficult to obtain, although unemployment remains close to zero. In the past it was possible to obtain seasonal work on the large sheep stations, but agrarian reform has nearly eliminated this option. Despite the Falklands' position as a British colony, even with a British passport you cannot simply turn up and look for work. Visitors intending to work in the Falklands must obtain a work permit before arriving. On arrival you will be asked to specify your departure date, and you may be required to prove you have sufficient funds to cover your stay.

Transport

CONTENTS

GETTING THERE & AWAY

ENTERING THE COUNTRY

Visitors to the Falkland Islands must have an onward or return ticket and sufficient funds or credit cards to finance their stay; they must also have at least their initial night's accommodation booked. However, in practice, arrivals who don't have pre-booked accommodation are simply held in the arrivals area while rooms are found.

ENTERING SOUTH GEORGIA

There are no particular entry requirements to South Georgia, but you can get your passport stamped at the King Edward Point British Antarctic Survey (BAS) station. The only way to get to South Georgia is by sea (see p177).

Passport

All nationalities, including British citizens, must carry valid passports to visit the Falklands. See p174 for information on visas.

AIR
Airports & Airlines

In the Falklands, Mt Pleasant International Airport, the military airport built after the Falklands War, handles international flights

---

THINGS CHANGE...

The information in this chapter is particularly vulnerable to change. Check directly with the airline or a travel agent to make sure you understand how a fare (and ticket you may buy) works and be aware of the security requirements for international travel. Shop carefully. The details given in this chapter should be regarded as pointers and are not a substitute for your own careful, up-to-date research.

---

from England and Chile; Stanley Airport, built in 1978, handles domestic flights. (See p83 for information on getting to and from these airports.)

There are duty-free facilities at Mt Pleasant International Airport and at Wideawake Airfield on Ascension Island, but not at RAF Brize Norton. There's a £20 departure tax out of the Falklands.

If you wish to fly to the Falklands there are only two choices: the Royal Air Force (RAF) from Britain or LanChile from Punta Arenas in Chile. From the USA, Australia, New Zealand and other countries, including Britain, you can connect to the LanChile flight via Santiago.

Tickets

Good places to find bargain air fares include the better-known travel agents **STA Travel** (in Australia ☎ 1300 733 035, in the UK ☎ 020-7361 6262, in the USA ☎ 800-777 0112; www.statravel .com), Australia-based **Flight Centre** (☎ 133 133; www.flightcentre.com.au), Canada-based **Travel Cuts** (☎ 800-667 2887; www.travelcuts.com) and UK-based **Trailfinders** (☎ 020-7938 3939; www.trailfinder.com; 194 Kensington High St, London W8 7RG) and **Journey Latin America** (☎ 020-8747 3108; www.journeylatinamerica.co.uk; 12 & 13 Heathfield Tce, Chiswick, London W4 4JE).

Argentina

One LanChile Punta Arenas–Falklands flight per month, in each direction, goes via Río Gallegos in Argentina. There are regular rumours about Aerolíneas Argentinas starting a regular service between Argentina and the Falklands, but some Falkland Islanders have strong opposition to this.

Asia & Africa

Carriers serving Santiago from Asia, usually via North America, include All Nippon Airways (with LanChile) via Los Angeles and Varig (via Brazil). Varig also flies to Johannesburg via São Paulo.

Malaysia Airlines (with LanChile) connects Santiago with Kuala Lumpur via Buenos Aires, Johannesburg and Cape Town, while South African Airways (with British Airways) flies from Santiago to Johannesburg via Buenos Aires, São Paulo and Rio de Janeiro.

Australia & New Zealand

LanChile, code-sharing with Qantas, flies Sydney–Auckland–Santiago. Connections from Melbourne can be made at Auckland. From Sydney to Santiago fares range from A$2300 return. All the way to the Falklands and back count on around A$3900, slightly less from New Zealand.

Canada

Canadian Airlines offers good connections to Santiago from Toronto via Miami (US$600 to US$800) and from Vancouver via Los Angeles (US$700 to US$900).

Chile

LanChile operates a weekly flight between Punta Arenas in the south of Chile and the Falklands. The Airbus A320 flights depart on Saturday and take one hour and 40 minutes. The return fare from Punta Arenas is US$606 (US$566 Apex fare if booked seven days ahead). From Santiago the return fare

is US$786 (US$706 Apex). Children up to two travel free; from two to 12 they pay 75% of the adult fare.

There has been speculation about LanChile offering a second weekly service. Extra seats might attract more visitors but, equally important, the increased flexibility would make the Falklands more attractive as visitors wouldn't be locked in to the current one week, two week, no variation pattern. The Falklands' deal with LanChile requires a subsidy if the load factors fall below a certain level, but the service has been sufficiently successful and the subsidy is rarely required. The second service would probably be only in the peak November to April summer season.

International Tours & Travels (Map pp70-1; ☎ 22041; fax 22042; se.itt@horizon.co.fk; Beauchêne Complex, John St, Stanley) handles the LanChile flights from the Falklands.

The UK

RAF flights on a TriStar from **RAF Brize Norton** (☎ 01993-896 643; www.raf.mod.uk/rafbrizenorton/index .html) air-force base, near Burford, Oxfordshire, operate six or seven times a month. They depart England in the late evening, arriving in the Falklands late the next morning. Brize Norton is about 24km west of Oxford; you can get there by train and bus and the website has the full story.

The flights are one class with a standard one-way fare of £1280. There is an Apex fare of £790, but you must book and pay 30 days in advance or cancellation penalties apply: 25% penalty if you cancel from 28 to seven days before departure; 50% if you cancel in the last week. For a group of six or more people booking and travelling together there's a group fare of £670 per person. Children travel free up to the age of two, but ages two to 12 must pay 50% of the adult fare. For return fares simply double the one-way fare; although you can buy a one-way ticket you must have an onward or return ticket to enter the Falklands. RAF flights are not party to any international airline agreement; you cannot buy a round-trip ticket returning to Britain via Chile or include the RAF Brize Norton–Mt Pleasant sector as part of an international itinerary.

For more information check out the website of the **Falklands Tourist Office** (www.tourism .org.fk). For travel information from the Falklands to the UK with the RAF contact **Falkland Islands Company** (Map pp70-1; FIC; ☎ 27633; fax 27603; West Store, Ross Rd). Bookings from the UK can be made through the **Falkland Islands Government Office** (☎ 020-7222 2542; fax 7222 2375; travel@figo.u-net.com; Falkland House, 14 Broadway, Westminster, London SW1H 0BH). Payment can be by cash or by personal or bank cheque; credit cards are not accepted. On each flight only 28 seats are reserved for nonmilitary personnel; sometimes even those can be unexpectedly closed off. It's a wise idea to book well ahead, particularly during the peak summer season. The flight takes 18 hours, including a two-hour refuelling stop on tiny Ascension Island in the South Atlantic. The free baggage allowance is 27kg.

If you don't wish to travel with the RAF, you can connect with the LanChile flight from Punta Arenas in Chile to the Falklands. The most direct route would be to fly London–Madrid with British Airways or Iberian, and Madrid–Santiago with LanChile. Madrid is the only city in Europe with direct flights to Chile. You would then have to overnight in Santiago before continuing to the Falklands. Economy-class fares on this route start at £930 return; much cheaper than the RAF flight. An alternative would be to fly British Airways to São Paulo in Brazil and connect with LanChile from there to Santiago. This service still requires an overnight in Santiago or Punta Arenas. There are various other connections possible via Rio de Janiero, Buenos Aires and other South American cities.

The USA

Various airports have direct flights to Santiago to connect with the LanChile flight to the Falklands. The regular return fares start at around US$1400 from Miami, US$1800 from Los Angeles and US$1500 from New York City. Round-trip fares between US cities and Santiago are available for less than US$1000, so you may do better including the Santiago–Falkland Islands–Santiago flight as an add-on to a cheap flight from the USA.

SEA

Island Shipping (☎ 22346; iship@horizon.co.fk; Waverley House, Philomel St), opposite the Falklands Brasserie, operates the MV *Tamar* around the islands. Periodically it travels on supply trips to Punta Arenas in Chile. There are

only four berths, and at £180 single the fare is very similar to the LanChile fare – but it's certainly an interesting way of getting to or from the Falklands (so long as you're not prone to seasickness).

Cruises

The majority of visitors to the Falklands and all (apart from a handful of people on yachts) who get to South Georgia island will be on cruise ships. Antarctic tourism has grown enormously in the past 10 to 15 years and the Antarctic Peninsula, the Falkland Islands and South Georgia are the three main centres for these trips. The trips vary a great deal, from adventure-style expeditions at one end to luxury cruises at the other. It's only the smaller vessels, typically with a 200-passenger limit, that are able to make landings at most sites on the Falklands or South Georgia. In 2003, for the first time, a 500-passenger cruise ship visited South Georgia, but the only stop was at the abandoned Grytviken whaling station. Ships carrying 1000–2000 passengers visit the Falkland Islands, but they are only able to stop at Stanley. The residents call cruise ship visitors 'day trippers'.

The main factor for the big increase in Antarctic tourism since the late 1980s is the collapse of the Soviet Union. The USSR operated many ice-strengthened, or even ice-breaking, research vessels and supply ships to their Antarctic and Arctic bases. The straitened post-communism Russian economy enabled Western adventure travel companies to charter these ships at very favourable rates.

The operators of the smaller vessels are generally members of the International Association of Antarctica Tour Operators (IAATO), which works to ensure Antarctica remains a sustainable tourism destination. IAATO members agree that they will never have more than 100 passengers ashore at one time at any Antarctic site. The majority of expedition ships operated by IAATO members carry less than 200 passengers. Members with ships that carry more than 500 members are not permitted to make any landings; they can only cruise Antarctic waters.

CRUISE OPERATORS

Tour costs listed will usually be on a share-room basis and usually do not include air fares. If air fares are included a credit will be offered if you want to arrange your own air travel (if you were coming from a different starting point for example). Typically, the supplement for single-room occupancy will be 40% to 50%. Rooms on the ships are variable and range from triples with shared bathroom facilities to suites with separate living rooms and attached bathrooms. Many operators book tours on each other's ships or even charter the whole ship for certain voyages, so at a glance it looks as if numerous operators have a share in the same ships. Cruise lengths listed are generally the actual length of the voyage, and don't include days getting to or from the departure port.

Abercrombie & Kent (☎ 800-323 7308, 630-954 2944; fax 572 1833; www.abercrombiekent.com; 1520 Kensington Rd, Oak Brook, IL 60523-2156 USA) This company offers trips ranging from 14 to 20 days, covering the Antarctic Peninsula and Falkland Islands or South Georgia, on the *Explorer II* (which is more luxurious than its predecessor, the *Explore*, the original ice-strengthened ship commissioned by Antarctic tourism pioneer Lars-Eric Lindblad). Costs vary from US$5995 up to US$17,995.

Adventure Associates (☎ 02-9389 7466; fax 9369-1853; www.adventureassociates.com; mail@adventure associates.com; 197 Oxford St Mall, Bondi Junction, NSW 2022, Australia) Adventure Associates has 16- and 19-day trips on the *Professor Multanovskiy, Professor Molchanov* and MV *Orlova* from US$4750 to US$11,750. There's also an eight-day trip on the *Professor Multanovskiy*, which concentrates purely on the Falkland Islands and costs from US$2250 to US$5150.

Aurora Expeditions (☎ 800-637 688, 02-9252 1033; fax 9252 1273; www.auroraexpeditions.com.au; 182A Cumberland St, The Rocks, Sydney, NSW 2000, Australia) Aurora's voyages to the region include a South Georgia trip with, for suitably qualified walkers, a crossing following the Shackleton route. Aurora has specialised in active trips to Antarctica and the sub-Antarctic islands with kayaking, mountain climbing and scuba-diving possibilities from the *Polar Pioneer*. The 18-day tour to the Falklands and South Georgia, or similar-length tours to Antarctica and South Georgia, cost from US$6550 to US$10,250.

Cheesemans' Ecology Safaris (☎ 800-527 5330, 408-867 1371; fax 741 0358; www.cheesemans.com; 20800 Kittredge Rd, Saratoga, CA 95070 USA) Cheesemans' tours include a 20-day Antarctica, Falkland Islands and South Georgia trip on the MV *Polar Star*, with fares from US$10,950 to US$17,500.

Clipper Cruise Line (☎ 800-325 0010, 314-655 6700; fax 655 6670; www.clippercruise.com; 11969 Westline Industrial Dr, St Louis, Missouri 63146-322 USA) This company operates the *Clipper Adventurer* and its 17-day cruise to the Falklands, South Georgia and Antarctica costs from US$10,670 to US$16,900, including air fare from Miami.

LIFE ABOARD A POLAR SHIP

Voyages to polar seas are different from other sorts of sea travel; even seasoned 'cruisers' may need to make some adjustments. Some people find shipboard life claustrophobic, and this can be heightened in Antarctica because the ships are small and relatively spartan, especially compared to the lavish floating palaces that ply the Caribbean, Mediterranean and other seas.

It's also completely normal to feel lethargic during the several days of sailing required to reach South Georgia. Typically, a printed bulletin listing the next day's planned activities is distributed each night and it helps to attend the educational lectures and video screenings, which are given, in part, to relieve the monotony. Enterprising passengers will find plenty of distractions – watching sea-birds, spotting icebergs, visiting the bridge or engine room, diary writing, reading – although even these can get stale after three or four days; however, it's worth the wait.

International law requires that every ship hold a lifeboat drill within 24 hours of sailing. These drills are serious and mandatory for all passengers. Each cabin should contain a sign or card advising the occupants which lifeboat station should be used. There will also be a life vest for each person in the cabin; these are usually equipped with a whistle, reflective patches and a battery-powered beacon light, which starts flashing automatically upon contact with salt water. The universal signal to proceed to lifeboat stations is seven short blasts on the ship's bell or horn, followed by a long blast. This signal may be repeated several times for the lifeboat drill. Since there is only one such drill held during each voyage, if you ever hear the signal a second time during your voyage, it is the *real thing*. You should go immediately to your cabin to pick up your life vest and warm clothing, and then straight to your lifeboat station to await instructions from the crew.

Extra care is needed when moving about any ship, but passengers on Antarctic cruises especially should keep in mind the rule of 'one hand for the ship', always keeping one hand free to

Expeditions Inc (☎ 888-484 2244, 541-330 2454; fax 330 2456; www.expeditioncruises.com; 20525 SE Dorchester, Bend, Oregon 97702 USA) Expeditions books through most of the Antarctic cruise operators and claims its arm's-length relationship enables it to give good advice on which ship and company best suits individual travellers. Its website has excellent descriptions of many of the ships operating in Antarctic waters.

Hapag-Lloyd Kreuzfahrten (☎ 40-3001 4600; fax 3001 4601; www.hlkf.de; Ballindamm 25, 20095 Hamburg, Germany) Hapag-Lloyd operates two ice-strengthened ships: the *Hanseatic* and the *Bremen*. In the past, some *Hanseatic* cruises have been marketed in the USA by Radisson Seven Seas.

Lindblad Expeditions (☎ 800-397 3348, 212-765 7740; fax 265 3770; www.expeditions.com; 720 Fifth Ave, New York, NY 10019 USA) Lindblad uses the *Endeavour* on its trips, including a 17-day Antarctica, Falkland Islands and South Georgia cruise which costs from US$9990 to US$16,990. A longer 22-day trip costs from US$13,640 to US$24,990.

Mountain Travel-Sobek (☎ 888-687 6235, 510-527 8100; fax 525 7710; www.mtsobek.com; 6420 Fairmount Ave, El Cerrito, CA 94530-3606 USA) It has an 18-day Antarctica, Falkland Islands and South Georgia trip aboard the *Akademik Ioffe*. This trip is operated for Mountain Travel-Sobek by Peregrine Expeditions and costs from US$6890 to US$11,720.

Oceanwide Expeditions (☎ 118-410 410; fax 410 417; www.ocnwide.com; Bellamypark 9, 4381 CG Vlissingen, Netherlands) Oceanwide operates the *Grigoriy Mikheev* on an 18-day Antarctica, Falkland Islands and South Georgia trip, which costs from US$8500 to US$12,500.

Orient Lines (☎ 800-333 7300, 954-527 6660; fax 527 6657; www.orientlines.com; 1510 SE 17 St, Ft Lauderdale, FL 33316 USA) Orient Lines operates the *Marco Polo*, which takes around 500 passengers on its Antarctic trips, far less than its 845 passenger capacity. Nevertheless, this large number of passengers does make landings more difficult. It has a 12-day Antarctica and Falklands trip from US$4995 or a 12-day Antarctica and South Georgia trip from US$5495.

Peregrine Expeditions (☎ 03-9662 2700; fax 9662 2422; www.peregrine.net.au; 258 Lonsdale St, Melbourne, Victoria 3000, Australia) Peregrine has the two sister ships *Akademik Ioffe* and *Akademik Sergei Vavilov* operating in Antarctic waters. It has a 12-day Antarctica and Falkland Islands tour priced from A$10,165 to A$15,910. There are also 16- to 19-day Antarctica, Falkland Islands and South Georgia trips from A$12,760 to A$19,290.

Polar Star Expeditions (☎ 800-509 1729, 902-423 7389; fax 420 9222; www.polarstarexpeditions.com; 2089 Upper Water St, Halifax, Nova Scotia B3K 5S3, Canada) Operates a variety of cruises to Antarctica, the Falklands and South Georgia on the MV *Polar Star* lasting from 18 to 25 days and costing from US$5900 to about US$15,000.

grab a railing or other support should the ship suddenly roll. You may notice that some berths on the ship (usually those running fore and aft) are equipped with airline-style seatbelts for use when seas get heavy. Take care not only when climbing steep ladders and stairs, but when in wide-open 'flat' areas such as the bridge, dining room or lecture hall, where a sudden slam into a chair or table could result in a broken arm or leg. Although the rolling motion of a ship on the open ocean tends to be fairly regular and predictable, a vessel pushing through ice can lurch suddenly, pitching unaware passengers onto their noses. Doors can become dangerous swinging projectiles in high seas. Take care not to accidentally curl your fingers around door jambs, as a fractured finger can result if the door closes suddenly. Decks can be slippery with rain, snow or oil, and you can easily trip on raised doorsills, stanchions and other shipboard tackle.

Cameras or video equipment should be securely stowed in the cabin. The best place to put such valuables, especially at night, is either on the floor or at the bottom of the closet. You don't want the first noise that alerts you to the onset of a sudden storm to be the sound of your Leica hitting the floor after flying off your desk.

Antarctic tourist ships generally maintain an 'open bridge', welcoming passengers to the navigation and steering area. The bridge will be closed during tricky navigation and whenever a pilot is aboard or the ship is in port. Etiquette demands that no food or drink be brought to the bridge, especially alcohol, and going barefoot on the bridge is also not appreciated. Keep your voice down; excessive noise interferes with communication between the navigator and helmsman. The low humming sound audible on the bridge is the ship's gyrocompass. Of course, it's always unwise to touch any equipment without being invited to do so by an officer of the watch. One further warning: sailors are a superstitious lot, and whistling anywhere on a ship is considered bad luck. Tradition says that a person whistling is calling up the wind, and that a storm will result.

Quark Expeditions (☎ 800-356 5699, 203-656 0499; fax 655 6623; www.quark-expeditions.com; enquiry@quarkexpeditions.co.uk; 980 Post Rd, Darien, CT 06820-4509 USA) This company is well known for its powerful Russian-flagged icebreakers, but these are not used on Falklands or South Georgia trips. Its 19- and 20-day Explorers' Cruises visit the Antarctic Peninsula, the Falklands and South Georgia on board the *Professor Molchanov*, *Professor Multanovskiy* and the MV *Orlova*, and cost from US$6795 to US$11,495. It also has a 20-day South Georgia trip on the *Professor Molchanov*, which costs from US$7195 to US$11,495. Suitably qualified walkers can attempt the Shackleton route crossing of the island for an additional US$3350. Quark also has a unique nine-day trip on the *Professor Multanovskiy*, which concentrates purely on the Falkland Islands. The planned itinerary starts at Stanley and stops at New Island, Beaver Island, Staats Island, Steeple Jason, Carcass Island, Wespoint Island, Saunders Island, Keppel Island, Port San Carlos, Port Howard, George Island, Barren Island, Sea Lion Island, Volunteer Point and finally returns to Stanley having seen more of the Falklands than most Falkland Islanders will ever manage. Costs range from US$3895 to US$7,095. Quark also has an office in the UK (☎ 1494-464 080; fax 1494-449 739; enquiry@quarkexpeditions.co.uk; 19A Crendon St, High Wycombe, Bucks, HP13 6LJ, England).

Society Expeditions (☎ 800-548 8669, 206-728-9400; fax 728-2301; www.societyexpeditions.com; 2001 Western Ave, Suite 300, Seattle, WA 98121-2114 USA) Society Expeditions was one of the seven founding members of IAATO and operates the *World Discoverer*. Cruises to Antarctica, the Falklands and South Georgia last 18 days and cost from US$9509 to US$16,445

Victor Emanuel Nature Tours (☎ 800-328 8368, 512-328 5221; fax 328 2919; www.ventbird.com; 2525 Wallingwood Drive, Suite 1003, Austin, TX 78746, USA) This company specialises in birdwatching tours.

WildWings (☎ 117-9658 333; fax 117-9375 681; www.wildwings.co.uk; 577-579 Fishponds Rd, Bristol BS163AF, England) The company has an 18-day Antarctica, Falkland Islands and South Georgia trip on the *Akademik Ioffe* costing from £6450 to £8500.

Zegrahm Expeditions (☎ 800-628 8747, 206-285 4000; fax 285 5037; www.zeco.com; 192 Nickerson St, Suite 200, Seattle, WA 98109-1632 USA) Its 17-day Antarctica, Falkland Islands and South Georgia trip uses the *Clipper Adventurer* and costs from US$10,490 to US$17,890.

In addition to these companies operating the expedition-style ships and the dual-purpose expedition ships, there are also companies with larger cruise ships that call in at Stanley as part of a South American or Antarctic itinerary. Holland-America's 1380-passenger *Amsterdam* and Princess Cruises' 1200-passenger *Royal Princess* are examples.

EXPEDITION SHIPS & CRUISE SHIPS

Expedition-style cruise ships are like slightly larger and more luxurious versions of the research vessels. Typically they carry 100–180 passengers and feature ice-strengthened hulls. Lars-Eric Lindblad was the founding father of this style of trip and his original ship, later renamed the *Explorer*, was finally retired after the 2002–03 season. While offering the facilities (in reduced scale) of a luxury cruise ship, the vessels in this category also carry Zodiac landing craft and have lecturers, naturalists and expedition staff on board. Once you get larger than this you're moving into the regular cruise ship category, although the number of passengers may be kept to a lower level on Antarctic cruises.

Bremen Built in 1990 and carrying 164 passengers, this ship has a length of 110m.

Clipper Adventurer This vessel used to be the *Alla Tarasova*. A US$13 million refit was performed in 1998. It has all outside cabins and can carry 122 passengers. Its length is 101m.

Endeavour The *Endeavour* used to be the *Caledonian Star*. It was built in 1966 and has all outside cabins. It can carry 110 passengers and has a length of 90m.

Explorer II This vessel used to be the MV *Minerva*. It was built in 1996 and can carry up to 300 passengers, limited to 198 for Antarctic trips, all in outside cabins. It has an ice-strengthened hull. Its length is 133m.

Hanseatic The *Hanseatic* used to be the *Society Adventurer*. It was built in 1991 and has more luxurious accommodation than is usual in Antarctic ships. It can carry 180 passengers and its length is 123m.

Marco Polo This vessel used to be the *Alexandr Pushkin*. It was built in 1965 and refurbished in 1992. At 176m it is one of the largest and most luxurious ships cruising in these waters. It has an ice-strengthened hull.

MV Orlova This vessel was built in Yugoslavia in 1976 and refurbished in 1999. It can carry 110 passengers and has a length of 100m.

World Discoverer This ship used to be *Bewa Discoverer*. It was built in 1989 and refurbished in 2001. It has replaced the earlier *World Discoverer*. It can carry 150 passengers and has a length of 108m.

RESEARCH VESSELS

Ice-strengthened research vessels, carrying 50 to 100 passengers, were predominantly built in Finland in the 1980s for the old Soviet Union. Once upon a time they were used for 'research', which if you read as 'spying' wouldn't be too far off the mark. These days they're on charter to Western adventure-travel companies and will have

Russian crews (they're the ice experts) supplemented by Western lecturers, expedition crews, cooks, bar personnel and so on. While not luxurious these ships are quite comfortable. They generally have all outside cabins, although the cheaper rooms will probably have shared shower and toilet facilities. Some of the trips on these ships will have 'adventure' at the top of the list; the opportunity to go kayaking, trekking, mountain climbing or scuba diving may be the principal attraction for some of the passengers. Just because these activities are on the itinerary, however, doesn't mean you have to take part. On a trip to South Georgia, for example,

---

ZODIACS

Without Zodiacs, Antarctic tourism would be much more difficult and much less pleasurable. Popularised by the French oceanographer Jacques Cousteau, Zodiacs are small, inflatable boats powered by outboard engines. Their shallow draught makes them ideal for cruising among icebergs and ice floes and for landing in otherwise inaccessible areas. They are made of a synthetic, rubber-like material forming a pontoon in a roughly wishbone shape, with a wooden transom on the back holding the engine. The deck (floor) is made of sections of aluminium. Zodiacs are very safe and stable in the water and are designed to stay afloat even if one or more of their six separate air-filled compartments are punctured. Zodiacs come in a variety of sizes, but on most trips you can expect to share your boat with nine to 14 other passengers, a driver and one other cruise staff member.

Smoking anywhere near Zodiacs is prohibited – and dangerous – since the fuel tanks are exposed. Safety vests must be worn during Zodiac trips. Wet-weather jackets and pants are also critically important, because even in fine weather the boat's flying spray will give you a good shower. Personal items should be carried in a waterproof backpack (or in a waterproof bag inside the backpack); you can also tuck cameras, binoculars or bags inside your foul-weather jacket to keep them dry. Remember, there are no toilets ashore, so go before you leave the ship.

To ensure that no-one gets left behind, tours maintain a system for keeping track of passengers. On some ships, a staff member checks your name off a list when you leave the ship, and again when you leave the shore. On others, you are responsible for turning over a coloured tag on a large notice board inside the ship, indicating your departure and return.

Entering and exiting Zodiacs are probably the most hazardous activities in Antarctic waters – but with a little care, there is no need for anyone to get hurt. Passengers descend the ship's gangway to the Zodiac, which is held to the landing at the bottom of the gangway by a crew member and/or several lines. Since the Zodiac will be rising and falling with the swell, it's important to have both hands free. If you have a camera or a bag, the Zodiac crew will ask you to hand it to them. They will then take hold of your wrist while you seize theirs in a hold known as the 'sailor's grip'. This is much safer than a mere handshake grip, since if one party accidentally lets go, the other still has a firm hold. Move slowly: step onto the pontoon of the Zodiac and then down onto the deck or floor, before moving to your seat on the pontoon. Sit facing the inside of the boat, and hold onto the ropes tied to the pontoon behind you because the ride can be quite bumpy.

Only one passenger at a time should stand in a Zodiac. You should never stand while the boat is moving; ask the driver to slow the Zodiac down before you do.

Exiting is as simple as entering. Most landings are made bow-first and tour staff will be on hand to help you get out of the boat. Passengers sitting in the bow should swing their legs toward the *stern* of the Zodiac (taking care not to kick their neighbour), then over the side and down onto the beach. Swinging your legs to the front of the Zodiac would be more difficult, since the pontoon is higher at the bow, and you might well fall back into the Zodiac, presenting a great photo opportunity for your fellow passengers. If there's a large swell, landings may be made stern-first. In this case, passengers in the stern disembark first. Never try to exit over the transom, since a surging wave could knock you over or lift and drop the heavy engine – or even the entire Zodiac – onto you.

Zodiac landings are either 'wet', meaning you have to step into a bit of water before getting to the dry beach, or 'dry', in which case you can step directly onto a rock, jetty, dock or other piece of dry land. No matter what anyone may tell you, *all* landings are 'wet'.

some passengers may be setting out on a trek following Shackleton's route, while others continue on a circumnavigation of the island. The powerful icebreakers like the *Kapitan Khlebnikov* are a step up from the research vessels; they're the top dogs in Antarctic waters, but are not normally used for trips to the Falklands or South Georgia. Research vessels and icebreakers that visit the Falklands or South Georgia include:

Akademik Ioffe & Akademik Sergei Vavilov These near-identical sister ships were built in Finland (*Sergei Vavilov* in 1988 and *Ioffe* in 1989). They both carry 110 passengers and have a length of 117m.

Grigoriy Mikheev Built in Finland in 1990, this vessel was refurbished in the Netherlands. It carries 46 passengers and has a length of 68m.

Polar Pioneer This vessel used to be *Akademik Shuleykin*. It was built in Finland in 1982 and refurbished in St Petersburg in 2000. It can carry 54 passengers and has a length of 72m.

Polar Star This icebreaker was built Finland in 1969 but is used by Sweden, not the USSR. It was refurbished in 2000. It carries 105 passengers and has a length of 87m.

Professor Molchanov & Professor Multanovskiy These near-identical sister ships were built in Finland in the 1980s. *Professor Molchanov* was the first of these Russian-flagged research vessels, all named after Russian academics, to cruise Antarctic waters, back in 1991. It has been extensively refurbished over the years and can carry 50 passengers. It has a length of 70m.

Yacht Voyages

Every year more private yachts visit the Falklands and South Georgia. For some reason Antarctic yachting seems to have a particular fascination for the French. For a flavour of yachting in Antarctic and sub-Antarctic waters check Sally and Jérôme Poncet's excellent 60-page *Southern Ocean Cruising* and Tim and Pauline Carr's evocative *Antarctic Oasis: Under the Spell of South Georgia*. These are extremely testing waters, not to be approached without careful consideration.

In the Falklands Stanley is, of course, the main destination for visiting yachts and the only port with immigration and customs facilities. Yachts usually tie up either at the FIPASS (Floating Interim Port and Storage System) floating dock or at the public jetty in the centre of town. At most other settlements around the island yachts will have to anchor offshore.

Yachts visiting South Georgia should apply to the **Commissioner for South Georgia & the South Sandwich Islands** (☎ 500-27433; fax 27434; gov.house@horizon.co.fk; Government House, Stanley, Falkland Islands via UK). Various regulations apply to visitors and landing on Cooper, Bird and Annenkov Islands requires special permission. Vessels en route to South Georgia must contact the marine officer at King Edward Point by radio (VHF Channel 16) or fax (Inmarsat ☎ +874 811 440 165).

Yachts can use the old whaling station jetties at Prince Olav Harbour, Leith Harbour, Stromness, Husvik and Grytviken, although captains are warned that the jetties are old and decrepit, and any use is at their own risk. Water is available alongside the Harpon Grytviken's main jetty. There's a great deal of useful information about yachting in South Georgia at the website of the **Royal Cruising Club Pilotage Foundation** (www.rccpf.org.uk).

YACHT CHARTER COMPANIES

Apart from the companies and charter operators listed below there are a number of individual operators. In addition, it's often possible to pick something up by simply hanging around in Ushuaia or, less frequently, Punta Arenas.

Croisieres Australes (☎ 2-99-23-67-41; fax 2-99-23-67-39; www.nature-sailing.com; croisieresaustrales@nature-sailing.com; 3 allée de l'Oseraie, 35760 St Grégoire, France) Operated by Eric Leyes this company organises yacht charters in many parts of the world, including the Falklands and South Georgia. There is even a 14-day charter around the Falklands.

Golden Fleece Expeditions (☎ /fax 42316; www.horizon.co.fk/goldenfleecexp) Golden Fleece is operated out of Beaver Island in the Falklands by Jérôme Poncet. For many years this has been the best-known Falklands charter operation using the 21m steel schooner *Golden Fleece*. It's been chartered by many film, TV and magazine operations, as well as for expeditions and adventure travel programmes. *Golden Fleece* can accommodate up to eight passengers and three crew. Charter rates start at around US$1000 per day.

Ocean Voyages (☎ 800-299 4444, 415-332 4681; fax 332 7460; www.oceanvoyages.com; 1709 Bridgeway, Sausalito, California 94965, USA) This company organises charters and cruise bookings on yachts and cruise ships all over the world, including the Falklands and South Georgia.

Pelagic Expeditions (☎ 1962-862 361; fax 1962-620 225; www.pelagic.co.uk; 75 Christchurch Rd, Winchester,

Hants SO23 9TG, England) Pelagic has been chartering in Antarctic waters, including the Falklands and South Georgia, for more than 10 years. *Pelagic Australia* does a Falklands tour at a cost of £2500 per person for eight passengers.

Victory Yacht Cruises (☎ 61-621 010; fax 621 092; www.victory-cruises.com; Teniente Munoz 118, Puerto Williams, Cape Horn Commune, Tierra Del Fuego, Chile) Operated by Ben Garrett, Victory Yacht specialises in this area of the world with charters organised on 18 different yachts, including 42-day cruises to South Georgia at US$190 per person per day.

GETTING AROUND

Most travel around the Falkland Islands is done by air because the road network is limited and shipping connections between the two major islands and out to the many smaller ones are restricted and infrequent. In camp, motorcycles and, to a lesser extent, horses are still used but 4WD, especially Land-Rovers, are the transport of choice. Walking is feasible for adventurous travellers, but trekkers must be prepared for changeable and often extremely uncomfortable weather, and must always get permission before crossing private land.

AIR

Falkland Islands Government Air Service (FIGAS; ☎ 27219; figas.fig@horizon.co.fk) operates an on-demand service with four eight-seater Britten-Norman Islander aircraft. These high wing, twin-engine, fixed undercarriage aircraft are sturdy, reliable and offer excellent views – flights rarely climb above 600m and short flights and/or low clouds often mean you fly even lower. Two other Islanders operate on fishery patrols.

There are about 40 grass or beach airstrips around the Falklands, although some of them are rarely used and others can only be used with the aircraft partially loaded. Although the RAF flights from Britain and the LanChile flights from Chile operate to and from Mt Pleasant Airport (MPA), 56km from Stanley, the FIGAS flights generally operate from the Stanley airport, a surfaced airstrip just 5km from the town. The Stanley airport was completed in 1977, paid for by Argentina. Only 900m of the 1200m runway is used today.

Passengers arriving on international flights at Mt Pleasant can arrange to fly out directly to other locations around the islands rather than starting their visit with the drive to Stanley. Of course, visitors will want to spend some time in Stanley but saving that visit for the very end makes good sense. Flights around the Falklands are rarely cancelled (perhaps 10 days a year), either due to high winds or low visibility, but it still makes sense to get back to Stanley a day or two before final departure. Missing the LanChile flight to Punta Arenas could mean a one week wait for the next departure.

There is no regular schedule. Flight plans depend on demand; if only one or two people are headed to a destination, FIGAS

FLIGHT PROCEDURES

There are no definite flight schedules; FIGAS flights go pretty much to order and since it's a government-run organisation load factors aren't a big part of the picture. However, load distribution definitely is, so passengers, their baggage and their hand baggage are all weighed, carefully distributed around the aircraft and often shifted around at intermediate stops.

At the settlements a phone call comes from Stanley when flights depart, giving time to drive the Land-Rover out to the airstrip, put up the windsock, drive up and down the runway a couple of times to chase any sheep and geese off, and hook up the trailer of fire fighting equipment. There's often a second run down the runway when the cursed geese fly back and land a bit further along.

The big moment in the Falklands/FIGAS day comes at 6.15pm each night, right after the Archers and the weather, when the following day's flight schedule is read out on the radio. But it's not just the flight schedule – the announcer also reports who's on each flight and where they get off. Half the Falklands tunes in to find who's going where; just think of the April Fool's Day possibilities: '11am departure from Stanley to Fox Bay, passengers are X, Y and Z (probably going to see his mistress).'

may delay a flight until other passengers join the group. On rare occasions, usually around holidays, flights are heavily booked and you may not get on.

You don't have to return to Stanley to get to your next destination. If you're on Pebble Island and want to continue westward to Carcass Island you'll probably be able to do so, although there may be a stop or two on that 60km trip. The flight might arrive from Stanley (via Mt Pleasant) with five people on board; drop a couple of new arrivals off on Pebble; pick you and your companion up; hop across to Saunders Island and pick up two more people en route for Carcass and drop off the three who've come from Stanley; make the short flight across to Hill Cove on the West Falkland 'mainland' to pick up two people going to Stanley; and finally arrive at Carcass. A week or two around the Falklands can involve a lot of take-offs and landings.

Bookings made with FIGAS will specify a date but not usually a flight time. To find out when you're actually flying you can phone FIGAS, wait for the fax that goes out to each FIGAS destination each day listing the flight movements, or listen to the radio (see the boxed text on p183).

Luggage is restricted to a strictly enforced 14kg and excess baggage costs 60p a kilogram. If you're taking food to your destination, because you're 'self-catering' for example, you might be able to negotiate a lower freight charge. Some of the airstrips around the Falklands require payload restrictions, when the weight limits may be particularly closely enforced or the number of passengers may be limited.

Flights from Stanley Airport (STY)

	Distance	One-way fare (£)
Bleaker Island	92km	40
Carcass Island	201km	75
Fox Bay	162km	65
Darwin	83km	36
Hill Cove	164km	65
Pebble Island	134km	55
Port Howard	125km	60
Port San Carlos	87km	37
Salvador	49km	26
Saunders Island	165km	65
Sea Lion Island	120km	50
Weddell Island	215km	80

BICYCLE

Not many cyclists have attempted the Falklands on two wheels; the wind conditions can make bike riding hard work. There is a bicycle shop in Stanley but it's not terribly well equipped; you should bring any spare parts you may need as well as tyres and tubes. The stony gravel roads can be very hard on bicycle tyres. Ivan Viehoff talks about his bicycle trip to the Falklands on www.geocities.com/TheTropics/Island /6810/ivan/falklands. He stresses the importance of being well equipped with clothing to withstand cold, wet and wind or, at the other extreme, that ozone-hole sun. Having good camping gear is particularly important and cyclists should also be prepared for the lack of water which, when it is available, is quite likely to have been polluted by sheep or wildlife.

CAR & MOTORCYCLE

There are sealed roads in Stanley: at the Mt Pleasant military base, and some stretches of the 56km Mt Pleasant Hwy between Stanley and MPA. Other than that there are good gravelled roads connecting all the main settlements on both islands. Outside of Stanley none of these roads existed before the Falklands War; prior to 1982 getting anywhere in the Falklands by land was likely to be a slow, tedious process of crossing camp by 4WD, motorcycle or horse.

The road network is still being extended, but already runs from Stanley via Mt Pleasant to Darwin-Goose Green and on to North Arm on the Bay of Harbours at the southern side of Lafonia. Not far south of Stanley on the way to Mt Pleasant a road branches off west to Port San Carlos; various spurs branch off these two main routes (see p91). In West Falkland the main route runs west from Port Howard south and west to Fox Bay and on towards Port Stephens (see p112). In all there are about 400km of road. And not a single traffic light.

Although these gravelled roads are in good condition and traffic is light, driving still requires care and attention. It's easy to put a wheel over the edge and lose control. In the case of an accident it can be a long time before help arrives. Off road, driving across camp requires special expertise and local knowledge. Quite apart from the difficulty of crossing the soft and often boggy terrain, simply finding the appropriate route can be difficult.

Rental vehicles are available in Stanley, while lodges at Pebble Island, Sea Lion Island, Port Howard and Port San Carlos have 4WDs available with drivers/guides for guests. Visitors may use their own state or national driver's licences in the Falklands for up to 12 months. See p83 for information on taxis and car rental, and p78 for tours. Fuel in the Falklands is quite reasonably priced at 25p a litre for diesel and 35p a litre for petrol. The only petrol station in the Falklands is in Stanley.

SEA

Island Shipping (☎ 22346; iship@horizon.co.fk; Waverley House, Philomel St), opposite the Falklands Brasserie, can carry a small number of passengers on its freighter MV *Tamar* as it makes its rounds to deliver fuel and other goods to settlements around the islands and to pick up wool. The schedules vary with demand and tend to be announced a few weeks in advance. Berths are limited: there are just two twin cabins, so book well ahead; day trips cost £20 while overnights cost £25. Meals are included although in rough Falklands waters many passengers don't get much opportunity to digest them.

The 591-ton *Tamar* was built in Norway in 1979 and came to the Falklands in 1993. She can carry four passengers, 700 bales of wool and has refrigeration capacity for 100 sheep carcasses. The vessel makes occasional trips to Chile to collect stores. Check Island Shipping's website www.shipping.horizon .co.fk for the ship's current schedule.

There has been talk for some time of starting a ferry service across Falkland Sound from New Haven, to the west of Goose Green on the East Falkland side of Falkland Sound, to Port Howard on the West Falkland side. Justifying a ferry service to West Falkland, when the island's population has fallen below 100, is very difficult.

Jérôme Poncet's yacht the *Golden Fleece* can be chartered for trips around the Falklands or to further afield (see p182 for details).

TOURS
Tour Operators

There's a lot to be said for organising everything in the Falklands before you arrive. There's a great deal to be seen around the islands, much of it on the smaller islands that can only be reached conveniently by the flights on the small FIGAS aircraft. Plus many of the places to stay have only a very limited number of rooms or beds, and can be booked out for weeks ahead during the peak summer months. A local tour operator can save a lot of time making all the bookings and arrangements.

There's also a lot to be said for getting out of Stanley as quickly as possible; save the capital for the end of your trip, that way you won't risk being stuck on an outer island by bad weather and missing your departure flight.

There are two local agents who can book all your flights, accommodation and tours. They're both responsive and used to dealing with inquiries by email:

International Tours & Travel Ltd (Map pp70-1; ☎ 22041; fax 22042; se.itt@horizon.co.fk; Beauchêne Complex, John St, Stanley)

Stanley Services (☎ 22622; fax 22623; sslcab@ horizon.co.fk; Airport Rd, Stanley)

RAILWAY

Remarkably, the Falklands once had a railway! In 1915–16 a 5km-long, 24-inch gauge railway was built from the Navy Jetty on the Camber, the spit of land which forms the north shore of Stanley Harbour, to the naval wireless station at Moody Brook. It was used to transport coal to the wireless station to fire the steam boilers, which powered the station's state-of-the-art spark transmitter dynamos. Two 'Wren' class locomotives built at Stoke-on-Trent were used, but by the mid-1920s improvements in radio technology had made coal-powered transmitters obsolete and the railway's useful life ended. In the meantime the Falklands railway had provided entertaining picnic trips for Stanley residents and a contemporary photograph shows one of these engines pulling passengers in three open wooden carriages labelled 1st, 2nd and 3rd class. The line even prompted some interesting experiments in wind-powered rail travelling, utilising the prevailing westerlies.

Backpackers visiting the Falklands often find that Kay McCallum (p79) is also adept at getting seats on FIGAS flights and sorting out places to stay.

There are many specialist tour operators outside the Falklands that organise trips to the islands. Companies that specialise in birdwatching and wildlife tours are particularly interested in Falklands tours (see p178).

Cruise Ship Tours

Many Antarctic cruise operators include the Falklands on their itineraries either to the Antarctic Peninsula or to South Georgia, typically spending a half day or day in Stanley with a stop or two at one of the outer islands. Quark Expeditions has also operated trips on the Russian vessel *Professor Multanovskiy* purely covering the Falkland Islands (see p180 for more details).

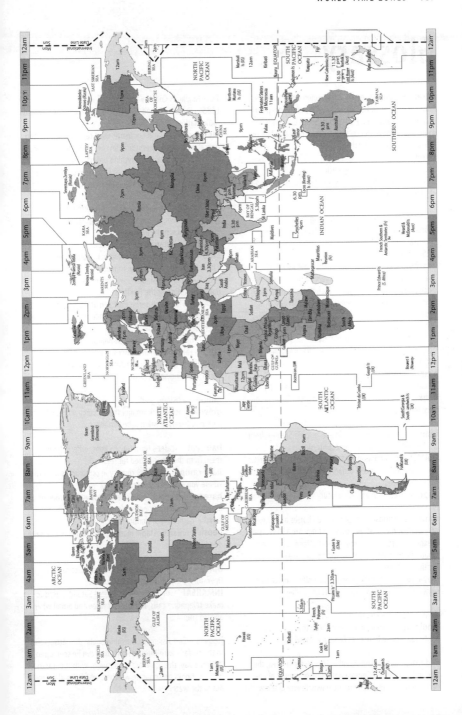

Glossary

Antarctic Convergence – the region where the cold Antarctic seas meet the warmer waters of the northern oceans; also called the Polar Front; South Georgia is south of the convergence, in the colder region, while the Falklands are to the north
arroyo – stream, from Spanish
asado – barbecue, from Spanish
ASTI – Areas of Special Tourist Interest; Grytviken and Bay of Isles on South Georgia

bachelors – immature, nonbreeding male seals
balsam bog – plant that forms a dense, hard, hemispherical green cushion
BAS – British Antarctic Survey
beachmaster – a large, dominant male seal who guards – and breeds with – a *harem* on a breeding beach
bergy bits – smaller than an iceberg but bigger than an ice cube, typically showing less than 5m above the surface
BFBS – British Forces Broadcasting Service; the Falklands TV channel provided by the military
bogged – a Falklands Land-Rover stuck in the mud in *soft camp*
bosal – a halter, from Spanish
brash ice – broken ice found among smooth first-year ice
bunk-ride – what many passengers prefer to do in rough seas; to sleep

camp – anywhere in the Falklands outside Stanley; from the Spanish word 'campo' for countryside
CCAMLR – Commission for the Conservation of Antarctic Marine Living Resources; organisation that manages Antarctic fishing
clapmatches – what 19th-century sealers called female fur seals
corral – an enclosure for penning up horses or cattle, typically built of turf or stone; some of them are 150 years old
crèche – a group of penguin chicks attended by a small group of adults while most of the parents are out at sea hunting for food
crevasse – deep crack or fissure in a glacier or ice field, sometimes covered by snow so it is not visible

demersal – deep water fish
diddle-dee – small, evergreen shrub that produces bright red, edible berries in February–March

endemic – something found only in a certain area; the Falklands and South Georgia both have a number of endemic birds and plants, ie found nowhere else in the world

FC – Falklands Conservation
FIBS – Falkland Islands Broadcasting Station; the Falklands radio station
FIC – Falkland Island Company; used to be the owner and operator of nearly everything on the islands and still owns at least half of nearly everything today
FICZ – Falkland Islands Interim Conservation & Management Zone; the islands' original fishing zone established in 1986
FID – a British Antarctic worker; this term is still in use today, even though the Falkland Islands Dependencies Survey, from which the name derives, was replaced by the name British Antarctic Survey in 1962
FIDC – Falkland Islands Development Corporation
FIG – Falkland Islands Government
FIGAS – Falkland Islands Government Air Service; the domestic airline of the Falklands
FIPASS – Floating Interim Port and Storage System; the 'temporary' floating dock system built just east of Stanley after the Falklands War
FITB – Falkland Islands Tourist Board
FOCZ – Falkland Islands Outer Conservation Zone; an extension of FICZ in 1990 to 200 nautical miles to the north, east and south of the islands

ghillie – a fishing guide
growler – ice chunk smaller than a *bergy bit*; usually awash or barely breaking the surface

hair seal – sealer's term for sea lions, differentiating them from the finer-haired fur seals
hard camp – rocky, dry country in *camp*; the sort of *camp* where you're unlikely to get *bogged*
harem – a group of female seals jealously guarded on a breeding beach by a *beachmaster*
herd – gathering of nonbreeding seals
hoosh – Antarctic staple made by mixing *pemmican* with dried biscuits

IAATO – International Association of Antarctica Tour Operators; the industry trade association
INMARSAT – International Maritime Satellite; used to make telephone calls and to send faxes and email when aboard ship

jiggers – East Asian squid fishing boats; they attract fish to the surface with intense lights that can be seen up to 100km away; the squid are then caught with thousands of barbless hooks on separate winches, which 'jig' the squid out of the water

kelpers – Falkland Islanders
krill – shrimp-like planktonic crustacean; occurs in sometimes enormous swarms south of the *Antarctic Convergence*

Lafonia – the southern part of East Falkland, a low-lying zone separated from the hillier northern part by the narrow isthmus at Goose Green-Darwin
laguna – pool, from Spanish
lemmers – the men who cut up whales after they have been flensed

maletas – saddle bags, from Spanish
mollymawk – another name for a small albatross; the 14 species of albatross are divided into two groups: the 'great albatrosses' and the 'small albatrosses' (mollymawks)
morro – bluff, from Spanish
MPA – Mt Pleasant Airport; although the international airport code is actually MPN

nelly – another name for either of the two species of giant petrel
nunatak – a rocky peak surrounded completely by ice

outside house – a house, usually for shepherds, situated well away from the buildings in a *settlement*

passerine – perching bird
pelagic – of the open sea; thus pelagic fish are fish found well away from shore
pemmican – ground dried meat mixed with equal parts lard; this concentrated food was a primary ration on early Antarctic expeditions
pod – group of seal pups, dolphins or whales
pup – newborn seal

rincon – corner, from Spanish; a lot of points and headlands in the Falklands are named 'something or other rincon'
rookery – gathering of breeding seals or birds

settlement – collection of farm houses and buildings in *camp*
SGSSI – British Dependent Territory of South Georgia & the South Sandwich Islands
shanty – another term for an *outside house*
smoko – Falklands term (also Australian and British) for tea break

soft camp – squishy, peat country in *camp*; if you don't drive carefully enough it's easy to get *bogged* in soft camp
SPA – Specially Protected Areas; areas in South Georgia for which special permission from the *BAS* is needed before entry
squaddies – British military servicemen
SSSI – Sites of Special Scientific Interest; areas in South Georgia for which special permission from the *BAS* is needed before entry
standing men – cairns marking hilltops
stinker – Falklands term for giant petrels; from their habit of ejecting a stream of vomit at intruders
stone run – 'river' or 'block stream' of loose stones and rocks, which are a notable feature of Falklands topography

tarn – small mountain lake or pool
The Ice – Antarctica
trypot – a cauldron on three legs for rendering ('trying out') the blubber of whales, seals or penguins into oil
tryworks/triworks – a place where *trypots* are operated
twitcher – obsessive birdwatcher

wallow – muddy, noxious-smelling hollow made by seals, especially elephant seals
warrah – extinct Falklands fox, closely related to the Patagonian fox
wellies – calf- or knee-high rubber boots (Wellington boots) worn by most Antarctic tourists to go ashore
white grass – common vegetation across the main Falkland islands, particularly in the *soft camp* areas where drainage is poor; white grass is indeed whitish to light brown in colour
wigs – what 19th-century fur sealers called male fur seals
wriggly tin – corrugated iron; the principal Falklands building material

yearlings – older seal pups, typically four or five months old
yomping – crossing rough country on foot carrying 'full kit'; this British army term, used when British troops 'yomped' their way across East Falkland in 1982 to confront the Argentines at Stanley, has become part of Falklands English

Zodiac – an inflatable rubber dinghy powered by an outboard engine; used for making shore landings from an Antarctic expedition ship

Behind the Scenes

THIS BOOK

Tony Wheeler's research and visits to the islands built on a great deal of earlier work in other Lonely Planet guidebooks. Wayne Bernhardson wrote the original Falkland Islands chapter used in various forms in Lonely Planet's *South America on a Shoestring*, *Argentina*, *Chile* and *Antarctica* guidebooks. Jeff Rubin's sterling work on Lonely Planet's *Antarctica* guide made major contributions to this book, particularly the South Georgia chapter. Dr John Cooper's *Wildlife Guide for the Antarctica* formed the basis for the Natural History section in this book. Robert Headland's book *The Island of South Georgia* remains the classic text on the island and he was very helpful with information for this new book. The Grytviken material is principally the work of Robert Burton, a past director of the South Georgia Museum. David Burnett contributed the boxed text 'Mt William & Tumbledown Walk'.

THANKS from the Authors

Tony Wheeler In the Falklands in camp thanks to Rob McGill, Ken and Auntie on Carcass Island; Russell Evans and Karen Taylor on Pebble Island; Suzan and David Pole-Evans on Saunders Island; Ron and Iris Dickson on Bleaker Island; Leslie Woodward and Jacqui Jennings at Port Howard; and Pat Pratlett and Patrick Berntsen, at the time the 'Ps in the Pod', at Port San Carlos. Travelling around the Falklands I met many other fellow travellers, some of whom realised I was working on this book but others who didn't; thanks for the info you passed on. In Stanley (and in camp from Stanley) thanks to Sharon Halford (Tenacres), Kay McCallum (Kay's B&B), Neil Rowlands (Hebe Tours), Robin Woods (Falklands Conservation), John Fowler (Falklands Tourist Board), Patrick Watts (Adventure Falklands) and Sally Ellis (International Tours & Travels). I've never worked on any LP project where I got such quick responses to queries as I did with the Falklands. I sometimes had the feeling that islanders were all sitting by their computers in the middle of the night just waiting for emailed questions to come through.

On my trip to South Georgia special thanks to Greg Mortimer and Margaret Werner of Aurora Expeditions and to all the other hard workers from Aurora; and, of course, the expert crew – Russian, Australian, New Zealander and British – of the sturdy *Polar Pioneer* (aka *Akademik Shuleykin*) and my fellow passengers (especially the Shackleton walkers). Finally Stan Armington, Bob Pierce and David Burnett travelled south just before we went to press and came back with some last-minute corrections and suggestions. Thanks also to bird-watching expert Brent Stephenson who cast an expert eye over the Natural History text, and to Pete and Debbie from the Channel Islands.

CREDITS

This book was commissioned and briefed in Lonely Planet's Oakland office by Wendy Smith and Erin Corrigan. The project managers were Kieran Grogan and Andrew Weatherill. Editing was coordinated by Martine Lleonart. David Andrew assisted with editing. Julia Taylor steered the manuscript through layout. Thanks to Maryanne Netto for assistance. Cartography was coordinated in turn by

---

THE LONELY PLANET STORY

The story begins with a classic travel adventure: Tony and Maureen Wheeler's 1972 journey across Europe and Asia to Australia. There was no useful information about the overland trail then, so Tony and Maureen published the first Lonely Planet guidebook to meet a growing need.

From a kitchen table, Lonely Planet has grown to become the largest independent travel publisher in the world, with offices in Melbourne (Australia), Oakland (USA), London (UK) and Paris (France).

Today Lonely Planet guidebooks cover the globe. There is an ever-growing list of books and information in a variety of media. Some things haven't changed. The main aim is still to make it possible for adventurous travellers to get out there – to explore and better understand the world.

At Lonely Planet we believe travellers can make a positive contribution to the countries they visit – if they respect their host communities and spend their money wisely.

Laurie Mikkelsen, Celia Wood and Anthony Phelan. Michael Ruff designed the colour pages and Sally Darmody laid the book out. The cover was designed by Tamsin Wilson and the artwork was done by Nic Lehman. Overseeing production were Kerryn Burgess (managing editor) and Alison Lyall (managing cartographer).

ACKNOWLEDGMENTS

Many thanks to the following for the use of their content:

Globe on back cover © Mountain High Maps 1993 Digital Wisdom, Inc.

SEND US YOUR FEEDBACK

We love to hear from travellers – your comments keep us on our toes and help make our books better. Our well-travelled team reads every word on what you loved or loathed about this book. Although we cannot reply individually to postal submissions, we always guarantee that your feedback goes straight to the appropriate authors, in time for the next edition. Each person who sends us information is thanked in the next edition – and the most useful submissions are rewarded with a free book.

To send us your updates – and find out about LP events, newsletters and travel news – visit our award-winning website: **www .lonelyplanet.com**.

Note: We may edit, reproduce and incorporate your comments in Lonely Planet products such as guidebooks, websites and digital products, so let us know if you don't want your comments reproduced or your name acknowledged. For a copy of our privacy policy visit www.lonelyplanet.com/privacy.

BEHIND THE SCENES

Index

000 Map pages
000 Location of colour photographs

000 Map pages
000 Location of colour photographs

000 Map pages
000 Location of colour photographs

INDEX

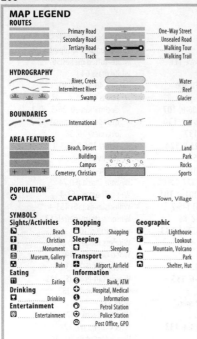

MAP LEGEND

ROUTES

Primary Road	One-Way Street
Secondary Road	Unsealed Road
Tertiary Road	Walking Tour
Track	Walking Trail

HYDROGRAPHY

River, Creek	Water
Intermittent River	Reef
Swamp	Glacier

BOUNDARIES

International	Cliff

AREA FEATURES

Beach, Desert	Land
Building	Park
Campus	Rocks
Cemetery, Christian	Sports

POPULATION

CAPITAL	Town, Village

SYMBOLS

Sights/Activities
- Beach
- Christian
- Monument
- Museum, Gallery
- Ruin

Eating
- Eating

Drinking
- Drinking

Entertainment
- Entertainment

Shopping
- Shopping

Sleeping
- Sleeping

Transport
- Airport, Airfield

Information
- Bank, ATM
- Hospital, Medical
- Information
- Petrol Station
- Police Station
- Post Office, GPO

Geographic
- Lighthouse
- Lookout
- Mountain, Volcano
- Park
- Shelter, Hut

LONELY PLANET OFFICES

Australia
Head Office
Locked Bag 1, Footscray, Victoria 3011
☎ 03 8379 8000, fax 03 8379 8111
talk2us@lonelyplanet.com.au

USA
150 Linden St, Oakland, CA 94607
☎ 510 893 8555, toll free 800 275 8555
fax 510 893 8572, info@lonelyplanet.com

UK
72–82 Rosebery Ave,
Clerkenwell, London EC1R 4RW
☎ 020 7841 9000, fax 020 7841 9001
go@lonelyplanet.co.uk

France
1 rue du Dahomey, 75011 Paris
☎ 01 55 25 33 00, fax 01 55 25 33 01
bip@lonelyplanet.fr, www.lonelyplanet.fr

Published by Lonely Planet Publications Pty Ltd
ABN 36 005 607 983

© Lonely Planet 2004

© photographers as indicated 2004

Cover photographs: Rockhopper penguin perched on rock, Tim Davis/APL Corbis (front); Anchor and building, Westpoint Island, Juliet Coombe/Lonely Planet Images (back). Many of the images in this guide are available for licensing from Lonely Planet Images: www.lonelyplanetimages.com.

Printed through Colorcraft Ltd, Hong Kong.
Printed in China